ALBRECHT RITSCHL AND THE PROBLEM OF THE HISTORICAL JESUS

ALBRECHT RITSCHL AND THE PROBLEM OF THE HISTORICAL JESUS

Clive Marsh

Mellen Research University Press
San Francisco

Library of Congress Cataloging-in-Publication Data

Marsh, Clive.
    Albrecht Ritschl and the problem of the historical Jesus / Clive
Marsh.
      p.   cm.
    Includes bibliographical references and index.
    ISBN 0-7734-9822-2
    1. Jesus Christ--History of doctrines--19th century. 2. Bible.
N. T. Gospels--Criticism, interpretation, etc.--History--19th
century. 3. Ritschl, Albrecht, 1822-1889. I. Title.
BT198.M385   1992
232'.092--dc20   92-3639
                                                      CIP

Editorial Inquiries:

Mellen Research University Press
534 Pacific Avenue
San Francisco
CA 91433

Order Fulfillment:

The Edwin Mellen Press
P.O. Box 450
Lewiston, NY 14092
USA

Printed in the United States of America

To James and Margaret

who have encouraged me from the start to
explore what all this abstract stuff might look
like in lived-out form

Albrecht Ritschl and the Problem of the Historical Jesus

A study in the relationship between historical-critical research into the canonical Gospels and Christian theology with special reference to the theological method of Albrecht Ritschl

Contents

Foreword

Albrecht Ritschl and the Problem of the Historical Jesus is a carefully written, clearly delimited, and skillfully argued assessment of the biblical basis for Ritschl's Christology.

The monograph is important, first of all, because it addresses a topic of ongoing contemporary concern: identifying clearly the appropriate role for historical-critical methods when constructing a Christian theology. Marsh utilizes Ritschl's treatment of Jesus and the Gospel writers as a case study and affirms many of the features found in Ritschl's approach. For example, Ritschl correctly understood that biblical interpretation is both a theological and a historical task and that interpreters must pay attention to the Gospel accounts themselves. Ritschl's dual concerns of historical inquiry and canonical context continues to be important for contemporary biblical theology, even if some of his specific exegetical conclusions have been altered by subsequent research. Difficulties are not lacking, however, and Marsh identifies several. For example Ritschl ascribed to Jesus themes which belong more to the theology of the particular evangelists than to Jesus himself, assumed a unity of Christology not actually present in the New Testament, and underestimated the problems of constructing a theological assessment of Jesus which is controlled by historical study rather than orthodoxy. We can learn from Ritschl's mistakes as well as benefit from his constructive insights.

Marsh's book is important, secondly, because it examines a central, but often overlooked, dimension of Albrecht Ritschl's theology. Ritschl regarded himself to be a "biblical theologian" but is seldom referred to in this way. As Marsh correctly points out, scholars have often approached Ritschl's theology through the third volume of xiv

The Christian Doctrine of Justification and Reconciliation (the positive development)
rather than, as he intended, through the first (which examines the history of the
doctrine) and second(which examines the biblical materials). Indeed, although
volumes one and three were translated into English, the second never was; to this day
the omission functions as both a symptom of past misreadings and a contributing
cause for continued neglect of the exegetical bases of Ritschl's theology. During the
last thirty years several interpreters have emphasized the importance of Ritschl's
"turn to history," but few have examined in any detail his use of the Bible. This
omission is significant, Marsh asserts, because scholars misunderstand the overall
thrust of Ritschl's theology whenever they overlook its exegetical components or
misconstrue its exegetical approach (by placing him, for example, into a straightforward
"Jesus of history" movement). Marsh counters both tendencies by examining how
Ritschl actually worked with the New Testament materials. His study explains the
importance of exegesis for Ritschl's Christology and carefully analyzes the
complexities, difficulties, and lasting contributions of Ritschl's interpretation of the
Gospels.

Lastly, this monograph helps us understand the development of nineteenth-
century biblical studies. Unless Ritschl's exegetical procedures and priorities are
understood, it is difficult to perceive how biblical studies evolved from Ferdinand
Christian Baur's seminal work in the 1830s and 40s to Ritschl's many successors at
the turn of the century. The approach to the Bible proposed by Albrecht Ritschl was
a crucial step in those developments.

Clive Marsh's investigation is important, therefore, because it addresses a topic
of ongoing theological concern, emphasizes a neglected aspect of Ritschl's own
work, and contributes to our understanding of New Testament exegesis and its
development since 1840.

Darrell Jodock
Muhlenberg College
Allentown, Pennsylvania

Preface

Work on this study began ten years ago. Initially, I was exploring Bultmann's New Testament work. But in the course of that initial exploration, I was drawn to the importance of the nineteenth century for our understanding of theological traditions in the twentieth century.

It is always easy, of course, to point out that the present depends on the past in some way. Even if the present is a reaction against the past, or even if the dependence is not itself easy to pinpoint, the past remains significant. In making my own discovery of the nineteenth century's importance in theology, however, I was drawn largely to the plethora of unanswered questions and loose ends. I was drawn also to the forgotten figures. Taught at a time when the sociology of knowledge was highlighted in education, I began to question the filter through which the nineteenth century was being presented to me. In the midst of all this I stumbled upon Ritschl.

Ritschl seemed to bring together many of my interests: the German language; the interpretation and use of the Bible; theological construction; practical Christianity; the historical Jesus; the liberal tradition. He was, I now see, a figure who helped me tackle theology in a scholarly fashion at the same time as giving me the chance to address questions which had a direct import in my own spiritual pilgrimage.

What resulted from the more academic part of my enquiries was a dissertation accepted for a D.Phil in the Faculty of Theology at the University of Oxford, England, in 1987. It was a thesis located somewhere "on the borderlands" between New Testament study, systematic theology and the history of theology. The writer of such a work always runs the risk of having expertise in no field rather than all three. Where expertise lies, others must judge. In my career work, at any rate, I have moved from New Testament to systematics, and the importance of historical study remains common to my approach to each.

I offered the work then, as I do now, primarily as work which assists the interpreter of Ritschl. Its originality lies in its angle of approach to Ritschl, and in its pointing to the possible consequences of this angle of approach for the understanding of his work. If I am right in my basic thesis, two things follow:

i)   Ritschl is not simply the "nineteenth century liberal" he may at first seem to be;

ii) some of the criticisms still launched in his direction are at best misleading, at worst a scandalous distortion of what he set out to achieve.

That Ritschl didn't have all the answers goes without saying. What critical engagement with his thought produces, in my estimation, is a series of challenges;

i)   To take real, concrete, lived religious experience seriously without making all theology dependent on it alone;

ii) To ensure that attention paid to religious experience is primarily to corporate, rather than individual, experience (in Christian terms: to the Church !);

iii) To ensure that the Church is always distinguished from the Kingdom of God, so that the latter remains primary;

iv) To continually find new ways of expressing the meaning of the revelation of God in Christ;

v)   To acknowledge the necessity of searching for norms and principles by which the adequacy of those new expressions may be assessed;

vi) To acknowledge, therefore, the importance of history and tradition to evaluate experience, without playing down the significance of new learning and experience.

Any influential theologian's work would provoke a similar list of challenges. I have no desire to allow an encounter with Ritschl to get out of proportion. On the specific topic with which this study deals, however, - the interplay of reading the Gospels, grappling with the problem of the historical Jesus and constructing a Christology - I maintain that a conversation with Ritschl is especially fruitful.

I have not made major changes to the content of the dissertation for publication, though I have (I hope!) polished up the style a little and gone some way towards translating it from Academic into English. Footnotes betray how my own thinking has developed since completing the work. I have realized that there were other important conclusions to be made on the basis of the material I was handling than I was able to see at the time. The very useful - helpfully ambiguous - term "picture of Jesus", which allowed me to smudge historical fact and theological interpretation together whilst attempting to unravel what Ritschl was up to, has proved to be even more important than I appreciated at the time. Since then, I have plotted the fluctuating meaning of the term in German (*Bild Jesu*) and can now see more clearly how the impact of historical research took effect in the late nineteenth and early twentieth centuries in Christology in Western Europe. Furthermore, through turning my attention most recently to Tillich, and interpreting him at a time when the turn away from history and towards literary theory in New Testament study is widespread, I have been able to discern the significance of the task of "picturing Jesus" in theology, in relation to ecclesiology, sociology, aesthetics, ethics and ontology.

I considered writing a detailed theological postscript to the work to take account of these developments in my thinking and to position the work more directly in relation to other current works in Christology. Inevitably, the moment I began to give thought to what such an additional chapter might include, I had the makings of a second book. I would have been trying to say too much. I concluded that the work is best left largely as it stands. Some indication of, if not full justification for, how the work relates to more recent thought can, however, be given.

I am conscious that there are limits to how many hard and fast rules there can be in Christology. Christology is not about sticking to rules, but about giving expression to the significance of a particular personal encounter. I am conscious too that it is (relatively speaking) easier to write books about method than about content. And there are many complaints in theological circles that there are already too many books on methodology! But Ritschl has, at least, given me some clues - often through his making mistakes - as to "how to do Christology". He has helped me see that all Christians are responsible for giving an account of their communal experience of who God in Christ is for them. Critical conversations between those diverse expressions then are vital for the ongoing life of the Church. As part of those conversations - in order to keep the question of truth alive - attention to the criteria by which those expressions are judged must be maintained. Theology therefore links with the congregational and confessional (or denominational) and seeks to transcend it in the interests of a greater truth. This quest for greater truth hopes and trusts, and can do no more, that God is there in the midst of the process.

A second book would therefore have to explore more from a systematic angle the significance of Christological diversity. It would keep alive the question of norms and offer proposals to amend Ritschl's rigid (and ultimately untenable) position on history. And, more than that, to overcome the preoccupation with method, it would offer a Christology for the present.

Allowing for the fact that such a book is a long way off being written (!), I can only point the reader, in the mean time, to works by established scholars which begin the process of the sort of task I have in mind. Jaroslav Pelikan's study <u>Jesus Through the Centuries</u> (1985) is both excellent and exasperating. It has rightly been called (by Marcus Borg) "a masterful survey" of a number of interpretations of the figure of Jesus down the ages. As a study in cultural history it eschews theological evaluation. Therein lies the exasperation. Pelikan's work stops at precisely the point where the profoundest theological questions begin.

Anton Wessels' <u>Images of Jesus</u> (1986, E.,T. 1990) is less thorough than Pelikan's work in its description, and more limited in scope, being a study of "how Jesus is perceived and portrayed in non-European cultures". To his great credit, however, Wessels begins to tackle the hard questions; how do we make some assessment of "pictures of Jesus"? is there such a thing as a "right" picture ? how do these pictures relate to practical action ?

From a different, but telling, perspective, Alan Davies' <u>Infected Christianity</u>, subtitled "A Study of Modern Racism" (1988), examines the abuse of the figure of Jesus in Christian history. His work highlights precisely what my own conversation with Ritschl discloses: that the quest for norms is necessary, even if no-one speaks from an absolute position, in order to prevent misconstrual of what God in Christ means.

The identification of the need for norms in theology keeps in check the ever-present tendency in liberalism towards a "lazy pluralism" (the phrase is David Tracy's). Pluralism has to be welcomed because it is inescapable. But to acknowledge that radically different views are held even within Christianity (not to mention the greater and yet more profound complexities of inter-faith dialogue) is not to claim that all are really saying the same thing. Nor is it to claim that everything said is of equal value. It is in the thick of the many voices that the quest for norms keeps the interest in truth alive. The need for such a qualification to the general drift of the liberal tradition in Christianity is now widely recognised. George Lindbeck's excellent account The Nature of Doctrine (1984) has rightly proved influential in this regard. I find myself unable to follow Lindbeck's critique of the "experiential- expressivist" approach to doctrine (his term for the liberal tradition) all the way. But his call for rigorous questioning of experiential-expressivism and its assumptions and influence merits the careful attention it has been receiving. I believe that Ritschl represents one who, whilst clearly standing within that tradition, noted the difficulties and tried to tackle them. My suspicion is that many other "liberals" have, in fact, tackled the question of norms in their own ways. Lindbeck would no doubt accept that the "experiential-expressivist" tradition he identifes is not as uniform as it may first appear. I would contend that the existentialist tradition in theology is simply not as blatantly subjective or as indifferent to theological conflict as, from a post 1960-1970 perspective, appears to be the case.

Be that as it may, in Christology in the present there is no escaping the recognition of the importance of the subjective: people put a lot of themselves into their Christologies. There is also no escaping the importance of the historical. "Jesus as he was" can't be dispensed with from the kerygma, even if we know that we can't know precisely who that Jesus was. A "historical" Christology is also a Christology which takes present history-making seriously: what happens to people now and what people choose "in Christ's name" to do becomes built into what people make of the figure of Jesus. If the Christologies we create are not quite fact, not quite fiction, then so be it.

It has been quite a struggle to get there, but we can now acknowledge that the figure of Jesus - who he was/is, what he stood/stands for, and how he imparted/imparts the power of God - is communicated via pictures about him. Pictures, all sorts of pictures, preserve and foster rediscovery of the power of God. That doesn't mean that Christianity is primarily a mental, intellectual exercise. Far from it. Questions about aesthetics and ontology, and about the emotional content of Christology must still be posed. But the easy link between Jesus the Christ "back there" and present faith in him "here and now" just can't be made as simply as was once thought. To quote Keith Ward:

> ...Jesus, the man, by the intention and will of God, has become a paradigm image of the infinite God in relation to us and to our salvation. But this means that it is the images flowing from the completed historical life, developed in the community of the church, which are the present vehicle of our relationship to God. A Vision to Pursue SCM: London 1991 p116.

Tillich used to say he learnt more about the figure of Jesus the Christ from paintings than books. He was touching on something important. Words will never be sufficient. They are, however, vital, even in their insufficiency, as we try and work out what Christology is all about. It is to this end that I offer the words that follow.

Clive Marsh, Sheffield
November 1st (All Saints' Day) 1991

Acknowledgements

Countless people have helped to bring this study to print. Philip Hefner, Wilhelm Linss, Rick Busse, Gerry McCulloh all read sections of the work in its early stages. Jonathan Draper helped me knock the thesis into an acceptable shape for offering as a D.Phil.. His practical help at that stage was invaluable. The British Academy supported my postgraduate studies in Oxford and attendance at the 1989 AAR Meeting in Anaheim, where the ideas contained here were taken a stage further. Wesley Memorial Church, Oxford, provided financial support towards three months' study at the Lutheran School of Theology at Chicago in 1984. My current employer, the Church Army have provided assistance both through sensitive management - enabling me to keep my research up to date - and practical help for attendance at important conferences. Students and staff at the Wilson Carlile College of Evangelism continually keep me on my toes. Their enthusiasm has ensured that this work didn't have chance to gather dust. Chris Roles and Joanne Rippin have helped with proof-reading. Paul Marsh has put in many hours preparing the final manuscript. Jill Marsh has lived with this for as long as she has known me. That in itself is worthy of thanks. But she has also put in many extra hours of child care in the past few months - far beyond the call of duty - to give me the opportunity to get it finished. We both look forward to the day when Philip will appreciate what it was all about. Claus, Ute, Niko, Katja, Zik and Frithjof Jönsson have all played a vital role; they, above all, helped me grasp hold of Ritschl's first language. Dr. Darrell Jodock of Muhlenberg College (Allentown, Pennsylvania) and Dr. Sarah Coakley of Oriel College (Oxford) deserve special thanks for supporting the publication of this work. Mention should also be made of the American Academy of Religion Nineteenth Century Theology Group which has, in particular, given me encouragement in my work and provided a forum in which to try out some ideas. Last, and by no means least, I wish to express thanks to Robert Morgan of Linacre College (Oxford). I first wrote to Bob back in 1981, asking for some ideas about how to take an interest in German and theology further. He remains a loyal supporter and trenchant critic of my work: I am very grateful to him.

Abbreviations

A.D.T.	*Anfänge der dialektischen Theologie* (ed. J.Moltmann; I 1962; II 1963; Munich)	E.R.	Epworth Review
		E.T.	English Translation
		Ev.Th.	*Evangelische Theologie*
		Ex.T.	Expository Times
A.J.T.	American Journal of Theology	H.B.T.	Horizons in Biblical Theology
A.N.R.W.	*Aufstieg und Niedergang der Römischen Welt* (eds. W.Haase and H.Temporini; Berlin and N.Y)	H.T.R.	Harvard Theological Review
		H.Z.	*Historische Zeitschrift*
		ICR	Instruction in the Christian Religion (see bibliography under Ritschl 1886)
A.K.Z.	*Allgemeine Kirchenzeitung*	I.D.B.	Interpreter's Dictionary of the Bible
A.T.R.	Anglican Theological Review	J.A.A.R.	Journal of the American Academy of Religion
B.J.R.L.	Bulletin of the John Rylands Library	J.B.L.	Journal of Biblical Literature
B.R.	Biblical Research	J.D.T.	*Jahrbücher für Deutsche Theologie*
BT	Ritschl's lectures on the Biblical Theology of the New Testament : Göttingen 1877-78 (see under 1877-8 in bibliography)	J.R.	Journal of Religion
		J & R I	Justification and Reconciliation Vol. 1 (see bibliography under Ritschl 1872).
C.H.	Church History	J & R III	Justification and Reconciliation Vol. 3 (see bibliography under Ritschl 1900).
C.Q.	The Church Quarterly		
C.U.P.	Cambridge University Press		
C.W.	*Christliche Welt*	J.S.N.T.	Journal for the Study of the New Testament
E50	*Die Entstehung der altkatholischen Kirche* (1st ed.)	J.T.C.	Journal for Theology and Church
E57	*Die Entstehung der altkatholischen Kirche* (2nd ed.)	J.T.5.	Journal of Theological Studies
E.Q.	Evangelical Quarterly	K.u.D.	*Kerygma und Dogma*

L.Q.	The Lutheran Quarterly	S.J.T.	Scottish Journal of Theology
M.Q.	McCormick Quarterly		
N.D.T.	New Dictionary of Theology (eds.A.Richardson and J.Bowden; SCM:London 1983)	S.R.	Studies in Religion/ Sciences Religieuses
		S.B.	H.L. Strack and P. Billerbeck *Kommentar zum Neuen Testament aus Talmud und Midrasch*
N.T.	Novum Testamentum		
N.T.S.	New Testament Studies	T.J.	*Theologische Jahrbrücher*
N.Z.S.T.R.	*Neue Zeitschrift für Systematische Theologie und Religionsphilosophie*	T.L.Z.	*Theologische Literaturzeitung*
		T.S.K.	*Theologische Studien und Kritiken*
O.U.P.	Oxford University Press		
P.S.	Process Studies	T.Z.	*Theologische Zeitschrift*
"Q"	Material common to Matthew and Luke (but not necessarily in written form).	T.Z.T.	*Tübinger Zeitschrift der Theologie*
		Z.K.G.	*Zeitschrift für Kirchengeschichte*
R.E.P.T.K.	*Realencyklopädie für protestantische Theologie und Kirche*	Z.N.W.	*Zeitschrift für die neutestamentliche Wissenschaft*
R.G.G.	*Die Religion in Geschichte und Gegenwart*	Z.Th.K.	*Zeitschrift für Theologie und Kirche*
R.S.	Religious Studies	Z.W.T.	*Zeitschrift für wissenschaftliche Theologie*
R.T.R.	Reformed Theological Review	Z.Z.	*Zwischen den Zeiten*
R u V	*Rechtfertigung und Versöhnung*		
R u V II	*Rechtfertigung und Versöhnung* Vol.2 (see bibliography under Ritschl) 1889		

Chapter I

The Purpose and Context
of the Present Study

1. THE POINT OF THE PRESENT STUDY

Albrecht Ritschl is not known as a biblical scholar. If he is known at all it is in terms of his theology being based on value-judgments [1], of his reductionism [2], of his inadequate understanding of sin and atonement [3], his dependence upon Kant [4] or his lack of eschatological perception [5]. He is, in short, viewed more as a systematic theologian or philosopher of religion, and often viewed negatively at that.

The pattern of negative reception of Ritschl and his work is changing, albeit very slowly [6]. What requires fresh analysis, however, is his method in theology from the perspective of the biblical scholar. Ritschl's attempt to be a biblical theologian has rarely been respected or explored [7]. As far as reception of Ritschl in the English-speaking world is concerned, furthermore, one cannot help feeling that the failure to assess Ritschl on his own terms may in part be quite accidental. That is to say, though the first and third volumes of his magnum opus _Rechtfertigung und Versöhnung_ were translated into English, the second volume never was. On this basis, a one-sided understanding of both the content and method of Ritschl's theology has inevitably resulted.

For this reason alone, a study of the place of biblical study in Ritschl's theology is justified. This reason aside, Ritschl's place in the history of the development of New Testament study requires that his work be assessed from this perspective. Here the historian of New Testament study enters a vicious circle. Precisely because Ritschl has scarcely been viewed as a New Testament scholar, his work does not on the whole receive treatment outside of particular studies of that history or general surveys [8].

There are some notable exceptions to this rule, and these should be highlighted.

W.R. Farmer clearly has his own point to prove in all that he writes on the question of the Synoptic Problem. That he perceives the need to keep open some important questions about the nineteenth century context of the debate over the Griesbach and Marcan hypotheses is, however, an important contribution. In this regard he has been insistent in drawing attention to the dogmatic significance of Ritschl's change of mind on the Synoptic Problem [9]. Farmer is thus respecting Ritschl's New Testament work.

A second exception is J.D.G. Dunn, who in his work Unity and Diversity in the New Testament pays brief attention to Ritschl in locating the origins of the discussion of "Early Catholicism" [10]. Admittedly the reference is more to Ritschl as a historian of early Christianity. Yet as it goes against the grain of so much of Ritschl-reception and as it refers to a work - namely, Ritschl's *Die Entstehung der altkatholischen Kirche* - which this present study makes use of, it is only proper that attention be drawn to Dunn's reference to Ritschl.

Farmer's and Dunn's reception of Ritschl apart, Ritschl is taken up by and large only by systematic theologians and philosphers of religion, who are keen to concentrate upon the finished product of Ritschl's theology from their own individual perspective, rather than to view Ritschl's method in reaching that finished product. Pannenberg [11], Calvert [12] and Gunton [13], for example, figure in this category.

The failure to deal with Ritschl's biblical work thus proves detrimental on a number of fronts. Ritschl himself is not properly understood, nor his insights used. A gap is left in the discussion of the development of New Testament study between Baur and Schweitzer which leaves a major omission as far as the discussion of the inter-relationship between biblical study and dogmatics in that period is concerned. On these bases, Ritschl's carrying through of a programme mapped out by Schleiermacher is clearly perceived, without it being perceived also that he carries on a programme mapped out by F.C.Baur. Ritschl's own theological method seeks to fuse both strands, one which tackles the question of the theological responsibility of New Testament study in a striking fashion.

Given this historical context for Ritschl's undertaking as a theologically responsible biblical scholar, the question of the appropriateness of this study of an aspect of

Ritschl's New Testament work within the wider context of current concern for the theological use of the New Testament arises.

Respect for Ritschl's own New Testament work should lead the interpreter in one of two major directions: to focus either upon his use of the Gospels or his use of the Pauline Epistles. Both these areas are prominent in his work, the latter perhaps more so given the ecclesiastical tradition within which Ritschl stands and to which he seeks consciously to refer [14]. Ritschl's theology is, however, clearly "Christocentric" in the sense that focus upon the person of Jesus is paramount in his theology [15]. Such an approach, therefore, requires that attention be given to how he uses the Gospels. It is this angle of approach - his Gospel study - that this present study adopts in its treatment of Ritschl's New Testament work.

The precise form of the enquiry thus derives ultimately from the fabric of Ritschl's own theological method. It is, however, worthy of note that four areas of current concern in New Testament study relate to the enquiry being undertaken. In expounding and appraising Ritschl's own approach, questions about the validity and efficacy of historical-critical method, the canon, the historical Jesus and New Testament theology, as they feature in present New Testament research, will never be far away.

The purpose of this present study is therefore primarily to make a contribution to a growing movement striving to "reappraise" Ritschl [16]. But it is also a feature of the enquiry to understand Ritschl as a theological interpreter of the canonical Gospels and to locate him in the history of the development of New Testament study. I proceed with the assumption that failure to respect him in this light not only does an injustice to Ritschl himself, but also misses out a key aspect in the development of New Testament study in Germany in the latter half of the nineteenth century, the repercussions of which are not only to be felt by the historian. Failure to view Ritschl as a New Testament scholar is, I contend, intrinsically bound up with a tendency to pay lip-service to the nineteenth century heritage of theological enquiry, even though the questions posed and highlighted in the period in which Ritschl was working remain with us [17].

This critical reappraisal of Ritschl is thus undertaken on the grounds that the concerns expressed and dwelt upon in the period in which Ritschl worked remain pressing concerns, and that answers given in that period may have been more easily cast aside than they should have been [18]. The reappraisal of Ritschl from whatever perspective is thus also a means of asking in what way Ritschl's work is of value for current enquirers into the questions posed by the New Testament itself - ultimate questions about human existence.

Both because of the way Ritschl construed his theology and the way he grasped the subject-matter of the material with which he was dealing in interpreting the New Testament, an enquiry into Ritschl's handling of a part of the New Testament is also an enquiry into Ritschl's theology itself. On this basis the present study, though essentially a historical study, moves away from its historical context in posing questions about the nature of theological enquiry within the context of the study of the New Testament. The adequacy of Ritschl's own theology is thus in question at the same time as his study of the New Testament is brought under scrutiny.

2. THE CURRENT STATE OF RITSCHL RESEARCH

Karl Barth attempted to sign the death-warrant for interest in Ritschl and his theology. Some of his statements about Ritschl are well-known: "Ritschl has the significance of an episode in more recent theology, and not, indeed not, that of an epoch." "Ritschl...stands with incredible clearness and firmness upon the ground of his 'ideal of life', the very epitome of the national-liberal German bourgeois of the age of Bismarck." [19] The whole chapter from which these quotations are taken is an attempt by Barth to deter his readers from spending time on Ritschl: Ritschl's whole approach is to be seen, in Barth's estimation, as symptomatic of the erroneous nature of the general direction of theological thinking in nineteenth century Europe [20]. Though published in 1947, the chapter merely summarized what Barth had held since the 1920s [21]. On this basis, and given also the fact that Barth's own thought has exerted such a powerful influence upon English-speaking theology in the immediate post-war period, it is not difficult to appreciate the effect of such a curt verdict on the reception of Ritschl and his theology.

The questions with which Ritschl grappled, however, will not go away [22].

However inadequate Ritschl's own answers to the questions of his day might have been, the fact that the same questions remain is ground enough upon which to base an argument for the legitimacy of an enquiry into Ritschl's own theology. Though there is just cause to be highly critical of Ritschl, even along the lines Barth himself suggested, Barth's own criticism cannot be allowed to stand unchallenged. Barth's verdict is based on, and incorporates, a parody of Ritschl's position, and makes him a scapegoat for a tendency in theology with which Barth had little sympathy.

The realization of this state of affairs is now well established: Hefner, Schäfer, Mueller, Lotz, Richmond, Draper and Ringleben have all drawn attention to this turn of the tide in the understanding of Ritschl [23]. It is now possible to look beyond Barth and attempt a fairer assessment of Ritschl and his work, building upon more positive voices from the past (e.g. A.T.Swing 1901). Indeed, over the past twenty-five years many attempts have been made not only to redress the balance of Barth's verdict on Ritschl by seeking to understand Ritschl on his own terms, but also to build upon Ritschl's work in a constructive way, striking out in a positive fashion at the negative assessment of Ritschl made by Barth. In addition to the writers cited above, one need only mention the writings of Deegan, Foster, Haenchen, Vorster, Timm, Jodock, Metzler, Livingston, McCulloh, Barnett and Welch [24].

The present reader of Ritschl is thus in a much better position to see Ritschl for what he was: much more than a mere slave of Kant's (or Lotze's) philosophy; more than a mere exponent of an ethical system; more than a mere systematician of pre-conceived ideas who paid lip-service to biblical tradition. He can now be understood as a theologian striving to maintain the momentum of the Reformation through a biblically-controlled critique of the tradition in which he stood.

In the process of reaching this revised appraisal of Ritschl's intentions and achievement, Hefner in particular has drawn attention to the extent to which Ritschl undertook *historical* work; Lotz and Mueller to the *Reformation context* of Ritschl's theology (from historical and systematic viewpoints respectively); Deegan, Vorster, McCulloh and Barnett have approached Ritschl's *Christology* from a more constructive angle than earlier studies; and Koenig and, most recently, Draper have sought to portray Ritschl as the *biblical theologian* he understood himself to be.

Gaps remain, however, in the overall picture of Ritschl's work. There are still, for example, no full assessments of Ritschl's work on Pietism, his work on non-Reformation Church History or his understanding of Pauline theology. It is one such gap that this present study seeks to fill.

3. THE PLACE OF THE PRESENT STUDY IN THE CONTEXT OF RITSCHL RESEARCH

Four particular aspects of Ritschl's work which have received specific attention - namely, his historical work, his interest in the Reformation, his Christology and his use of the Bible - were mentioned above [25]. One scholar who has made a major contribution to the understanding of both F.C.Baur and Albrecht Ritschl, however, was not mentioned. Yet Darrell Jodock's F.C.Baur and Albrecht Ritschl on Historical Theology is both a major study and unique in its manner of procedure. For though other writers have made use of manuscript material (e.g. Hök, Schäfer, Draper) to reach an assessment of Ritschl which seems on the whole fairer than a seemingly customary over-dependence upon J & R III [26], the particular value of Jodock's enquiry is that it seeks to do justice to the early period of Ritschl's development. The seminal period of Ritschl's career in the period around 1850 is viewed from the perspective of his relationship, both personal and academic, to his teacher F.C.Baur. This is a fruitful and important line of enquiry, in that it recognizes the significance for Ritschl of the ideas and person of his teacher. It can probably be stated that any assessment of Ritschl which fails to do justice to Ritschl's relationship to Baur will inevitably prove inadequate.

This present study seeks to follow a similar approach in viewing as important the first stage of Ritschl's academic career. Distinct from Jodock's study, however, the present work looks not at a comparison of Ritschl's early work with Baur's work of the same period, but views rather Ritschl's early work in relation to his later work and traces the development in Ritschl's thinking with respect to the particular question under scrutiny i.e. Ritschl's encounter with the Gospels.

This study differs methodologically from Jodock in one other significant respect.

It can legitimately be claimed that Ritschl's "mature period" begins in 1857 with his final public break with Baur through the second edition of *Die Entstehung der altkatholischen Kirche* [27], or that at most reference back to the 1850 edition of the same work is permissible and necessary. For a study of Ritschl's work on the Gospels, however, it is clear that one must delve deeper and take into consideration the two published works of 1846 and 1847, namely Ritschl's book and article on Marcion and Luke. Thus, though Jodock explores Ritschl's work back to 1850 with great effect, this present study takes the enquiry one step further.

In subject matter the present study is very different from Jodock's enquiry. Whereas Jodock concentrates more particularly upon the historical aspects of Ritschl's work *vis-a-vis* Baur, this study dwells upon the biblical aspects of Ritschl's work. In this respect, it builds upon the work of Koenig and Draper, both of whom deal with the question of Ritschl's biblical work as systematic theologians in terms of the "use of the Bible". In other words, the first steps in the enquiry into the *content* of Ritschl's biblical study remain to be taken. It is these steps that the present study attempts to make [28]. In opting to look in some detail at Ritschl's encounter with the four canonical Gospels, then, one aspect only of Ritschl's biblical work is touched upon. This study is therefore by no means a New Testament study *per se*, any more than it is a study which does justice to the full extent of Ritschl's own dealings with the New Testament (a study of his understanding of Paul would be a wholly separate enterprise). It is, rather, an attempt to determine what Ritschl makes of the Gospels. As stated above, the topics which demand scrutiny derive from this primary interest. The concern for the person of Jesus, the question of canon, history and theology in the Gospels and the method(s) used to interpret them all become part of the enquiry because of the nature of Ritschl's own interest. The recent enquiries into Ritschl's Christology in particular (e.g. McCulloh, Barnett) thus feature alongside Koenig and Draper as the background and context in Ritschl research for the present study. For christological considerations must feature prominently. The reasons for this are clear: the Gospels themselves demand that Christology be high on the Christian theological agenda; the construal of the theological task by Ritschl himself places Christology at the heart of the theological task. In this regard, the "Christocentricity" of Ritschl's

8

theology again comes to the fore. The enquiry thus builds on studies into Ritschl's biblical interests and his Christology as far as subject-matter is concerned, and extends two aspects of the method used by Jodock to determine Ritschl's understanding of the theological task, i.e. it places great stress on detailed scrutiny of a limited range of primary source-material and takes the early period of Ritschl's development as a scholar as of especial importance. But it goes beyond Jodock in tracing back the roots of that development to 1846.

4. THE PRESENT STUDY : A SUMMARY OF PROCEDURE

The study focusses upon the "quest for Jesus" because such a quest appears to be at the heart of Ritschl's system. The definition of the "Jesus" here referred to cannot, however, yet be determined. Whether Ritschl in practice understands "Jesus" as "Jesus of Nazareth", the "historical Jesus", the "earthly Jesus", the "biblical Christ", or in some other way, the study must show. Furthermore, the precise relationship between Ritschl's interest in Jesus and the so-called "Quest of the Historical Jesus" must yet be clarified. Yet the expression "quest for Jesus" remains useful in indicating a possible link with the so-called Quest, without suggesting identity.

That this should be the resultant focus of such a study, however, is something which must first be established on the basis of Ritschl's own procedure as evident in his writings. This is done by considering the two aspects of Ritschl's understanding of the theological task inextricably related to the issue of the "quest for Jesus", namely the questions of the definition of "biblical theology" and the point of the study of the Gospels. The exposition of these three interrelated questions follows a chiastic structure, with an exposition of Ritschl's "picture of Jesus" at the centre. The exposition thus proceeds in the following manner. After specifying in general terms the sources upon which the present enquiry is based (II.1.1), the study continues to examine in brief what Ritschl understands by "biblical theology" (II.1.2 and 1.3). It becomes clear in what context in Ritschl's theology his work on the Gospels must be understood. Moving from formal considerations to considerations of content, the study then explores the questions in what sense and to what extent the "New

Testament theology" which Ritschl's biblical theology shows itself to be is to be termed and understood as "christocentric" (1.4). A survey of Ritschl's New Testament work is then provided, showing with the help of Otto Ritschl's biographical account of his father Albrecht's development how this work fitted into his career as a theologian as a whole (1.5). From the New Testament work is then extracted what seems, on the basis of Ritschl's own understanding of "Christocentricity", of particular relevance to his construal of the theological task, namely his work upon the Gospels (II.2). Again the base of Ritschl's sources is determined (2.1) before methodological considerations are extracted from Ritschl's work in an attempt to expound his answer to the question "what is the main point of studying the Gospels?" (2.2).

Moving once more from form to content, Ritschl's "picture of Jesus" is then presented (3.1). At this point the heart of the exposition is reached. A more analytical treatment of the "picture of Jesus" at the formal level is then offered, demonstrating the relationship between the critical work on the Gospels undertaken by Ritschl and the content of the "picture" itself (3.2). The degree of importance of Ritschl's understanding of the figure of Jesus is spelled out in the next section, where the relationship between Ritschl's picture of Jesus and his theological system as a whole is presented (3.3). Chapters III and IV focus respectively on the problems and assets of Ritschl's approach. Chapter III begins with a brief critique of Ritschl's use of the Gospels (III.1). Section III.2 then provides the chapter's core, being a critique and assessment of Ritschl's picture of Jesus. The critique continues by highlighting two particularly problematic aspects of Ritschl's presentation of Jesus in relation to his construal of the task of Christology (III.3 and III.4). In the fourth chapter more positive notes are sounded. General remarks are made about the value of Ritschl's angle of approach (IV.1 and IV.2), before particular strengths of his picture of Jesus are considered more closely (IV.3 and IV.4). The final section of the work (IV.5) summarizes the value of respecting Ritschl's actual procedure with regard to the exposition of a picture of Jesus and the articulation of a Christian theology.

Notes to Chapter I

1. This was especially the case with the older secondary literature on Ritschl; see e.g. Garvie 1918.

2. E.g. Hamilton 1965 p89

3. E.g. Garvie 1918 p819

4. E.g. Macquarrie 1963 p76f.

5. E.g. Schweitzer 1968 p250; Walther 1961 ch.7 esp.p139f.

6. See below I.2 and I.3

7. There are problems of definition, as will become clear below in chapter II of the study. However, regardless of the question whether Ritschl's theology can legitimately be called a "biblical theology", the fact that he sought to be a "biblical theologian" deserves respect cf. Foster 1965 esp. pp.51 and 61. Foster remarks (p61): "As a biblical scholar he (Ritschl) is tendentious, and his work now dated; but no adequate assessment has yet been given of Ritschl's pioneering effort to combine historical and theological exegesis." For assistance in the clarification of terms through an exposition of the two clearest possible understandings of the term "New Testament theology", see J.L.Houlden's article in A.E.Harvey (ed.) 1985; cf.esp. p122.

8. As in e.g. Stoldt 1980, Tuckett 1983a and Kümmel 1975.

9. See Farmer 1961 p35 (n46) and 1976 p29. An important qualification must, however, be added. Tuckett's argument (1983a) that one should not point to dogmatic motives behind the nineteenth century debates on the Synoptic Problem still stands. The difference between the two arguments is that Tuckett is concerned to banish dogmatic *motives* from the discussion, whilst Farmer wishes to draw attention to the dogmatic *implications*. Both intentions may stand alongside each other.

10. Dunn 1977 p342.

11. Pannenberg 1968.

12. Calvert 1983.

13. Gunton 1983.

14. *R u V II* pp23-5 esp. p24.

15. See further below II.1.4.

16. E.g. Richmond 1978, Parsons 1979 and Ringleben (ed.) 1990.

17. As stressed e.g. by Lotz 1974 p15.

18. This applies especially to the negative verdict cast on Ritschl by Karl Barth. See

further below I.2..

19. Barth 1972 pp654 and 656.

20. ibid. p656.

21. Richmond 1978 pp32-6.

22. One need only consider the recent three-volume production under the editorship of N.Smart, S.Katz, P.Sherry and J.P.Clayton: <u>Nineteenth Century Religious Thought in the West</u> to perceive the significance and relevance of this period for modern discussions. It is sad that there is no chapter devoted to Ritschl and his work.

23. Hefner esp. 1966; Schäfer esp. 1968; Mueller 1969; Lotz 1974; Richmond 1978; Draper 1984; Ringleben (ed.) 1990.

24. Deegan esp. 1962; Foster 1965; Haenchen 1965; Vorster 1965; Timm 1967; Jodock 1969; Metzler 1971; Livingston 1971; McCulloh 1973; Barnett 1976 and 1979; Welch 1985.

25. Other areas of Ritschl's work which have been covered in the secondary literature, but which are not dealt with here, include his epistemology and philosophy of religion (esp. his rejection of metaphysics). See e.g. Wrzecionko 1964 and Busse 1984.

26. This charge counts also against some positive receptions of Ritschl, however, e.g. Richmond 1978, which is little more than an assessment of Ritschl based upon *R u V III* and *Theologie und Metaphysik*. The references to other works are very scanty indeed.

27. As e.g. Richmond 1978 assumes p18ff.

28. Some past studies have clear relevance to the present enquiry (e.g. some of the studies looking at Ritschl's understanding of the Kingdom: Metzler 1971; also Deegan on the historical Jesus 1964). These are but partial treatments, however, and do not attempt to look at the topic from the perspective of seeking to understand Ritschl's theology as biblical theology.

Chapter II

Ritschl's Christocentric Theology: the Context for his Picture of Jesus

1. BIBLICAL THEOLOGY AND NEW TESTAMENT STUDY

1.1. Ritschl's Biblical Theology : the Sources

It is necessary, first, to establish which of Ritschl's writings are of particular relevance to the study of his biblical work. A more detailed survey of Ritschl's New Testament work, as it relates to his theological development, is to be undertaken below and a more specific presentation of the source material to be used in the scrutiny of his work on the Gospels will be offered (II.1.5 and II.2.1). At this point it is important to present in more general terms the essential sources with which the interpreter must come to terms if (s)he is properly to understand Ritschl. This both clarifies the writings upon which this present enquiry depends and justifies the exclusion of other writings of Ritschl's not immediately relevant. For the purposes of clarity, the Ritschl material drawn upon is best divided into four categories.

First, there is the material most commonly referred to when Ritschl receives a passing mention in studies not devoted solely to his work. This represents the material for which he is best known, namely *Die Entstehung der altkatholischen Kirche* and, more especially, the three-volume work *Rechtfertigung und Versöhnung* [1]. To this can be added his *Unterricht in der christlichen Religion* [2]. References to Ritschl's work usually confine themselves to the first two works cited, however, and furthermore to the 1857 edition of the former work [3] and the third volume of the latter [4].

To his great credit Colin Gunton, a recent writer on Ritschl, does draw on two other works namely *Theologie und Metaphysik* [5] and the first volume of *Rechtfertigung und Versöhnung* [6]. The fact that the second volume of the latter work is missing from Gunton's list, however, is instructive. For it betrays the manner in which Ritschl's theological undertaking has been misunderstood by not being viewed in its entirety, omitting in particular a consideration of its biblical dimension. It certainly reflects what appears to be a common fault of the reception of Ritschl in the English-speaking milieu, namely that Ritschl's *magnum opus* is studied on the basis of only two of its three volumes, the second - the biblical volume - being left unconsidered [7].

A second category of Ritschl material would include *Theologie und Metaphysik*, the three-volume *Geschichte des Pietismus*, his works on Christian perfection, Schleiermacher's speeches, conscience and, above all, the second volume of *Rechtfertigung und Versöhnung* [8]. These works are taken up by specialists in particular fields. As was seen above, *Theologie und Metaphysik* has been made use of by both Gunton and Richmond [9]. This is right and proper for philosophers of religion, and each can legitimately justify their lack of consideration of some aspects of Ritschl's work on this basis, Ritschl's range of writing across the board of theological disciplines being unusually wide by modern standards (though not, it has to be admitted, by the standards of his own day). Assessing Ritschl's ability as a Church historian would naturally include a consideration of his work on Pietism [10]. One would have to draw also on a number of other writings in this field, not least *J & R I* [11].

A study of Ritschl as biblical scholar and biblical theologian requires a careful reading of *R u V II*, a text which is rarely used in Ritschl research [12]. To *R u V II* should be added the 1851 essay on the Synoptic Gospels [13], and also the essays of 1861 and 1862 recording the exchange between Ritschl and Zeller [14].

A third category of Ritschl material is brought into play by the nature of the methodology of this present study. Given that the enquiry lays great store in the attempt to locate Ritschl's biblical work within the framework of Ritschl's emerging theology as a whole, it is imperative that early work be considered.

Under this rubric the 1850 edition of *Die Entstehung der altkatholischen Kirche* and, to a lesser extent, the 1846 work *Das Evangelium Marcions und das kanonische Evangelium des Lucas* come into consideration.

A fourth category of Ritschl material is an amalgam of shorter writings and material not easily obtainable. In the former category come articles and even book reviews which prove of relevance to the enquiry. In the latter comes especially the manuscript of Ritschl's 1877-78 Göttingen lectures, as noted down by S.Eck [15].

This categorization of the material used in the course of the enquiry is presented for the purposes of formal clarity only. No judgments implicit or explicit about the content of material in each category are being made by this categorization. Even in the case of the third category, where there will clearly be material superseded by later material as far as Ritschl's development is concerned, it should be stressed that the material is no less valuable for that, given that it is the present study's concern to explore that development.

The bibliography appended to this study includes all the works that are deemed to be essential to a consideration of Ritschl as a biblical theologian, a task which demands that one does not rest content simply with *R u V II*, important though its "rediscovery" undoubtedly is, but that one also delve deeper into Ritschl's other biblical work.

Having clarified the sources, it is therefore now necessary to begin the exposition of Ritschl's theology from this perspective, commencing with broad methodological considerations about the definition and place of "biblical theology" as a theological discipline.

1.2 Ritschl's Theology as Biblical Theology

The topic of Ritschl as a "biblical theologian" is in some ways a new one. Though brought to the fore most recently by Draper (1984) and to some extent anticipated by the work of Schäfer (1968) and Koenig (1953), the task of understanding Ritschl's theology as "biblical theology" is, by and large, not one which has been undertaken by interpreters of Ritschl.

The main reasons for the failure to approach Ritschl from this perspective are easy to determine. Given the context of the reception of Ritschl outlined above (I.2), it is easy to see how Barth's verdict on Ritschl, when coupled with the influence Barth has exerted upon theological thinking in this century, has prevented a full understanding of Ritschl's aims and achievements. Not least of the aims was to formulate a theology which was at once biblical and in keeping with the tradition of the Reformation (and indeed on that very basis biblical) [16]. Where Barth's verdict has determined or at least influenced twentieth-century reception of the theological heritage of the nineteenth-century, it is thus no surprise to find that the topic of Ritschl as a "biblical theologian" has rarely figured on the agenda.

The reasons for the failure to deal with the topic are not solely to be found in the writings and opinions of Ritschl's negative critics. The way both Ritschl's own school and his more distant disciples took up Ritschl's ideas in a positive way had the lasting effect of limiting a proper understanding of Ritschl on his own terms. Wherever Ritschl's thinking on "value-judgments" in theology, on the importance of "the mind of Christ" or on the exclusion of metaphysics from theology is taken up [17], or wherever a stress upon ethics or an ethical understanding of the Kingdom of God is traced back to Ritschl [18], the danger exists that at that point Ritschl is being understood on the basis of his followers' thinking and emphases and not on his own terms. The problem is the proverbial one of a teacher being viewed solely on the extent to which her/his pupils or followers have comprehended their words.

A return to the sources - in this case Ritschl's own writings - is thus imperative. As this study tries to show, the question of Ritschl as a "biblical theologian" lies at the heart of his understanding of his own role as a theologian.

The failure to consider Ritschl from this angle has had two consequences: i) What Ritschl was trying to do has been misunderstood. His flight from metaphysics, from mysticism, from pietism, his Christocentricity, his emphasis upon ethics, his stress upon the importance of the Kingdom of God have been too easily attributed to Kantianism or Neo-Kantianism irrespective of potential links to other spheres of influence [19]; ii) The understanding of the development of the term and discipline "biblical theology" amongst historians and theologians has been deficient. Thus, to cite one major example, Otto Merk fails to mention Ritschl in his study *Biblische Theologie des Neuen Testaments in ihrer Anfangszeit* [20]. Hans-Joachim Kraus (1970) is more perceptive, therefore, in including a section on Ritschl. What is more, his treatment of Ritschl alongside Kähler proves ultimately most appropriate [21] even if he fails to get to the heart of Ritschl's understanding of "biblical theology". For Kraus over-concentrates on Ritschl's narrow understanding of the background to the New Testament in terms of the Old. As the discussion below proposes to demonstrate, Ritschl's weakness at this point cannot be allowed to have the final say in the matter [22].

It is the great merit of Draper's recent work (1984) that the author opens up discussion on the question of Ritschl as a "biblical theologian". Draper's work makes a positive contribution to both aspects of the question's consequences as outlined above, though to the second more by indirect means. His discussion of this second aspect could thus be sharpened by closer reference to Ritschl's more immediate contemporaries. Ritschl's understanding of "biblical theology" would then indeed be better "placed" [23].

It is necessary, in short, to fill out with greater clarity and with closer reference to Ritschl's contemporaries the significance of the distinction between understanding "biblical theology" as a historical discipline (i.e. effectively equivalent to *Religionsgeschichte* - the History of Religion) and as a dogmatic discipline (i.e. as the foundation of dogmatics) [24].

Bernhard Weiss, for example, clearly adopts the former understanding of the term in defining the "biblical theology of the New Testament" as "the scientific representation of the religious ideas and doctrines which are contained in the New Testament." [25] He states further, "Inasmuch as our science has to do only with the objective representation of the religious ideas and doctrines which are to be found in the New Testament, excluding all subjective criticism, it is a purely historical discipline." [26] As such, "biblical theology" is to be distinguished from "biblical dogmatics", which aspires to a systematic presentation of a (seemingly) unified New Testament truth [27]. The discipline of "biblical theology" is thus in a position to encounter the diversity of the New Testament in a way that "biblical dogmatics" cannot and should not [28].

Martin Kähler, on the other hand, follows the latter of the two understandings of "biblical theology" sketched above. In his 1897 article on *"Biblische Theologie"*, for example, he argues that "biblical theology" does away with itself if it simply describes the religious ideas to be found in the Bible. He claims that a sifting and evaluation process must inevitably occur [29].

To this very basic tension in the understanding of the term "biblical theology" can be added one further observation. When one considers that alongside B.Weiss in the camp of those deeming "biblical theology" to be a historical discipline stand F.C.Baur before him and William Wrede after him, it becomes immediately apparent that even to define "biblical theology" simply as a historical discipline is insufficient.

The matter may be expressed in this way: that B.Weiss, a conservative, and Baur, the notorious radical, should be placed alongside each other and contrasted with Kähler and that all three can be contrasted with Wrede is demonstrative enough of the fact that diverse definitions of the term "biblical theology" as a historical discipline abound [30]. That such abundance was prevalent in Ritschl's own day only highlights the difficulty both in perceiving Ritschl's own meaning and in being able to conclude that Ritschl himself saw precisely in which direction he was heading.

The clarification which these references to Ritschl's contemporaries call for, therefore, is a basic one: where does Ritschl stand with respect to this methodological tension ?

At first sight it appears that Ritschl's most explicit responses to the question of the meaning of "biblical theology" bring him close to B.Weiss. He appears to perceive the discipline to be historical along the lines suggested by Weiss. Ritschl states, *"(Die) biblische Theologie...(ist) nicht System oder Reihenfolge von loci theologici...sondern sie stellt eine Reihe religiöser Gedankenkreise dar."* [31] "Biblical theology" thus provides the "material" (*Stoff*) with which the dogmatician operates [32].

As such, "biblical theology" is thus the immediate prerequisite of "dogmatic theology", a discipline which seems identical in meaning to "systematic theology" as far as Ritschl is concerned [33]. "Systematic/dogmatic theology" thus builds upon the findings of "biblical theology", though is not simply a summary of those findings [34].

To this understanding of "biblical theology", however, is to be added a second understanding of the discipline, an understanding which seems closer to Kähler than to B.Weiss.   In the third paragraph of ICR Ritschl writes: "...it stands as the fundamental principle of the protestant church that Christian doctrine is to be obtained from the Bible *alone*." [35] At first glance these words sound quite innocuous. When viewed within the context of the discussion of the meaning of the term "biblical theology" for Ritschl, however, they take on considerable importance. For on the meaning of the word "obtained" (*schöpfe*) depends much about Ritschl's basic ideas about the role of the Bible in theology, and thus the precise definition of "biblical theology".

Two reservations must be overcome. The first is that Ritschl does not actually use the term "biblical theology" in the paragraph referred to, and in part cited, above. The second reservation concerns the fact that the work from which the quotation is taken, Instruction in the Christian Religion, is by no means an "academic work". Can such stress be placed upon such a "popular" piece of writing ? [36]

In response to the first reservation it need simply be said that Ritschl does not refer to "dogmatic theology" by name though this is clearly in view where discussion of the means of "obtaining" Christian doctrine is concerned. There is thus no reason to suppose that Ritschl's understanding of "biblical theology" is not also being considered at this point, given that the function of the Bible in theology is in question.

The second reservation can be countered if there is sufficient reason on the basis of other (more self-evidently "academic") writings to suppose that Ritschl did in fact complicate his understanding of "biblical theology" by demonstrating that he viewed it not simply as a historical discipline in the sense suggested by B.Weiss, i.e. that the base for this claim in the sources is broader than the quote from ICR. Though not as explicit as one would wish there is material in Ritschl's writings which demonstrates that this is indeed the case.

Ritschl refers a number of times in his works to the Bible as the "*Quelle*" (source) for Christian theology. It is essential to determine in what sense he means this. At the start of §4 in the introduction to *R u V II* he states: "*Die heilige Schrift...bewährt sich als die Quelle für die positive Theologie durch die Auslegung*" [37]. §14 of the Dogmatics lectures deals exclusively with the question of "*Die Heilige Schrift die ausschließliche Quelle der theologischen Erkenntnis der christlichen Offenbarung"* [38]. Clearly, it is possible to claim that when Ritschl talks in terms of the biblical material being the "source" material for Christian theology he means no more than that it provides the "*Stoff*" for the dogmatician in the sense described above. But it is highly unlikely that this is what Ritschl does mean, given the way he develops his understanding of the Bible as the "*Quelle*" for theology.

In the paragraph of the Dogmatics lectures just referred to, for example, Ritschl shows that he believes there is a sense in which theology may only reproduce what is found in the biblical records [39]. This sounds staggering in the light of what has been looked at so far. "Biblical theology" had the task, as was shown, of presenting the religious ideas to be found in the Bible; the dogmatician then had the task of appraising and using the material. What had seemed at first a task to be undertaken responsibly, but with considerable freedom, now appears rather restricted.

Of course, the two views are in no way mutually exclusive if one permits an element of selection to be brought into play; the dogmatician may select from the biblical records (though the question of criteria must arise) but cannot begin elsewhere than the Bible for her/his material. In that sense, one can only reproduce what is found in the biblical records.

Ritschl does not introduce this element of selectivity at the level of methodology into his presentation, though it lies implicit in his appeal to the Reformation tradition as the background against which he sets about his task as a theologian (on which basis, a key role is granted to the Apostle Paul) [40].

What is clearly not intended by the reference is that one may not creatively reinterpret biblical ideas. The whole of *R u V III* is proof enough of this. Indeed, it is precisely the historical dimension brought into critical reflection upon Christian doctrine by Schleiermacher - but not seen to the fullest extent even by Schleiermacher himself - which demands the creative reinterpretation of religious ideas in Christianity [41].

The question of the nature of the continuity between that which is to be found in the biblical records and that which is to be understood now as the faith of Christians remains, however. Ritschl makes the claim of a clear line of continuity between the faith of the first Christians and the faith of present-day believers. One form in which this claim finds expression is Ritschl's understanding of the theologian's use of the Bible. One must therefore conclude that Ritschl's understanding of the Bible as the *"Quelle"* of Christian theology is more complex than it first appears.

Ritschl does not understand the Bible as *"Quelle"* in a simplistic way as the provider of all Christian understanding and language. Nor does he view it simply as the *"Stoff"* for the dogmatician, adopting thereby an understanding of "biblical theology" then current, that is, as the historical task preceding dogmatic/systematic theology. In other words, the question of the theological continuity between the first Christian believers and the present Christian community renders the task of the interpretation of the Bible a theological and not simply a historical or literary-critical task [42].

In summary, then, it can be seen that the topic of Ritschl as "biblical theologian" is important both for the understanding of Ritschl and for the history of the development of the discipline. Working back from that history it is possible to locate Ritschl between the two main traditions of understanding, "biblical theology" as a historical discipline and as a dogmatic discipline. Ritschl makes his approach from the perspective of his interest in seeing "biblical theology" as a historical discipline [43]. The historical approach which he adopts with regard to the history of Christian doctrine, and which he carries through logically into the sphere of biblical study, enables and causes him to treat "biblical theology" equally as a dogmatic discipline. The question of theological continuity being constantly in Ritschl's mind, he recognizes (positively expressed) the theological responsibility of biblical study and discloses (negatively expressed) the restrictions placed upon the historian by the nature of the biblical material.

1.3 Ritschl's Biblical Theology as New Testament Theology

In addition to the clarification about Ritschl's understanding of the term "biblical theology" with respect to some of his near contemporaries, Ritschl's understanding of the term must be explored further to show that the term "biblical" means in practice

"New Testament" rather than "the Bible". Ritschl as a biblical theologian is first and foremost a New Testament theologian.

Even citing quotations referred to in the previous section shows that Ritschl offers precisely this definition of "biblical theology" at a number of points. Thus: *"Die heilige Schrift, insbesondere das N(eue) T(estament), bewährt sich als die Quelle für die positive Theologie durch die Auslegung."* [44] Or again: *"...die biblische Theologie, insbesondere die des N(euen) T(estaments), (ist) nicht System oder Reihenfolge von* loci theologici...*sondern sie stellt eine Reihe religiöser Gedankenkreise dar."* [45]

To these quotations more can be added:

...direkt ist die Theologie berufen, zum Zwecke der Leitung des kirchlichen Unterrichts, die authentische Kenntnis der christlichen Religion und Offenbarung zu gewinnen; diese aber kann nur aus Urkunden geschöpft werden, welche der Stiftungsepoche der Kirche nahe stehen, und aus keinen anderen. [46]

And further:

...die Theologie, welche die christliche Religion aus den ursprünglichen Quellen zu erkennen hat, (ist) nur an die Schriften des Neuen Testaments gewiesen. [47]

Ritschl thus appears to be quite insistent on this point; the task of (Christian) theology as he sees it, and thus his own theology, depends upon and is concerned primarily with the New Testament. The great stress Ritschl placed upon the Old Testament is, however, widely known and cited [48]. It is thus imperative that some account be given of how the claim can be made that Ritschl strives to construct, in fact, a New Testament theology, when his stress upon the Old Testament seems equally strong.

It is important to observe that the stress upon the Old Testament is of only relative significance as far as the end-product of Christian theological formulation is concerned. Though it is undoubtedly true that Ritschl excludes the so-called "intertestamental literature" as of value to the interpretation of the New Testament [49], it should not on this basis be assumed that his theology is therefore based equally upon both Testaments. There appear to be, indeed, quite explicit denials that this is the case [50].

The complementary consideration to the above emphasis upon the primacy of the New Testament, in other words, is the acceptance that though both Testaments are seen as of greater importance than other literature of the corresponding periods, the Old Testament is to be seen as the necessarily exclusive background material for the understanding of the New. The two Testaments are not, however, of equal relevance. Distinction between the two Testaments is very necessary.

Denn direkt kann der Gedankeninhalt des Christentums nur aus dem NT geschöpft werden, und die Nichtunterscheidung beider Testamente im Schriftbeweis ist unstatthaft, weil auch ganz gleichlautende Begriffe oder Sätze an beiden Orten Glieder eines verschiedenen Zusammenhanges sind und weil die Religion Israels bei aller Verwandtschaft eben doch eine andere war, als das Christentum ist. [51]

The Old Testament is to be distinguished from the New, yet remains nevertheless important because "the religion of the prophets does not simply present the historical presupposition for Christianity, but at the same time provides the key for the right understanding of all Christian ideas." [52]. This is a lofty claim for Ritschl to make, and one which, when coupled with his stress upon the *canon* in isolation from other literature of the Old Testament and inter-testamental periods helps account for assumptions made about Ritschl's conservatism. The distinction made between the Testaments referred to above, when seen in the light of the manner in which Ritschl then goes on to express formally how he views this distinction, should force the reader to qualify such assumptions.

Ritschl sees the New Testament as the "source of knowledge" (*Erkenntnisquelle*) for Christianity, the Old Testament being the "auxiliary document" (*Hilfsurkunde*) [53]. In making this distinction Ritschl accepts that he is adopting a critical stance towards the Reformation heritage within which he seeks to operate. He trusts, however, that in claiming that theology only reproduces what is found in the biblical records, he is making no move beyond the Reformation. Indeed he is picking up what the Protestant tradition took as valuable from the early Catholic tradition.

The realization that Ritschl's biblical theology is in practice a New Testament theology is ultimately not affected by the stress he places upon the Old Testament. As has been shown, though he isolates the Old Testament as the exclusive background for the New Testament, the two Testaments are seen on two different levels. Ritschl's theology is therefore "biblical" in the sense that he refers to the whole of the Christian Bible (thus standing firmly in the Protestant tradition) in formulating his theology, whilst accepting that the New Testament carries an inevitable priority in the interpretation of the text as a whole for the purposes of a Christian theology.

Before taking the argument one step further and looking more particularly at how the christological core of Ritschl's theology relates to his understanding of theology as New Testament theology, it is necessary to summarize the findings of the last two sections, linking these findings together.

In the previous section it was seen how Ritschl's theology is to be undersood as "biblical" not simply in a historical sense. Ritschl is not interested in the Bible for the sake of gaining theological ideas second-hand. We noted also Ritschl's concern for the question of the theological continuity between the faith of the first Christian believers and Christians today. Already implicit in such a conclusion was a necessary preference for the *New* Testament, given that Ritschl is concerned with the faith of the followers of Jesus as reflected by the earliest communities (whose writings the texts of the New Testament are taken by Ritschl to be).

On the basis of further probing at the methodological level, it has been shown that Ritschl does indeed show a distinct preference for the New Testament writings in construing his theology as a "biblical theology".

Ritschl's biblical theology is therefore to be understood as an enterprise caught in the tension between being the exposition of the diverse religious ideas of the first Christians (New Testament theology as a historical discipline) and being the attempt to articulate a Christian theology for the present continuous with the faith of those first Christians (New Testament theology as a dogmatic discipline). Any reference to Ritschl's "theology", "biblical theology" or "New Testament theology" from this point on in the enquiry will inevitably require a recollection of that basic tension.

1.4 Ritschl's New Testament Theology as Christocentric Theology

Ritschl's theology has been called "christocentric" [54]. This is a correct designation but it requires clarification. For a recognition of the Christocentricity of Ritschl's theological system should not lead one to assume that the reasoning on Ritschl's part behind such an emphasis was merely a negative intention, that is, to exclude natural theology [55]. Rather, there is a positive side to the emphasis: Ritschl perceives the importance of the person of Jesus for Christian theology. This positive aspect must now be considered. The term "Christocentricity" will be viewed from both historical and dogmatic perspectives.

What does it mean to talk of "Christocentricity" from a "historical perspective"? For Ritschl it means that a significant role must be played in theology by the earthly Jesus, whose story as founder of the Kingdom of God and divine Son is narrated in the Gospels [56]. It means also noting a direct link between Jesus and the believer in the present. Though the Gospels are the writings of the earliest Christian communities [57] they ultimately do not, in Ritschl's estimation, prevent the present-day reader having Jesus available to him/her in the sense that (s)he can know what Jesus was like.

This link between Jesus and the present believer via the faith of the earliest Christians in Jesus is important for Ritschl. For in this link, Ritschl sees a guarantee that Christian theological formulation is grounded in and focussed upon Jesus. Christianity's religious ideas in some sense derive from Jesus; they are certainly influenced by his effect. The danger is ever-present that Christianity could lose its "concreteness" and its expression of faith become a flight of fancy. This will not happen, Ritschl maintains, if the earthly Jesus functions as a control for Christian theology. This aspect of Ritschl's theological methodology finds expression in two ways. First, he places emphasis upon the "historical Jesus" as distinct from the "ideal Christ" [58]. At this point, therefore, Ritschl enters the arena in which most nineteenth century theologians have met their end at the hand of their twentieth century critics, namely that of the Jesus of history/Christ of faith debate.

Second, this "historical norm" for theology is at one and the same time a historical norm for Christology. As a norm for Christology, this historical norm finds expression persistently and consistently in Ritschl's work. The following may serve as examples:

...every form of influence exerted by Christ must find its criterion in the historical figure presented by His life. [59]

Or again:

...it is necessary...that Christ's activity *in statu exaltationis* be conceived as the expression of the abiding influence of his historical manifestation. [60]

Already implicit in these observations is the answer to the question to what extent Ritschl views "Christocentricity" from a dogmatic perspective. For Ritschl has already introduced into the discussion the recognition that just as appeal to the earthly Jesus functions as a norm in Christology (a Christology which is thus historically controlled), so also the appeal to the earthly Jesus is the foundation upon which the construction of a *theo*logy is possible. Ritschl's theology is, in short, christologically-controlled [61].

The implications of this methodological approach of Ritschl's need to be spelt out. Drawing upon the findings of the previous two sections of this study, it becomes apparent that certain assumptions are being made about the New Testament, the Christian theologian's primary text. (For, as was noted, it is Ritschl's claim that the Christian theological task is a task of the theological interpretation of the Bible, especially the New Testament.) The Christian theologian's interpretative task is not to be understood simply as the isolation and articulation of a number of diverse religious ideas as found in the Bible, though theology does build upon these ideas. The matter at issue is the theological continuity between past expression of Christian faith and current expression. If, as we now see from further analysis of Ritschl's perception of the theological task, theology is to be understood as a christologically-controlled operation - this Christology in turn being historically-controlled - then two things follow. In Ritschl's estimation, the New Testament is able to provide reliable historical material about Jesus, for without this there would exist no possibility of perceiving the historical control upon Christology at work. This interest in historical material about Jesus lying behind the Gospel tradition should, however, be kept separate from the task of "biblical theology" understood as a historical discipline in the sense used in II.1.2 above. For the latter may still be seen simply as the recovery of the religious ideas of the first Christian communities (as indeed it is so seen by Ritschl [62]) independent of the question whether there is historically reliable material about Jesus available as part of the tradition incorporating those ideas [63]. An interest in the "historical Jesus" is required once the theological importance of the earthly Jesus is maintained [64]. In other words, Ritschl undoubtedly places himself to some extent in the camp of the "Quest of the Historical Jesus" in the sense that his theological stance commits him to an interest in what can be known historically about Jesus.

The question which will occupy us throughout this study is whether Ritschl's position is *in fact* so neat and tidy. If it is, then it would seem that his position is not tenable today even in modified form. The bankruptcy of many "Quests" and the persistent unclarity about what data about Jesus in the New Testament may be deemed historically reliable appear to render Ritschl's position highly problematic.

If Ritschl's position is not as neat as these first discoveries indicate, then the places where Ritschl can be seen doing theology related to but not directly dependent on the findings of historical research may well be the places his approach can be taken up once more.

One thing at least is clear; when one begins to respect the approach adopted by Ritschl - the biblical character of his theology, its New Testament focus, its Christocentricity - the importance of the Gospel material and Ritschl's use of it in his theology cannot pass unnoticed.

To summarize, then, the question of the christocentric character of Ritschl's theology subdivides into two separate considerations: the historical character of his Christology; and the christological character of his theology. Both rely ultimately upon the use made of the Gospel tradition, particularly with regard to the extent to which one is able to isolate from them historically reliable material about Jesus. How Ritschl uses the Gospels to construct a "picture of Jesus" and what sort of "picture" he produces feature as the focal point of this present study (II.3 and III). Prior to that it is necessary to examine Ritschl's New Testament study as an integral part of his overall undertaking as a theologian, and to consider, in the light of that general survey, how his work on the Gospels features as part of it.

1.5 Ritschl as a New Testament Scholar

1.5.1. Introduction

Having specified in general terms the sources which figure as the basis of the present enquiry and examined with reference to them Ritschl's theology as christocentric New Testament theology, it is now necessary to be more specific and focus upon the New Testament work relevant to an understanding of his theology. This section, therefore, is an introduction to Ritschl's writings either exclusively on New Testament topics, or at least including some reference to a New Testament theme. It will be of major interest throughout this survey to locate these writings in Ritschl's overall development and to adumbrate some lines along which later discussion of his "picture of Jesus" might develop.

What follows is in some ways a literary biography. It is, however, incomplete, particularly since the focus of attention rests heavily upon the earlier period of Ritschl's career, the period in which the works of most immediate interest were written. It is also incomplete because it does not look at the entire corpus in any given period. Yet the undertaking is biographical in the sense that it seeks not to view the works in isolation from Ritschl's overall intellectual development.

As in part a biographical undertaking, the survey to be conducted draws heavily upon Otto Ritschl's biography of his father, Albrecht. It has rightly become commonplace to accept that biographical reference to Ritschl must come to terms with Otto Ritschl's work [65]. The survey does, however, seek to make a relatively independent judgment based on Ritschl's writings. In this respect it strives to be more analytical than Otto Ritschl seems to have been able to be about his father's work [66]. As becomes clear, an assumption that is often made about Ritschl - that he moved from New Testament study to systematics [67] - is only a half-truth. Such an assumption attaches too much significance to the titles of the academic posts held by Ritschl and pays too little heed to the content of his writings throughout the whole of his academic career and to such attendant facts as the date of his first Dogmatics lectures (1853) and his last New Testament lectures (Introduction 1871 and Theology 1888) [68]. If, as this study attempts to suggest, Ritschl's overall understanding of the nature of the task of Christian theology better integrates the disciplines of biblical study and dogmatics than is often supposed, then the assumption referred to above may prove to be at best misleading and at worst contributing to a serious misconstrual of what Ritschl was trying to achieve.

1.5.2   Up to 1850

Ritschl went to Tübingen in 1845. It is at this point in Ritschl's career that it is most fitting to begin. For even though Ritschl had already spend periods of study in Bonn (1839-41), Halle (1841-3), Berlin (1843-5) and Heidelberg (February-August 1845), it was on his arrival in Tübingen that Ritschl reached his own "promised land" [69]. F.C.Baur continued to be a key figure in New Testament studies at this time, having turned his attention to the Gospel literature since 1844 after first making an impression upon the academic world with his work in the fields of Pauline studies, the philosophy of religion and Christian doctrine [70]. Ritschl had first come across Baur's work two years previously and been much impressed [71]. From Baur he had picked up the importance of historical understanding [72]. There is no reason to suppose that Ritschl ever lost this basic perception emerging in his thinking in his early twenties, despite his "break with Baur" some time in the mid 1850s [73]. Though the significant break with Baur occurred over a question in which historical considerations featured prominently - the question of continuity and normativity in Christian theology - the importance of historical considerations for both men cannot be understated. Indeed, it was Ritschl's firm conviction that he was being more true to Baur's own emphasis upon historical understanding than Baur himself [74].

The move to Tübingen can be regarded as significant as it represented Ritschl's clear preference for the new movement in New Testament studies emanating from there. The move opened him up, in short, to still greater influence from the Tübingen School, a "member" of which, in the late 1840s at least, he can be said to have been [75]. The immediate influence of Baur upon Ritschl after the latter's move to Tübingen was of a quite specific nature. As Baur himself was working on the Gospels, producing his three-part treatment of the Gospel of John entitled *"Ueber die Composition und den Charakter des johanneischen Evangeliums"* for the *Theologische Jahrbücher* for 1844, Ritschl was drawn to the Gospel material himself. His first major published work, his *Habilitationsschrift*, appeared a matter of months after his arrival in Tübingen and dealt with a Gospel topic.

Ritschl soon rejected the central thesis of the work in question *Das Evangelium Marcions und das kanonische Evangelium des Lucas* (Tübingen 1846). Though he explored further the possibility that Marcion may indeed have preserved a more original version of Luke in his own canon after 1846 [76], it was not a thesis which could stand too much scrutiny. Ritschl therefore soon accepted that Volckmar's work on Luke rendered his own thesis highly questionable [77]. The 1846 work is, however, important in a number of respects. It displays the extent to which Ritschl was already concerned both with some key questions of New Testament study (especially the study of the Gospels) and questions of ultimate dogmatic importance, even if somewhat indirectly. There is therefore in this early work material of relevance for this present study.

Four aspects can be highlighted: i) Ritschl accepts the argument for Matthean priority [78]. As will become clear, this fact is of particular significance in the question of how he establishes a "picture of Jesus" with which to work; ii) Ritschl makes some important observations on the character of the Gospel material. Of particular importance is his observation that the Gospels are "in no way simply historical documents" (*gar nicht rein historische Dokumente*) [79]. This must be looked at in detail in the next section of this present study, in particular with respect to the questions of what precisely Ritschl meant by this observation and whether he remained consistent in his application of the observation throughout his career; iii) The implicit, but consistent, concern to locate material in the Gospels pertinent to the "Quest of the Historical Jesus" should be stressed [80]. Though it proves not to be Ritschl's intent to write a "Life of Jesus", two questions nevertheless become both legitimate and necessary. First, there is the question whether this had *always* been Ritschl's understanding. Second, there is the question what effect any different understanding of, or ambiguous attitude to, what the Gospels might yield in the way

30

of historical material about Jesus might have had on Ritschl's construal of the relationship between historical-critical study of the New Testament and Christian theology at this crucial point of contact, the problem of the historical Jesus; iv) More negatively, the denigration of the third Gospel, though tied to the rejected central thesis, can be perceived in the work. It could be argued that the third Gospel never received its full value in Ritschl's work, and that this early work may have contributed in no small way to this state of affairs [81].

It is clear that much which is of relevance to this whole question of Ritschl's understanding of the relationship between biblical study and theology is left untouched if one begins to look at Ritschl from the perspective of works written in 1850, let alone 1857.

1.5.3   1850-1856

A major new chapter in Ritschl's development as a scholar undoubtedly began in 1850. In this year the study of the early centuries of the history of Christianity that Ritschl had been working on for some years was published under the title *Die Entstehung der altkatholischen Kirche*. The general drift of the argument is now well-known; rather than Catholic Christianity being the product of a synthesis of Jewish- and Gentile-Christianity, it is to be seen solely as a development of Gentile Christianity. Clearly it is F.C.Baur's basic conception of the emergence of Catholic Christianity that is being opposed here. What is striking, however, is the extent to which the thesis which Ritschl develops is still dependent upon Baur's basic terms of reference. It was not, in other words, until the second edition of 1857 that Ritschl felt in a position to be able to break free from Baur in this respect. And even then - and this should be stressed - Ritschl still set off from the perception brought to the fore by Baur, namely that there was a basic tension at the heart of Christianity from its most primitive period, a tension caused - for want of better labels - by a distinction between "Petrine" and "Pauline" tendencies or traditions [82].

The seeds are nevertheless already being planted for a substantial break with Baur in this work. Ritschl is paving the way for the more penetrating analysis of early Christianity's inherent complexity which came in the later edition. Though some reserve may be felt about the manner in which Ritschl ultimately finds his way through that complexity, his contribution to that basic discovery, and the seeds of that contribution as found in this 1850 work, need highlighting [83]. As a study of the earliest period of Christianity's history, therefore, it can rightly be classed as monumental. It draws upon a wide range of material, dealing with the New Testament but then moving beyond it [84]. The work is subtitled "A Monograph in Church History and the History of Dogma" (*Eine kirchen- und dogmengeschichtliche Monographie*). As with much of Ritschl's work, however, precise classification, if not impossible, is ill-advised. For on the basis of Ritschl's emerging understanding of theology as a discipline - or more appropriately a collection of related disciplines - and in particular the application of historical insights to theological understanding, it is itself a theological work. This is the case because the history of doctrine, church history and biblical theology are all disciplines which use the techniques of historical work, dealing in ideas from the past, yet posing theological questions (seeking to be informed from the past). Inasmuch, therefore, as it deals in part with New Testament material it is of direct relevance to this present study providing essential clues to Ritschl's emergent New Testament theology. The main sections of interest are the introduction and the first two chapters of the work. Chapter Two would need to be followed up closely by an interpreter dealing with Ritschl's study of Paul. The introduction has much of historical interest (recording Ritschl's relationship to scholars of his own day).

Of prime significance for a study in Ritschl's use of the Gospels and in particular his encounter with the historical Jesus, however, is the first chapter of the work, entitled *Christus und das mosaische Gesetz* (Christ and the Mosaic Law). The precise extent to which this first chapter informs and provides source material for this present study will be looked at below (II.2.1). At this point it is necessary only to note that Ritschl places a chapter on Jesus at the head of his first major study on the history of early Christianity and that the chapter is very much concerned with the question of establishing what the "earthly Jesus" (though such terminological clarity is naturally not to be found in the chapter itself) was like, and saw his task to be.

Striking is the restriction under which the enquiry is placed because of its angle of approach. Because the chapter deals with *Christus **und das mosaische Gesetz*** (my emphasis), there is an implicit assumption at work in Ritschl's presentation that this issue - the issue of the Mosaic Law - was essential for Jesus himself. More must be said on this issue when the 1857 edition is considered [85]. For the time being it is important to stress only that Ritschl is at least presenting the material as an attempt to begin from the Jesus of history and grasp how Christianity developed in relation to him, posing the question where any break in continuity may have occurred. This observation is valid even when one allows for the fact that Ritschl may have been guilty of "reading back" a later set of questions into the situation of Jesus himself in his attempt to understand the nature of the continuity.

In the following year Ritschl published an essay which is of the utmost importance as far as the relationship between his New Testament study and his theological development is concerned. Entitled *"Ueber den gegenwärtigen Stand der synoptischen Evangelien"*, the essay does exactly what its title suggests; it reviews current opinions on the study of the Synoptic Gospels [86]. The main relevance of the essay is that it reveals Ritschl's shift of position on the Synoptic Problem from the Griesbach hypothesis, as favoured by Baur and the core of the Tübingen School, to the argument for Marcan priority [87]. In spite of the significance of this shift in Ritschl's thinking, this essay has received all too little attention [88]. Indeed, the lack of attention to it has in all probability contributed to the customary misrepresentation of Ritschl described earlier in this study. For as soon as the impact of the change of mind on Ritschl's part which the essay reveals becomes clear, its importance cannot be overstated. Tuckett's argument about the ground upon which the battle over the Synoptic Problem was fought in the mid-nineteenth century can be allowed to stand (i.e. it was a literary-critical battle and did not draw upon the dogmatic presuppositions of the respective combatants). But the fact remains that internal enquiries in the field of New Testament criticism nevertheless carried with them dogmatic implications [89]. As long as the disciplines of biblical and dogmatic theology were seen in such close interrelationship (as was the case despite the ambiguities already referred to above in section II.1.2), the fruits of New Testament research were bound to have implications for the Christian scholar seeking to construct a theology. Such was the case with Ritschl's shift of position on the Synoptic Problem.

1.5.4   1857-1860

The most direct and significant implication for Ritschl of this change of mind on the Synoptic Problem became evident when the second edition of *Die Entstehung der altkatholischen Kirche* appeared in 1857. In the chapter in which this present enquiry has particular interest (ch.1), the New Testament source-material is made use of in a distinctly different way by Ritschl. Though still entitled *Christus and das mosaische Gesetz*, and though still much concerned with the question of essential continuity between Jesus and Paul with respect to the question of attitudes to the Mosaic Law, the picture of Jesus now presented in the chapter differs from that of the 1850 edition. More importantly for our discussion, the difference seems to be directly related to the different use made of the source-material. Mark, not Matthew, has become the normative Gospel in Ritschl's presentation. Though Matthew remains the most frequently cited Gospel, it is Mark which now sets the tone and controls the presentation [90].

As a result of this shift (see further below II.3.2), it must be asked whether Ritschl is already moving significantly beyond the framework within which the chapter is set. In other words, though the chapter purports to deal with the question of Jesus and the Law, the move to Marcan normativity brings about a corresponding shift of focus in Ritschl's understanding of the figure of Jesus which is great enough to challenge the understanding which the framework of the first part of the work demands. At issue, then, is much more than a shift of focus on the Synoptic Problem and its implications lying somewhere in the background of Ritschl's thinking. Here the reader encounters the direct interplay between theological disciplines in a striking way.

Where does the framework within which Ritschl casts his understanding of Christianity's formative period come from? Initially it appeared to come from the Apostle Paul. Church history and doctrine are seen in interrelationship within Ritschl's method. Now, however, Ritschl's close inspection of the New Testament through the medium of the historical-critical approach (which he never detaches from an awareness of the theological responsibility accompanying such enquiry [91]) causes this Pauline angle of approach to be challenged by an understanding of what constituted the heart of Jesus' message. Gospel criticism, in other words, has led Ritschl to modify his understanding of Christianity's essence, an understanding which Ritschl believes derives from Jesus himself. The Kingdom of God rather than freedom from the Law is now the essence of Christianity. In this procedure, New Testament (particularly Gospel) study serves as a control for Church history and doctrine.

Jodock contends that there is little essential difference between the two pictures of Jesus in the respective editions of the work [92]. As will be shown in more detail below, this is correct only up to a point. Because Jodock's concern is to make an assessment of the whole of this specific work - an assessment which he makes very adequately - and not to delve behind the significance of seemingly minor changes, let alone explore the reasons for such changes, he is also not compelled to account further for the great leap which occurs in Ritschl's "picture of Jesus" from these two editions to that incorporated by Ritschl into *R u V*. In Ritschl's *magnum opus*, the question of obedience to and freedom from the Law has disappeared if not wholly from view, then at least from the centre of the stage. At this point I begin to antici-pate my conclusion. It appears the shift of focus on the Synoptic Problem has led to a significant change in Ritschl's understanding of Jesus, an understanding which itself proves decisive enough for him to change tack in the course of constructing his theology.

Turning to shorter writings in the period currently under consideration, it should be noted that the bulk of Ritschl's writing followed a similar pattern after 1857 to the period up to the publication of the second edition of *Die Entstehung der altkatholis-chen Kirche*. That is, Ritschl wrote mostly on topics in Church history [93]. The notable exception to this general pattern was the publication in 1859 of the Latin text of Ritschl's *Antrittsvorlesung* to the position of Professor Ordinarius in Bonn on the subject of the wrath of God [94]. As one would expect, this work offers little which is of direct relevance to this present enquiry, the New Testament interest Ritschl displays being primarily in the writings of Paul [95]. In one respect, however, it is important. As Otto Ritschl observes, the structure of *R u V* is here directly prefigured

[96]. The triadic structure of history of dogma - biblical theology - systematic theology is here seen used explicitly in actual practice.

1.5.5   1861-1873

The writings produced by Ritschl in the period from 1861 until the publication of *R u V II* include a more varied selection of material than in the two periods just considered. Writings on the Epistle to the Hebrews (1866) and the New Testament references to the saving significance of Jesus' death (1863) mingle with lengthy essays on dogmatics and the history of dogma [97].

Of particular significance for the present discussion, however, are the two essays of 1861 and 1862 bearing the titles *"Ueber geschichtliche Methode in der Erforschung des Urchristenthums* and *Einige Erläuterungen zu dem Sendschreiben 'Die historische Kritik und das Wunder'."* The former essay is particularly helpful in that in it Ritschl expounds the nature of his disagreements with Baur's attempts to explore Christianity's early history "purely historically" (*"rein historisch"*). In opposing Baur, Ritschl reveals more clearly how his own thought is developing. The essay is, in effect, a methodological "stopping-place" *en route* to *Rechtfertigung und Versöhnung*. Though the structure of the later work had, as noted above, been in Ritschl's mind for some time, it was clear that much more work had to be done both with regard to methodology and content.

In the essay, Ritschl enters into debate with the anonymous writer of an article published in the *Historische Zeitschrift* entitled *"Die Tübinger historische Schule"* and takes issue with the understanding of the methods and aims of the Tübingen School as presented in that article. In essence, Ritschl accuses Baur of not being historical enough and following Hegel too closely [98]. As far as Ritschl can see, the concreteness of Jesus as founder of a religion can be nothing but a problem for Baur the Hegelian philosopher of religion [99].

In the course of his critique, Ritschl makes frequent appeal to the contrast between the "ideal" and the "historical" Christ [100]. It is the latter which Ritschl feels is the more accurate and appropriate focus for the employment of historical research into early Christianity. Baur has, he maintains, simply not located the "historical" Christ as accurately as is possible [101].

In writing the essay, however, Ritschl was launching himself into a debate from which he did not emerge unscathed [102]. Furthermore, the realm into which the discussion moved once the anonymous writer had disclosed his identity in a riposte was not a wholly fruitful one [103]. There were, in other words, other aspects in the matters raised by Ritschl's essay which could have been taken up [104].

Be that as it may, it is perhaps no accident that the question of the miracles in the Gospels should arise at this point. Nor is the discussion without significance for an assessment of Ritschl's handling of the Gospel material. For the discussion about the philosophical dimensions to the question of miracles discloses that Ritschl had failed at this point adequately to come to terms with the New Testament source-material. Though dealt with in this exchange with Zeller on the philosophical - or seemingly at times, pseudo-philosophical - plane [105], the question remains of what understanding of the material's content Ritschl adopts and how he incorporates that understanding into his theology. This is especially the case given that Ritschl leaves the reader feeling that he resorts to some special pleading in his second essay. For in pressing the distinction between "religious" and "scientific" knowledge still further Ritschl is running the risk of creating a fissure between a strand of thinking which borders on historicism (or historical positivism) and a strand of thinking which renders the religious realm wholly detached from the historical world. At issue, in other words, is how the two strands are kept in tension without dissolving into one or the other.

The problem is that of the relationship between theology and history. It is therefore not surprising that the question of the "historical Jesus" should figure in the course of the debate between Zeller and Ritschl. Though raised at this juncture at a rather distant and somewhat abstract level, it is nevertheless clear that the debate has consequences for the understanding of Ritschl's approach to the problem of the historical Jesus. For here some key methodological issues are being clarified prior to Ritschl's embarking on the task of writing a New Testament theology in which the "historical Jesus" plays a significant part. Here, in other words, can be found the roots in the abstract of the reasons for the major disparity between Ritschl's "pictures of

Jesus" of 1850 and 1857, and the "picture(s) of Jesus" he builds into _Rechtfertigung und Versöhnung_.

It will also be clear by now that these essays have a direct bearing on the understanding of Ritschl's theological use of the Gospel material. For Ritschl is placing great stress upon the fact that the _"historische Christus"_ is determinable and can thus function normatively for Christian theology. At the same time he is building into his method the proviso that a particular type of understanding - religious understanding - is necessary to perceive this Jesus properly.

How such a method should be put into practice Ritschl did not reveal in published form until the publication of _R u V II_ and _R u V III_ in 1874. It is to these works that attention must now turn.

1.5.6   1874-1889

Even for an enquiry into Albrecht Ritschl's New Testament work, _Rechtfertigung und Versöhnung_ must figure prominently in the investigation. This is especially the case if, as is being maintained throughout this study, Ritschl's New Testament work is being viewed as more integrally a part of his theology than has often been thought. The point at issue in the understanding of _R u V II_ and _R u V III_, therefore, is how the two volumes relate to each other; how, above all, the Christocentricity of Ritschl's theological system finds expression within his construal of the relationship between the volumes. For at this point is located Ritschl's construal of the relationship between the biblical and dogmatic aspects of the theological task.

It is unfortunate for our enquiry that there is little in the way of methodological exposition in _R u V_. The introductions to each of the three volumes, the prefaces of the respective editions and other relevant occasional writings (such as the essays of 1861, 1862 and 1871 referred to above) barely provide sufficient clues to how Ritschl approaches his theological undertaking. The clues provided are helpful, but not ultimately adequate for a full understanding of Ritschl's procedure. Inference from actual practice is therefore necessary to uncover Ritschl's method.

The first thing to note is that Ritschl originally conceived the second and third volumes of _R u V_ as a single work. They became two volumes purely because of their sheer size [106]. This is at once significant and ironic. It is significant because it adds weight to the belief that Ritschl's New Testament work is to be seen as an integral part of the constructive piece of theology he produces. It is ironic because Ritschl is so often considered on the basis of *R u V III*. This is especially the case in the English-speaking world, where *R u V II* remains untranslated.

Nevertheless, there does seem to be a clear division between the tasks of the two works, a division which Ritschl himself is perhaps guilty of underplaying. This essential division - as was noted above (II.1.2 and 1.3) - is between *R u V II* as belonging to the discipline of "biblical theology" and *R u V III* as being "systematic/ dogmatic theology".

There are two significant aspects to the overall undertaking which are common to each volume, however. These are : biblicism and Christocentricity. Taking the former first, it is possible to point to critics of Ritschl's, old and new, who have drawn attention to his "biblicism" in a very negative way. Troeltsch, for example, had little time for this conservative Lutheran dimension to Ritschl's thinking [107]. More recently, Morgan, taking up Troeltsch's criticism, refers to Ritschl's "residual biblicism" as if it were something which belonged to a bygone era [108]. It is, however, important to explore the nature of Ritschl's "biblicism".

On examination, Ritschl's "biblicism" proves to be an attempt to stress the normativity of the New Testament in Christian theology in precisely the sense described in the sections devoted to the understanding of Ritschl's theology as "biblical theology" above. His biblicism may thus be understood as part and parcel of his reaction to Baur, his foresight in drawing out the implications of the position which Baur had reached, and the resulting choice to head in another direction [109]. If volumes two and three of *R u V* are thus viewed as a New Testament theology, a Christian theology formulated with a respect for the theological significance of the New Testament canon, then Ritschl's undertaking is perhaps better understood.

When tied with the second emphasis of the two volumes in question - Christocentricity - Ritschl's biblicism reveals itself as the theological interest in the New Testament's presentation of Jesus. For the christocentric focus of Ritschl's theology is, as was shown above (II.1.4), an interest in the earthly Jesus. And though

Ritschl, by virtue of his chronological place in the development of the study of the New Testament, was in no position to unravel the complexities of the problem of the historical Jesus, the position he takes up must be located in the course of the development of theological (esp. christological) understanding from Strauss to Kähler.

Ritschl stressed the importance of the earthly Jesus, yet rejected the writing of a life of Jesus. He placed an equal emphasis upon the importance of the New Testament canon, yet seemingly left some room also for diversity within the canon. In this way, Ritschl takes up a position as an immediate precursor of Kähler in showing his interest in the "canonical" Jesus [110].

In the light of these considerations, it is not at all surprising that *R u V II* should open with a chapter on Jesus and his effects on the first community. Indeed, it is of decisive methodological significance that the first paragraph of the chapter (paragraph 5, entitled *"Die Verkündigung des Reiches Gottes"*) should take up material from the Gospels to locate, in the ministry and message of Jesus, a key concept of Ritschl's own theology. Immediately, therefore, the procedure Ritschl aims to follow is clear; from the earthly Jesus to Christian theology. Of the six remaining paragraphs in that same opening chapter, two more (paragraphs 7 and 11) are devoted to further aspects of Jesus' own message and self-understanding as Ritschl interprets them on the basis of the Gospel material.

Ritschl's understanding of the task of New Testament theology is more complex, however, than the rather naive construal of his method just offered - from earthly Jesus to Christian theology - might suggest. His theology does not collapse into Christology any more than his Christology collapses into a record of a few known facts about Jesus. Nor does his theology, understood as New Testament theology, dissolve into a reading of the Gospels alone. That *R u V III* incorporates much more material than its christological core in chapter six is ample demonstration of the first of the observations just made. Furthermore, the coverage of Pauline and Johannine material in *R u V II* - in paragraphs 6, 13, 27, 28, 34-37 and 39-40 - shows that Ritschl seeks to do justice to the whole New Testament.

The way Ritschl construes the Christocentricity he believes should necessarily feature at the heart of one's understanding of Christian theology [111] does, however, require that one focus upon the Gospel material in the manner announced by the opening chapter of *R u V II*. On this basis, a tension within Ritschl's undertaking in these two volumes inevitably results. Interestingly, it is a tension similar to that which may be determined as emerging in E57. In short, Ritschl sets out with a Pauline framework and yet is compelled to adapt his procedure, if not his structure, because of competing claims between the "normativity of Jesus" for theology and the content of the "Pauline-Lutheran" tradition within which Ritschl stands and seeks to work [112].

To highlight Ritschl's inevitable focus upon the Gospels is in no way to be sufficiently specific about his use of the Gospels. This must feature as an aspect of the present enquiry [113]. It is important at this point to note only the general terms in which the discussion will take place, by observing the bare outline of Ritschl's use of the Gospels in *R u V II* and *R u V III*. In comparison to Ritschl's chapters on Jesus in the two editions of E50 and E57, it is striking to what extent *R u V II* and *R u V III* make use of the Fourth Gospel in putting together a picture of Jesus constructed on the basis of a historical-critical reading of the Gospels [114]. The presence of the Fourth Gospel in ch.6 of *R u V III* is particularly noticeable. Here it is not so much a matter of what is explicit, as what lies in the background of the presentation [115]. Ritschl fully respects the fact, however, that the Kingdom of God - which he himself has placed in such a prominent position in his own theological system - was not a key idea for John [116]. It is thus clear that the Synoptic evidence is vital as Ritschl begins his exposition of the biblical material in *R u V II* [117].

The outline of this present enquiry is therefore becoming clear. What is required is an account of how Ritschl can move from the two "pictures of Jesus" found in E50 and E57, themselves separated by a shift of position on the Synoptic Problem and articulated under the constraint of a pre-conceived framework (i.e. the question of Jesus and the Law), to a "picture" or "pictures" of Jesus built into a (New Testament) theology, where there would appear to be not only a tension between a focus upon the Gospel material and the Pauline material, but also a tension within the use of the Gospel material itself.

The question thus posed is not formulated simply from a present-day perspective (that is: "how can a historical-critical approach to the use of the Gospel material in Christian theology justify such widespread use of the Fourth Gospel ?") - though this question must ultimately arise too. It is, rather, a question arising from Ritschl's own reading and construal of the Gospel material (that is: "how can I depend heavily on John when John does not make much use of a symbol I perceive to have been central for Jesus and for Christian theology ?"). In short, how does Ritschl reach the theology of _R u V_ as far as his Gospel work and understanding of the Christocentricity of Christian theology are concerned ?

_R u V_ was to go through two further editions. The third volume of the work went to a fourth printing. Significant changes can be seen to exist between the editions, changes which have, to some extent, already been subjected to detailed study [118]. During this period, in which Ritschl's theology was proving irresistible to many [119], Ritschl himself moved on. He still worked on New Testament topics and small-scale works in the field of Church History [120]. But Ritschl was also working more explicitly in the realms of the philosophy of religion, practical theology and above all on his three-volume History of Pietism [121]. He thus continued to retain an interest in the broadest possible spectrum of theological disciplines.

Three things are clear from this survey:

i) The interrelationship of Ritschl's historical research, New Testament work, philosophical enquiry and systematic theology may at once be both more consistent and more complex than is often imagined. He kept as much interest in each discipline as was realistically possible;

ii) The New Testament interest is certainly not to be relegated to the margins of Ritschl's overall undertaking. If it is as integral to his theology as the methodological enquiry conducted above and the literary-biographical sketch just concluded indicate, then it needs more adequate treatment than has been the case;

iii) As far as the particular aspect of Ritschl's New Testament work which is of direct interest to this enquiry - Ritschl's work on the Gospels - is concerned, it would seem clear that the primary period of interest is 1846-1874. Only in a heavily qualified sense can it be deemed that Ritschl moved from being a Church historian and/or

42

biblical scholar to being a systematic theologian. It is pertinent to suggest, however, on the basis of the sketch undertaken, that the crucial fixed points in Ritschl's own theological development can be included within the timespan of 1846-1874.

1.5.7   Summary

To summarize: there are six fixed points which need to be highlighted. They are the years 1846, 1850, 1851, 1857, 1861-2 and 1874. 1846 was the year in which Ritschl published his first major work, and is found dealing with a Gospel topic - the Gospel of Luke - from a primarily literary perspective, yet with a clearly discernible underlying interest in material of relevance to the "Quest of the Historical Jesus". Of particular importance is that he answers the Synoptic Problem in the same way as Baur, that is, with the Griesbach hypothesis. In 1850 Ritschl's work on earliest Christianity's history was published. In it, his chapter on Jesus depended heavily upon the Gospel of Matthew. A year later, however, Ritschl's work on the Gospels was to undergo a major change of direction. For in 1851 he published an essay on the Synoptic Gospels, in which he declared his move from support for the Griesbach Hypothesis to support for the argument for Marcan priority. The effect of this major change of direction became particularly evident in 1857 when, in E57, the chapter on Jesus underwent significant alteration as a direct result of the Marcan material being brought more to the fore. The years 1861 and 1862 found Ritschl in debate with Eduard Zeller in connection with the very essence of historical study and its appropriateness as a tool for understanding Christianity's origins. In the course of this debate, conducted in large part at a very theoretical level, important aspects of Ritschl's emerging methodology are evident, particularly with respect to his understanding of Christology and thus, by implication, his understanding of the Gospels as used in Christology. By 1874 Ritschl had seen fit to give full expression to his theology in its final form. Though altered in detail, in essence the methodology used and the general thinking presented did not alter thereafter. The findings of studies undertaken in various theological disciplines are thus found crystallized into a single system in *R u V*. In this system, the role played by the Fourth Gospel, in particular in *R u V III*, should be noted.

The study of Ritschl as a New Testament scholar is thus the study of someone who strove to construct a theology with constant reference to the New Testament. The importance attached by Ritschl to Christology demands that special attention be placed upon the study of the Gospels.

It would be wrong to maintain that a study of Ritschl's use of the Gospels in _R u V_ is an exhaustive study either of his use of the Gospels *per se* or of the New Testament in that work. It can, however, be claimed that a study of Ritschl's use of the Gospels in _R u V_ does focus upon a key aspect of Ritschl's theology and theological method given the christocentric focus of his theology and his understanding of the relationship between New Testament study and the overall theological task. It is now necessary to turn to Ritschl's Gospel work in more detail, beginning first with his understanding of the sources in terms of their genre and intent, before moving on to consider their content. In the latter case, the focus will be upon the christological interest in the Gospels which controls Ritschl's theological concerns.

2. GOSPEL STUDY AND THE QUEST FOR JESUS

2.1 Ritschl's Gospel Study: the Sources

Building on the earlier sections II.1.1 and 1.5, this brief introduction to the question of how Ritschl views the Gospels clarifies the particular source material which is of importance for the study of Ritschl's use of the Gospels in Christology. In short; where does one turn in order to become clear about what Ritschl thinks about the Gospels, and about how he uses them to create a picture of Jesus for his theology ?

The main primary material which should be consulted in the consideration of the question posed numbers eight works in particular. They are, listed in chronological order, as follows.

1. *Das Evangelium Marcions und das kanonische Evangelium des Lucas*. This 1846 work is of particular importance for its second half (*Zweites Buch* pp172-301), in which, though built upon an unsound thesis which Ritschl himself later rejected,

44

Ritschl reveals aspects of his early views upon the nature of the Gospel material. Abandonment of a particular thesis need not, of course, entail alteration of an overall verdict upon the Gospels as literary and/or historical documents. Part of the task of interpreting Ritschl from the perspective of his work on the Gospels is thus to determine these early views and to see if he altered them or remained consistent in them. The significance in the light of his own "quest for Jesus" can then be assessed.

2. *Die Entstehung der altkatholischen Kirche*. The first edition of this important work (1850) contains Ritschl's first major attempt to treat the question of the details of Jesus' life and teachings. The first chapter of the work - in which the attempt is made (E50 pp27-52) - is thus of immense importance. It is related to Ritschl's 1846 work on Marcion and Luke, in that it starts from the premiss of the historicity of the Matthean portrayal [122].

3. *Ueber den gegenwärtigen Stand der Kritik der synoptischen Evangelien*. The importance of this 1851 essay of Ritschl's has already been mentioned. The contents of the essay have a considerable bearing upon the attempts made by Ritschl to piece together a picture of Jesus. The move to the argument for Marcan priority as a solution to the Synoptic Problem, in other words, carried with it major implications for Ritschl's approach to the "quest for Jesus" and the "picture" he creates. It is necessary both to appreciate the significance of the essay as a turning-point for Ritschl and to pay attention to the content of the section dealing with the Gospel of Mark (pp25-43 in the 1893 edition).

4. *Die Entstehung der altkatholischen Kirche*. The first chapter of the second edition of this work (1857) brings the full effects of the 1851 essay to expression (E57 pp27-51). The seemingly normative role now played by the Gospel of Mark (in contrast to Ritschl's thinking in 1846 and 1850) must be explored and its importance for Ritschl's later work assessed.

5. *Rechtfertigung und Versöhnung: Band II* (1874; 3rd ed. 1889). As this present study dwells heavily upon the findings of closer examination of this particular volume of the three-volume work *R u V*, it is inevitable that major sections of this work will figure prominently in the enquiry. Of especial relevance are, in ch.1, paragraphs 5-7 and 11; in ch.2, paragraph 13; in ch.3, paragraph 28; and in ch.4, paragraph 31. In these paragraphs Ritschl's understanding of the Gospel material, in particular with respect to his understanding of the person of Jesus, becomes evident.

6. *Rechtfertigung und Versöhnung: Band III* (1874; 3rd ed. 1888 = 4th ed. 1895; E.T. Justification and Reconciliation). Chapter 6 of this, the third volume of *R u V* (J & R III paragraphs 44-50, pp385-484), is concerned with Christology. Given Ritschl's method in Christology (i.e. using a historical norm), the fruits of the historical-criticial work undertaken by Ritschl are here built into the theological assessment being made of the life of Jesus. Simultaneously, as we shall see, the theological interest which controls the entire work causes Ritschl to exceed the bounds of his own approach. On either level, however, the sixth chapter is of decisive significance.

7. *Unterricht in der christlichen Religion* (1875; 3rd ed. 1886; E.T. Instruction in the Christian Religion). This more popular work of Ritschl's is a helpful summary of his position on a number of fronts. The first section of the work (paragraphs 4-25) is especially useful, dealing with the topic "The Doctrine of the Kingdom of God". Other paragraphs are also important (e.g. 44f), as are the footnotes to the whole work, which provide Ritschl's biblical support for the positions he takes up.

8. *Biblische Theologie des Neuen Testaments*. Ritschl's lectures delivered throughout the period in which his three-volume *magnum opus* was coming to birth are naturally useful in that they provide information about Ritschl's emergent thinking. Clearly, the lectures of 1877-8 are but repetition of much that had already been published [123]. But their relevance is beyond question, particularly the second section of the work (paragraphs 11-24; pp107-232 in the Eck manuscript), in which Ritschl deals

with the proclamation of Jesus. Here, the material which must be gleaned somewhat piecemeal from the published material is found recorded in more sustained fashion.

From these eight works in particular, then, the reader of Ritschl is able to gain clarity both about Ritschl's stance with regard to the Gospels and his actual use of the Gospel material in the construction of his "picture of Jesus". Upon this foundation, therefore, it is now possible to build. The task must be one of probing this material, drawing upon subsidiary and more incidentally relevant sources where necessary, to present the two expository aspects of the enquiry: Ritschl on the Gospels, and Ritschl's "picture of Jesus".

2.2. The Gospels: their Genre and Purpose

What sort of texts are the Gospels ? Ritschl offers no simple, straightforward answer to this question. More precisely, he is most explicit in suggesting an answer in the earliest period in his academic career. As his career developed, however, he apparently saw no need to reflect upon the matter further. Ritschl's answer is thus to be found via an answer to the question "to what extent, in later life, does Ritschl deviate from the explicit understanding of the nature of the Gospel material suggested early in his career ?" This is a question to be answered on the basis of observation of how Ritschl uses the Gospels in practice.

The clearest expression Ritschl gives to his understanding of what the Gospels are is to be found in his work on Marcion and Luke, published in 1846. As if becoming a mouthpiece for the views of F.C.Baur, he comments on recent enquiry into the reliability of the Synoptic Gospels, noting that it had become clear *"dass diesselben gar nicht rein historische Dokumente zu liefern gesonnen waren, sondern ihre Sammlungen von Traditionen über das Leben Jesu bestimmten dogmatischen Partheitendenzen unterordneten"* [124]. Ritschl thus clearly takes up Baur's observation that the Synoptic Gospels are not simple, or simply, "historical documents" which record details about the life of Jesus in a neutral fashion. Admittedly, for the present-day reader, the nature of the unhistorical aspects of the Gospel literature is left insufficiently explored. That is to say: the absence of neutrality in the particular presentation of Jesus offered by each Synoptist (the *Tendenz* of each Synoptic Gospel) is not explored a) with respect to the question of the creation of new material or alteration of traditional material, or b) in terms simply of the selection of material. (In all probability the latter, rather than the former, is in view [125].) Nevertheless, Ritschl has at least acknowledged that the Gospels do not simply allow details of Jesus' life to be "read off" from them.

The question then arises whether Ritschl maintains this perception - itself acceptable to the present-day reader: it could indeed be said it is a prerequisite for a present-day critical reading of the Gospels - and, if so, how this affects his approach to Christology. For as has been shown already, it is important for Ritschl's method, that historical data be discernible in, or through, the Gospels. That is to say: the extent to which Ritschl could nevertheless "read off" historical data about the life of Jesus from the Gospels is both apparent and surprising. The tendency is evident in the first chapter of E50. The Gospel of Matthew is here used in a manner which to the present-day reader seems naively uncritical. Essentially an unpacking of the saying of Jesus recorded in Mt 5.17, the authenticity of which is not questioned, the chapter presents a Jesus in the Matthean mould, working on the assumption that Matthew's presentation of Jesus is historically reliable [126].

The possibility of questioning the authenticity of some of the Matthean material is by no means excluded by Ritschl. He thereby respects the fact that Matthew may have created some of the material in his Gospel. The one prime example of this in the chapter is, however, left unresolved by Ritschl. He thus suggests that Mt 19.9 is "either a momentary lapse on Jesus' part from his otherwise strictly consistent premiss" with regard to obedience to the Law or that its authenticity must be questioned [127]. What is clear is that Ritschl cannot bring himself at this point to conclude that Matthew's portrayal may be historically unreliable.

It would thus seem that though there is no reason for Ritschl to have altered the stance taken up in 1846 with respect to the nature of the Gospels, in the practical use of the Gospel material there remains the underlying assumption that there is more than adequate historical data available for the interpreter to be able to put together an impression of what constituted Jesus' teaching and character. This would seem only to confirm the speculation ventured earlier that the selection of the available material, rather than the specific creation of new material, is what determines the *Tendenz* of each Gospel [128].

The question whether Ritschl maintained his perception that the Gospels are not "purely historical documents" therefore receives a refined form; did this observation really have any effect at all on his use of the Gospels? The question is rendered more complex by developments in Ritschl's thought as recorded in the publications of the years 1851 and 1857. For included in his shift of position on the Synoptic Problem is a highly significant argument adduced in favour of Marcan priority. Rounding off a series of arguments for Marcan priority, Ritschl refers finally to Mark's "neutrality", its "dogmatic indifference" [129]. This is a telling expression. Ritschl seems here to show that either he fails to allow the full implications of his perception that the Gospels are not "purely historical documents" to take effect, or that he has changed his mind since 1846. For the Gospel of Mark at least, the *Tendenz* of the Gospel has no real significance. The explicitness cannot be overstressed. Ritschl states quite categorically:

> *Freilich entbehrt das Evangelium eines solchen dogmatischen Typus, wie*
> *ihn Matthäus und Lukas unverkennbar tragen, aber wenn man bedenkt, wie*
> *in diesen Schriften gerade die dogmatischen Tendenzen zur Verdunkelung*
> *oder Verkürzung des geschichtlichen Bildes Christi beitragen, so kann die*
> *vorgebliche dogmatische Indifferenz durchaus nicht als Merkmal sekundären*
> *Charakters, sondern nur als Kennzeichen höheren geschichtlichen Werthes*
> *erscheinen* [130].

Ritschl thus takes up the label of "dogmatic indifference" and claims that if this is indeed the case with Mark, then it is a sign only of its historical reliability. He does consider too, however, that the Gospel of Mark may nevertheless have its own *Tendenz* and yet still be the most historically reliable Synoptic Gospel. For he still refers to the "dogmatic indifference" as "alleged" (*vorgeblich*).

There is thus a highly complicating factor being brought at this point into the discussion of the consistency of Ritschl's perception of the nature of the Gospel material. Ritschl's change of mind on the Synoptic Problem brings with it a major shift of focus in Ritschl's use of the Gospels: Mark rather than Matthew becomes the main Gospel upon which Ritschl rests for the picture of Jesus he creates. Implicit in this shift is the assumption that Mark, not Matthew, is the most historically reliable of the Gospels. This is confirmed, as was shown above, by what Ritschl himself states in the 1851 essay on the Synoptics concerning Mark's relation to the other two Synoptic Gospels. The interpreter may begin to assume, therefore, that Ritschl has effectively removed Mark from the context of his general observation that the Gospels are not "purely historical documents". As has, however, become clear, Ritschl still leaves room for the recognition that all Gospels have a *Tendenz* and that the label "dogmatic indifference" may ultimately be illegitimate.

There is nevertheless no reason to suppose that Ritschl did not then proceed in his Gospel interpretation/ quest for Jesus on the basis of his observation of the greater reliability of the Gospel of Mark. As scrutiny of E57 shows, it is quite clear that Mark has become the major source of interest in the chapter on Jesus. And once more, there seems at work a clear tendency to "read off" details from the Gospels in a rather uncritical way. The content of the first chapter of E57 will be considered in more detail in the course of the exposition of Ritschl's "picture of Jesus" below (II.3.1). Here it is necessary only to relate what can be gleaned from the chapter with respect to Ritschl's understanding of the nature of the Gospels to the present discussion of the consistency of his approach.

The ease with which Ritschl can turn to Mark's Gospel and find readily to hand the historical material he requires is once more immediately apparent. He readily finds material sufficient to answer the question he poses, namely, "what was Jesus' attitude to the Mosaic Law ?". Furthermore, much Matthean material is accepted as authentic and remains of use [131]. Striking now, however, is Ritschl's willingness to be more committed in the pinpointing of inauthentic material. The practice is not one which is prominent in the chapter by any means. But where it is apparent, as for example in Ritschl's conviction that Mk 10:2-12 and not Mt 19:3-9 preserves an authentic account of Jesus' teaching on divorce [132], it becomes clear that Ritschl is ready to ascribe material to the hand of the Evangelist (or his source) and sees the need for criteria on the basis of which one is able to "get back to Jesus".

Clearly, the prime criterion here operative in Ritschl's case - i.e. Mark is the first Gospel - is much too simple. Yet the intent may be respected nevertheless. A major problem is emerging, however. For in the employment of this basic criterion, the stress being placed upon Mark's historical reliability is enormous. The extent to which Ritschl cannot realistically carry through his perception that Mark has a *Tendenz* in the same way that the other two Synoptic Gospels betray a particular theological interest becomes apparent. Though Ritschl may, and indirectly does, appeal to the fact that Mark has less of a dogmatic interest than the other Synoptists, in actual practice, his procedure scarcely allows that interest to come into play.

One must therefore conclude that Ritschl attempts in this period 1846-57 to continue with Baur's perception of the Gospels as writings which portray Jesus from particular dogmatic viewpoints, but is prone to reading first Matthew, and then, to a much greater extent, Mark as having a propensity to greater historical reliability [133]. One can only surmise that there is a theological motivation behind this interest in historically reliable data.

Other factors yet to be considered do, however, suggest that Ritschl may in fact ultimately have left greater space for the *Tendenzen* of the Gospels to play a role than seems first to be the case. The first of these is the straightforward but decisive observation that as Ritschl's career progressed he made increasing and more explicit use of the Fourth Gospel in his theology [134]. This use appears not different in kind to the use he makes of the Synoptic Gospels. It is different only in degree and is easily documented [135]. One need only refer to *R u V II* and *J & R III*, drawing attention in particular to where such topics as the "sonship" of Jesus are under consideration [136]. One could also point to Ritschl's biblical backing for the presentation of Christianity given in ICR, where considerable use of the Fourth Gospel is made.

It could be claimed that Ritschl here compromises in his use of the Gospels. Either he demonstrates quite clearly that he jeopardizes the possibility of his adhering to the historical norm he has built into his Christology. For if he uses the Synoptics and John *in the same way*, then he has misread at the very least the possibility of the Fourth Gospel delivering the kind of historical material that Ritschl feels able to glean from the Synoptics. Or, alternatively, Ritschl lets go of the basic perception he had originally held concerning the Gospels by using the Fourth Gospel in the same way, on the grounds that in making no distinction between the Synoptics and John he discloses the nature of the uncritical approach to the former he had adopted throughout.

This is a serious criticism. Yet it presupposes much. In particular the assumption is made that the use of the Fourth Gospel for any historical purpose with respect to the life of Jesus will be illegitimate [137]. Be that as it may, the criticism cannot be allowed to have the last word even though there is sufficient reason to suppose that this area of Ritschl's use of the Gospels must be explored more fully. At this juncture it is possible only to suggest in anticipatory fashion that what is betrayed by this observation is the fact that Ritschl's historical norm should not be seen as wholly in control of Ritschl's Christology. His use of the Fourth Gospel may, in other words, prove complementary to the claim that Ritschl maintained a perception that the Gospels - all four of them, even including Mark - are more than "purely historical documents".

A second aspect yet to be considered seems to support this conjecture. Ritschl's stress upon the role of the Christian community in the creation of theology extends not only to include the Church present but also the Church past. What is more, Ritschl recognizes that the Church past must be seen as including not only one's own explicit ecclesiastical tradition but must incorporate an understanding of the apostles as "the first Christian community" [138].

The importance of this now commonplace perception both historically - in the development of the study of the New Testament [139] - and for an understanding of Ritschl's use of the Gospels cannot be over-stressed. For in making the rather general understanding quite specific in tracing it back to a very concrete early community (or, more importantly still, concrete communities [140]), Ritschl opens up the way for the *Tendenzen* of the Gospels to be viewed as diverse theological expressions deriving from different social contexts.

As with the first aspect which called for consideration, this second aspect demands a qualifier. For there remains in Ritschl's writings a lack of clarity about how far back he would take the possibility of discerning diversity in theological expression, i.e. whether he would trace it back into the "apostolic situation" [141]. Though potentially Ritschl allows for the *Tendenzen* of the Gospels, and the diverse religious ideas in the New Testament he refers to, to be one and the same, it is not altogether clear that he is prepared to make the equation. Indeed, such an equation would perhaps be unlikely so long as the conviction remained that one encountered first and foremost Jesus, rather than the Evangelists, in the Gospels [142]. It may therefore be claimed that Ritschl does not really have the Gospels in mind so long as he has quite optimistic opinions concerning the ease with which it is possible to "get back to Jesus". The diversity of the apostolically-derived theological ideas may thus only be seen, in Ritschl's thinking, in the non-Gospel writings found in the New Testament [143].

Nevertheless, the point is worth making that, potentially at least, the stress placed by Ritschl upon the role of the Christian community in theology, when viewed from the perspective of Ritschl's construal of the community's role in Christianity's primitive period, leaves room for the creatively theological role of the earliest community/communities at the level of the primary interpretation of the life of Jesus. This means that Ritschl potentially leaves scope for the recognition of the Gospels as themselves distinct interpretations of Jesus. This lasting perception of Ritschl's may thus, as with the first aspect mentioned above, serve to suggest that Ritschl did indeed maintain his perception that the Gospels are more than "purely historical documents".

It can thus be seen that though Ritschl presents no direct and succinct summary of how he views the Gospels - What is their literary genre ? What is their purpose ? - there is nevertheless sufficient material in his writings to suggest what the answers to the questions might be. It was suggested that Ritschl can be said to have maintained his basic perception that the Gospels are more than purely historical documents. This can be claimed even though an added complication was introduced into Ritschl's thinking by his change of mind on the Synoptic Problem, a change of mind which seemed initially to remove the Gospel of Mark from the discussion altogether. When other factors were brought into the discussion - namely Ritschl's use of John, and Ritschl's stress upon the Christian community's role in theological formulation - it became clear that there is further reason to adhere to the claim for Ritschl's essential consistency in this matter.

Ritschl's understanding of the nature of the Gospels - what sort of texts they are - thus requires that serious questions be posed concerning the approach he adopts to constructing a Christology. In discussing his "picture of Jesus", therefore, it will at all times be necessary to ask whether he is simply "reading off" material from the Gospels in the manner which the superficial glance at his work on Jesus suggested (as evidenced in the first chapter of E50 and E57 respectively) or whether he is paying full attention to the observations about the character of the Gospel material that he appears to make.

There is, in short, a hiatus existing between the way Ritschl construes Christology - as more than, but controlled by historical data about Jesus - and the understanding of the character of the Gospels with which he operates. He reveals in practice that he does not view them as biographies in the modern sense, or histories in the sense of "objective accounts". They are, for Ritschl, prototypes of the theological assessment of Jesus for his own day to which Ritschl himself aspires.

2.3. The Study of the Gospels and the Problem of the Historical Jesus

The question of the main "point" of Gospel study overlaps with the considerations just made concerning Ritschl's identification of the nature of the Gospel material. It also relates directly to the methodological enquiry conducted earlier concerning Ritschl's understanding of theology as New Testament theology, and especially his construal of Christian theology's Christocentricity. Given, in other words, that Ritschl lays great stress upon locating historically reliable material about Jesus not simply for its own sake, but rather for theological ends, the agenda for Ritschl's study of the Gospels is set. Ritschl's interest in Jesus has to go beyond that displayed by the Apostle Paul, since material about Jesus' life appears to be available [144]. It is Ritschl's claim that this material cannot but be of decisive significance. On this basis, the canonical Gospels become a focal point for Ritschl's theology. Because his theology is christocentric, and because his Christology functions in accordance with an historical norm, the "quest for Jesus" in the canonical Gospels takes on considerable importance.

The "quest for Jesus" thereby required and embarked upon, however, is a problem in itself. Ritschl's own central perception is that a "Life of Jesus" cannot be allowed to stand as a substitute for a theological assessment of the life of Jesus, and it is only the latter which will do justice to, and fully grasp the significance of, that life (i.e. which will satisfactorily answer the truth question being posed) [145]. His "quest for Jesus" is thus not at one with the "Quest of the Historical Jesus" admirably documented, if not in a wholly unbiassed fashion, by Schweitzer, and often referred to in twentieth-century discussion ever since [146].

On this basis alone, therefore, Ritschl evades the criticism launched at the Nineteenth Century Quest and should not be numbered easily among the "Questers" of that period. The position he has taken up, however, clearly does bear some affinity with the Nineteenth Century Quest. The fact that he attaches such significance to what can be known as a result of historical enquiry into the life of Jesus shows that if not a blood-brother then he is at least a distant cousin of the Questers. Ritschl is clearly operating in the context of the nexus of questions surrounding the historical Jesus by virtue of his construal of the nature of theology, and his understanding of the historical norm operative in Christology. For this reason, it must be a central feature of this present study to determine which "Jesus" is being spoken about when Ritschl sets about the writing of his christocentric theology. In short, his position vis-a-vis the Nineteenth Century Quest requires clarification.

It was evident from the previous section that Ritschl finds historical data about Jesus with ease in the Gospels [147]. The question which ultimately concerns the interpreter of Ritschl, therefore, is the relationship between this interest in historical data about Jesus, the recognition of such data's importance for a theological assessment of Jesus' life (i.e. in some sense functioning as a norm) and the complementary facts that Ritschl recognizes: i) that the Gospels are not "purely historical documents"; and ii) that historical data assembled into a "Life of Jesus" will not suffice as a theological assessment.

Distilling these concerns, and relating them to the conclusions of the previous section in particular, but also the thrust of the enquiry conducted above in II.1.2-4, it becomes possible to perceive the following with regard to Ritschl's approach; his concern is to construct a theology for his own day. As Ritschl perceives the theological task, such a construction in some way revolves around a theological assessment of the life of Jesus. The task of portraying Jesus in a theology for his own day causes him to run the risk of "modernizing Jesus". His concern in his Gospel study is thus a concrete one; to deal with the question of criteria for a theological assessment of Jesus. Ritschl turns to the historical basis which is clearest behind the Gospels - the earthly Jesus. He has, however, allowed in his methodology a role for the second pole of the historical basis behind the Gospels, namely the communities which produced the four respective pictures of Jesus found in the Gospels. Where Ritschl appears to fail - a failure to be pinpointed below - is in the clarification of the relationship between the two poles and the acceptance that the question of criteria must involve also the role played by the earliest Christian communities. At root, therefore, his attempt is to do the Gospels justice by treating them as more than historical documents and dealing with the theological questions they seek to raise. His own attempt at theological construction follows their own example; Christian theology as the self-expression of a Christian community whose self-understanding is determined by a theological assessment of the life of Jesus. When it comes to the question of criteria, however, he has sought to detach the "purely historical" from the Gospels in order that this material might operate normatively. With hindsight, it is possible to see that this presents great problems for the reception of Ritschl's theological method. He has not, in short, solved the problem of the historical Jesus. It is, however, necessary to go into detail about how Ritschl uses the Gospels to produce his own "picture of Jesus" before it can be determined whether, with substantial modification, Ritschl's own approach to the task of Christian theology may have something to offer, in the present. Here it has been the intention solely to point out the implications of Ritschl's "Christocentricity" with respect to his study of the Gospels and the particular series of problems into which his manner of approach leads him.

3. RITSCHL'S PICTURE OF JESUS

3.1. Ritschl's Picture of Jesus: an Exposition

3.1.1 Introduction

It is now necessary to consider what use Ritschl actually makes of the Gospels. It is necessary to present the "picture of Jesus" he feels able to create on the basis of his enquiries into the Gospels [148]. It must be stated at the outset that the picture of Jesus to be described is in no way to be seen as a "Life of Jesus" [149]. Furthermore, it must be stressed that the picture presented is an abstraction; Ritschl nowhere draws together all the strands of his picture of Jesus to produce a single, clear image for the benefit of his readers [150]. It is possible to glean aspects of Ritschl's own picture of Jesus only from their positions as constituent parts of his overall theological system. His picture is, as it were, "built into" his theology, and must be extracted from it if it is to be studied closely [151].

The very fact that this is the case suggests that he has successfully avoided the temptation to write a "Life", or make do with historical data about Jesus, as a substitute for a theological assessment. Ritschl does at times specifically undertake a historical task, and thus delineates more clearly what he perceives as "hard evidence" about Jesus' life. But his procedure in Christology allows a detachment of historical from theological interest in a way conducive to this present enquiry, whilst simultaneously reminding readers that it is the relationship between theology and history that is important, rather than their distinction and separation.

When seen within the overarching construct of Ritschl's theology it becomes clear that the early, more explicitly historical work itself has an ultimately theological purpose (i.e. as being prolegomena for a biblical or systematic theology; E50 and E57 are thus to be understood as history of dogma [152]). The persistent theological purpose behind Ritschl's work thus justifies the claim made above that Ritschl's picture of Jesus is "built into" his theology.

Given, however, that Ritschl's own procedure in Christology links historical data about Jesus with theological assertions, in some respects the work of extraction is done for us. Yet we should noted from the start what is happening. The term "picture of Jesus" is being directed to the historical data which Ritschl highlights as the controlling data of his Christology. This is limiting and inaccurate. For it is the purpose of this study to probe the nature of Ritschl's historical norm for Christology in his use of the Gospels and the adequacy of his historical-criticism in this respect. The term "picture of Jesus" must therefore retain an element of ambiguity until clarity is gained.

Two further factors should be noted: i) first, there is an inevitability about the fact that his use of the Gospels is likely to be less critical than a present-day reader would wish - his picture of Jesus will thus include much more material which he is prepared to label "historical" than is the case today. It is precisely this aspect which must figure prominently in the critical appraisal of Ritschl's picture - how adequate is Ritschl's understanding of the historical base for a Christology? [153]; ii) second, it is necessary to observe that little allowance is being made for inconsistency in Ritschl's approach. There may, in other words, be points - significant or not - at which Ritschl's picture of Jesus is not "warranted" by the historical data, not simply from the perspective of present-day scholarship, but on the basis of Ritschl's own procedure. He may, in other words, have failed to support his Christology with the historical warrants required by his own methodology [154].

With these considerations in mind, therefore, the exposition of Ritschl's picture of Jesus can begin. It has become clear that the exposition will be of Ritschl's theological assessment of Jesus. At each point that assessment is ostensibly warranted by an appeal to historical evidence for an aspect of the life of the earthly Jesus as found in the canonical Gospels. The exposition is presented under six headings; Jesus the Son, Jesus the Teacher, Jesus the Lord, Jesus the Obedient One, Jesus the Founder of the Kingdom of God, and Jesus as Prophet and Messiah.

3.1.2   Jesus the Son

Ritschl does not distinguish between Jesus as "Son" and Jesus as "Son of God", where the latter expression has something of the quality of a technical term about it, as thoroughly as contemporary discussion would wish. In practice, therefore, he does not do justice to the latter aspect of the question of the sonship of Jesus. He does, however, attach immense significance to Jesus' sonship understood in terms of Jesus' filial consciousness with respect to God; Jesus is Son because he believed God to be his own Father and there is firm evidence to show that Jesus believed this to have been the case.

For Ritschl there is no question that Jesus saw himself in these terms. In ICR he states the following:

> Christianity claims to have...perfect knowledge of God because its community derives itself from Jesus Christ who, as the Son of God, ascribes to himself perfect knowledge of his Father...[155]

The matter is stated more clearly later in the same work:

> ...the complete name of God (i.e. 'The God and Father of our Lord Jesus Christ') means that he has assumed this special relationship to this particular community (i.e. the community directed towards the Kingdom of God) only because he is already and first of all the Father of Jesus Christ, who is recognized as Lord by his community. In this capacity, however, Christ stands nearer to God, nearer than any other, because he shares in God's attributes of being the end of creation and recognizes himself as set apart from the world in his position of sonship to God the Father. [156]

The notion of the divine sonship of Jesus, in the sense already outlined, stands at the heart of Jesus' understanding of himself and his mission:

> Man renkt...alle Glieder der quellenmäßigen Selbstdarstellung Jesu aus, wenn man leugnet, daß er in demselben Sinne Gott seinen Vater nennt, in welchem er sich selbst als den Sohn des Menschen bezeichnet...[157]

Even allowing for the lack of clarity concerning what Ritschl means by the term "Son of Man" here, in the light of what precedes this present passage in the context of the discussion in R u V II (i.e. the "Son of Man" is not to be seen solely in the sense of a future figure belonging to the Endzeit), it is clear that Ritschl is keen to root his understanding of Jesus as divine Son firmly in Jesus' own understanding of himself.

According to Ritschl, it was Jesus' intention to draw others into the same kind of relationship he himself enjoyed with God the Father: his followers too should share in the sense of sonship. Ritschl states:

> ...beyond all doubt Jesus was conscious of a new and hitherto unknown relation to God, and said so to his disciples; and his aim was to bring his disciples into the same attitude toward the world as his own, and to the same estimate of themselves...[158]

Shortly afterwards, Ritschl expresses the identity of relationship in terms of sonship:

> ...the disciples of Jesus take the rank of sons of God (Matt.xvii.26), and are received into the same relation to God in which Christ stands to his Father (John xvii.21-23). [159]

Despite this sharing in the sense of sonship by his disciples, Jesus' sense of sonship can nevertheless be regarded as unique:

> Since he is the first to actualize in his own personal life the final purpose of the kingdom of God, Jesus is therefore unique, for should any other fulfill the same task as perfectly as he, he would be unlike him because of his dependence upon Jesus. [160]

More can be said: the work of Jesus as Son is the work of God himself, for every action of Jesus arises out of the intimacy of the relationship he enjoyed with God:

> ...Christ stood in the highest possible relation of fellowship with God, and exercised this fellowship at each moment of his life, since every act and word of his vocation arose out of his religious relation to God. [161]

The motivation and action of Jesus and God may be seen as one.

> The task assigned to Jesus...is a course of conduct in which the content is conceived as the work of God himself, because the aim represents God's innermost purpose. [162]

The "spiritual interaction" between God the Father and Jesus the Son is the key to this relationship [163].

To be able to claim, as Ritschl does, that Jesus saw himself in such terms demands that one see in the Gospels readily available historical material to substantiate the assertions made. At best, of course, Ritschl can only be said to have reasserted that the divine sonship of Jesus was a prominent strand in early Christian interpretation of Jesus. This is an observation which must be taken up later, however.

Inevitably, the Fourth Gospel features heavily in the background to Ritschl's presentation of Jesus as the Son, given that it is in this Gospel in particular in the New Testament canon that the motif gains prominence [164]. It is, however, Ritschl's use of the Gospels in this way which must be put to the test. His findings and the theological expression incorporating these findings cannot be cast aside without a more rigorous critique (III.2 below).

3.1.3   Jesus the Teacher

The educative role of Jesus is for Ritschl so important a part in his picture of Jesus, that one might be forgiven for thinking that Jesus as "educator" or "law-giver" may be more appropriate as headings. Yet these are loaded terms and are more misleading than helpful. "Jesus the Teacher" thus introduces in a more neutral fashion a key aspect of Jesus' activity as perceived by Ritschl.

Because the Gospels depict the disciples as the most direct - though not necessarily the only - immediate recipients of Jesus' teaching, it is for Ritschl essential to see Jesus as teacher in relation to Jesus' understanding of and relationship to his disciples. From the early perception of the Sermon on the Mount as teaching material delivered solely to the disciples [165], Ritschl moves on to spell out the teaching role of Jesus in terms of the strategic and systematic education of a loyal group of followers:

...es kam...für Jesus darauf an, einen bestimmten Kreis von Menschen durch regelmäßige Einwirkung zu dem Gottesreiche zu erziehen... [166]

Yet in this context of a close relationship between Jesus and his disciples, Jesus does not function either as a new law-giver or as the one who imposes a moral code. Ritschl quite explicitly rejects both options:

Also wie es falsch ist, wenn Jesus hauptsächlich als Gesetzgeber aufgefaßt wird, so ist es falsch...zu behaupten, daß er das Ceremonialgesetz abgeschafft, das Sittengesetz bestätigt habe;... [167]

...Jesus is not concerned to provide a moral code for the details of life; that is not his business. Any estimate of his person that has this for its starting-point is historically unjust. [168]

Ultimately, then, the main context of the teaching of Jesus is to be found not with respect to the Jewish Law, but rather with regard to the ways of the Kingdom:

Indem Jesus weiß, daß er selbst als Messias durch sein eigenthümliches Wirken die Herrschaft Gottes ausübt, so hängt für ihn die Verwirklichung derselben in einem Reiche von gehorsamen Unterthanen davon ab, daß er eine Gemeinde bildet, welche zu der sittlichen Aufgabe des göttlichen Reiches unter der Bedingung geeignet wird, daß sie in ihrem Meister den Sohn Gottes und Träger der Herrschaft Gottes anerkennt. [169]

The founding of this Kingdom is Jesus' own purpose [170] and the establishing of it - if such a subtle distinction may be drawn - becomes the disciples' task. "Jesus the Teacher" is a key aspect of Ritschl's picture of Jesus. Yet Ritschl has no wish to give this particular aspect a disproportionate amount of attention. Jesus is, in other words, more than a teacher in a way that he invites his readers, as readers of the Gospels, to move on to explore. In Ritschl's own words:

...he himself means more for his disciples than the passing occasion of their religion or a lawgiver for their conduct, who would be of no more account when once the law which he proclaimed was thoroughly learned. [171]

He continues:

(the)...religious vocation of the members of the Christian community is prefigured in the person of its Founder, and rests upon his person as its abiding source of strength for all imitation of him...[172]

"Jesus the Teacher" is thus inadequate as a category to grasp the abiding significance of Jesus. "Jesus the Lord" seems more appropriate to serve this purpose, and it is to Ritschl's understanding of the Lordship of Jesus that we turn next.

3.1.4   Jesus the Lord

Ritschl's exposition of Jesus as Lord is far removed from modern discussion [173]. There is in Ritschl's work no detailed discussion of the title *kyrios* as providing a background to an understanding of the "Lordship of Jesus". Rather, Ritschl begins with the Christian community, focuses upon the aspect of "headship" of the community - a role which in some sense Jesus obviously fills - and sees it necessary to determine the nature of Jesus' Lordship along this avenue of exploration.

Ritschl thus states:

> As Lord over the world, Christ is also Lord over His community. But the latter relation is the primary one, partly because the community acknowledges him as God, and partly because, in definite statements, the community, of which Christ is the head, is made to share his position toward the world. [174]

At this point, Ritschl's fusing of the "past Christian community" (in particular the earliest communities) and the "present community" is at its clearest. Lordship of the present community is, however, for Ritschl only possible on the basis of the historical warrant i.e. Jesus was "Lord" of his own particular community.

The link is spelt out once community and Kingdom are seen as correlates under the rubric of "Lordship":

> When we investigated the Kingdom of God as the correlate of the thought that God is love, it appeared that this organisation of men can be construed as the object and end of God's love only in so far as it is conformed to the type of its Founder, the Son of God. The harmony with God and likeness to him which the Kingdom of God must maintain in order to be understood as the objective of God's love, attaches to the said Kingdom only in so far as it is called into being by the Son of God, and bows to him as Lord...In other words, it is on the Son of God that in the first place the Father's love falls, and, only for his sake, on the community of which he is Lord. [175]

As the quotation indicates, community and Kingdom are to be seen as direct correlates, the relationship between them being that the former indicates particularity. This feature is highlighted in more explicit terms, and again in conjunction with the Lordship of Jesus, in ICR:

> In the complete name of God the fact that God is the Father of human beings is connected with Jesus Christ insofar as he is recognized as the Lord of a particular fellowship...The concept of God as love corresponds to that idea

of humankind which sees humanity destined for the kingdom of God and for

the activity directed toward this kingdom...This destiny, however, is realized

by human beings only in their union with the community of their lord Jesus

Christ.   [176]

A further aspect of the relationship between past and present communities is presented here. Just as every christological assertion, as far as Ritschl is concerned, demands historical warrant, so also what was true of Jesus should as far as possible be transferred to the community which refers back to him and be/become the task of that community. The Lordship of Jesus is thus a responsibility for that community. On this basis, the Lordship of Jesus as viewed in the life of Jesus in terms of ethical superiority over those around him becomes the demand placed upon the community —– which bows to Jesus as Lord to stand over against the world [177]. For in this way, claims Ritschl, Jesus' Lordship found expression:

Practical proof of sonship with God in spiritual freedom and dominion over

the world and labor for the kingdom of God fill out the Christian life... [178]

or again:

The Christian perfection which corresponds to the personal example of

Christ himself is shaped by the religious functions of sonship with God and

dominion over the world...and by the ethical functions of dutiful action in

one's particular vocation and the development of ethical virtues.   [179]

The topic of the Lordship of Jesus, then, whilst being highly unsatisfactory from the perspective of the modern discussion's expectations concerning the starting-point of the discussion, is, for Ritschl, an important concept bridging the past and present Christian communities. Ritschl takes the lead from Jesus' own ethical conduct and his attitude to the world around him and interprets his "Lordship" on this basis, transferring that understanding to Christian communities in the present.

3.1.5   Jesus the Obedient One

Jesus can carry out the task of founding the Kingdom of God only because he stands in a special relationship to God. That relationship, as was shown above, finds clearest expression for Ritschl in terms of a Father-Son relationship between God and Jesus.

Being God's Son, and being therefore given a specific task - the founding of the Kingdom - presupposes, however, that Jesus must be able to discern and carry out the will of God his Father. In that sense, Jesus is the "Obedient One", for he carries through his calling to the full, in the face of the possiblity of his refusing. "Vocation" is thus also a key concept for Ritschl.

The mutual understanding of Father and Son is the foundation for Jesus' carrying through his vocation:

> ...Jesus subordinates to himself the relation between himself and the world, in consequence of the mutual knowledge subsisting between the Father and the Son, even as on this same account He recognises his sufferings to be the yoke by which he is led of God, by whom he, the Son, is first recognised. [180]

The vocation was to form a religious community through which the Kingdom of God might be preached and be enabled to come into being:

> The idea of an ethical vocation serves...as a criterion for the public life of Christ as a visibly connected whole. When Christ presents himself as the bearer of God's moral lordship over men...He understands the name Christ as the expression of his individual vocation. His conduct within this sphere is as certainly in harmony with the universal moral law, as the end of the Kingdom of God, which he pursues in his special vocation as the founder, is the supreme end out of which the moral law arises. [181]

It was a vocation which would lead to Jesus' own death. Jesus' death, and the sufferings leading up to his death, are the hallmark of obedience, the proof of his adherance to his vocation:

> ...for Christ his sufferings served as a means of testing his faithfulness to his vocation - this and nothing else. [182]

It is on these terms that Ritschl feels best able to interpret the death of Jesus as a "sacrificial death":

> It is not the mere fate of dying that determines the value of Christ's death as a sacrifice; what renders this issue of his life significant for others is his willing acceptance of the death inflicted on him by his adversaries as a

dispensation of God, and the highest proof of faithfulness to his vocation. [183]

Yet such obedience is only real in view of the fact that it could have become disobedience: Jesus had a genuine choice not to fulfil his vocation. In a passage in which Ritschl also reveals his understanding of religion as an act of will, he writes:

> By His (i.e.Jesus') patience the suffering inflicted on him is as such made his own; and that, too, without any deadening of feeling, but rather with keen sensitiveness to suffering in every degree and throughout the whole course of his public life. For these considerations room is found in the formula, that the obedience of Christ in doing and in suffering is identical, obedience here being understood to mean activity of the will. [184]

In enduring suffering and death, however, Jesus resists the temptation to be disobedient to his call, gives full expression to his humanity, yet dies in a way which renders him unique:

> *Wenn Jesus voraussieht, daß er sein Leben auch im Tode nur seinem Vater hingiebt, daß er die specifische Zweckmäßigkeit seines Lebens für Gott im freiwilligen Sterben nicht nur beibehält, sondern sogar steigert, so steht das in keiner Gleichung mit dem Leben der anderen Menschen, deren Bestimmung zum Dienste für Gott durch das auf ihnen lastende Todesverhängniß durchkreuzt ist.* [185]

Through the obedience of Jesus Ritschl expresses how Jesus could persist with a lifestyle and course which could only result in his death. In linking it with the notions of sonship and Lordship he makes his exposition of Jesus consistent. As well as highlighting a particular aspect of his understanding of religion under this heading - that is, religion as an act of will - he also opens up the discussion to what extent his picture of Jesus is determined by his appeal to the Fourth Gospel. This latter aspect must inevitably figure prominently in the critique of Ritschl's understanding of the vocation of Jesus later in the present study.

3.1.6   Jesus the Founder of the Kingdom of God

The Kingdom of God became central both to Ritschl's understanding of Jesus and to

Ritschl's own theology after 1857 [186]. Calling Jesus the "founder" of the Kingdom of God is one way Ritschl chooses of describing Jesus' role with respect to the Kingdom of God. "Founder" is, of course, a far from unambiguous term. Indeed, one of the advantages of Ritschl's use of the idea is its inherent ambiguity. It may, however, be regarded as the most accurate summary term of Ritschl's understanding of Jesus' relationship to the Kingdom of God.

Jesus as "founder" of the Kingdom was one way of expressing the centrality of Jesus in a theology constructed around the Kingdom of God. It was especially appropriate to express the historical relation of Jesus to the Kingdom. The presence of Jesus brought something special. The ambiguity referred to above rendered the term useful for showing that the life and message of Jesus gave birth to something qualitatively different, something new.

In simplest terms, it denotes Jesus' founding/laying the foundations for the Kingdom of God (*Gründung* [187]) in the sense that in his own words and actions Jesus proclaims the presence of the Kingdom of God. The presence of the Kingdom, alongside the summons to repentance, is the most accurate means of summarizing Jesus' proclamation:

> *Der zusammenfassende Ausdruck der ursprünglichen Verkündigung Jesu*
> *knüpft an die Verheißung der unmittelbar bevorstehenden Offenbarung der*
> *Herrschaft Gottes die allgemein geltende Aufforderung zur Sinnesänderung*
> *(Mc.1.15; vgl.6.12; Lc.13.3; 15.7). Diese Zumuthung empfängt ihr volles*
> *Licht erst dadurch, daß Jesus in verschiedenen Abstufungen von Deutlichkeit*
> *den Gegnern wie den Zweiflern nahe legt, daß sein eigenthümliches*
> *berufsmäßiges Wirken selbst die Herrschaft Gottes verwirklicht. Indem er*
> *dämonisch Kranke heilt, also die Machtäbung des Teufels schmälert, so ist*
> *die Herrschaft Gottes in das Leben getreten (Mt.12.28). Indem er den Armen*
> *die Botschaft des Gottesreichs, den Gefangenen die der Erlösung bringt,*
> *indem er Blinde sehend macht, so beweist er sich als den Träger der*
> *Gottesherrschaft (Lc.4.17-21; Mt.11.2-6). [188]*

There were, however, other ways of expressing Jesus' relationship to the Kingdom. In the passage just quoted, Jesus is referred to as the "bearer" (*Träger*) of the Kingdom of God. He is also described as the "head" (*Haupt*) of the Kingdom of God [189]. He is described as being involved in "establishing" the Kingdom of God [190], which is to be viewed as "the first and highest task of Jesus" (*die erste und höchste Aufgabe Jesus*) [191]. If a distinction is to be made between the German words "*Stiftung*" and "*Gründung*" then it must be in terms of the degree of involvement in that which is "founded" by the "founder". What is clear is that though there would be room for subtle distinctions with respect to Jesus' relationship to the Kingdom (i.e. such that Jesus "founded" in the sense of "set in motion", but his disciples "founded" in the sense of "appropriated and set on the road to completion"), Ritschl himself makes no such use of the terms [192]. They should thus, in his usage, be seen as synonymous. It is quite clear from what he states throughout his exposition that Jesus is decisive for the Kingdom's appearance, and it is this which must be stressed by the use of the notion of the "founding" of the Kingdom of God.

The question how Jesus sets about the task of founding the Kingdom of God introduces other means of expression of Jesus' relationship to it. Jesus seems to "educate people into the Kingdom" [193]. He "realizes" (*verwirklicht*) the Kingdom in his own actions, and is thus its "bearer", as was seen above [194]. In seeking to fulfil his task he "forms" (*bildet*) a community around him [195].

The notion of "founding" should be viewed as the common denominator of all that Ritschl tries to express with regard to the relationship between Jesus and the Kingdom of God. Jesus is personally involved in its proclamation and its coming into being. This emphasis finds, according to Ritschl, considerable support in the Synoptic Gospels [196].

Ritschl remains consistent in this emphasis and also in his attempt to bring it increasingly, from 1857 onwards, to the forefront of his own theology. The notion of Jesus as the founder of the Kingdom of God should thus be seen as the heart of Ritschl's mature "picture of Jesus" and the manner in which his interpretation of Jesus directly influences Ritschl's own theological formulation should be observed [197].

3.1.7   Jesus as Prophet and Messiah

The terms "prophet" and "Messiah" also figure as part of Ritschl's picture of Jesus. It must, however, be admitted that Ritschl makes relatively little use of them. The most explicit references to the terms are in his earliest work and though they are seen as self-designations, i.e. Ritschl believed that Jesus used the terms of himself, because, in Ritschl's estimation, they were not central for Jesus, they receive little weight in the construction of Ritschl's overall picture [198].

It should also be said that Ritschl has few problems with the two terms. This should, at least in the case of "Messiah", cause questions to be raised about the adequacy of his understanding of the term and what he deems to have been Jesus' use of it, when the critique of Ritschl's picture of Jesus is undertaken.

Ritschl treats the terms "prophet" and "Messiah" as titles existing in continuity with each other; the meaning of "Messiah" derives from the Jewish prophetic tradition, being a specific extension of it [199]. Jesus stands, in Ritschl's understanding, firmly within that Jewish prophetic tradition, though the prophetic background is of itself insufficient to express fully what Jesus was about [200]. This should be stressed even though one influential strand of the history of doctrine focuses heavily upon the prophetic role of Jesus [201].

Beyond the fact that "Messiah" offers a way of understanding Jesus' role as prophet over and above the Jewish prophetic tradition up to that point, the term is left largely unexplored by Ritschl. It is apparent from his earliest work that he understands it to be virtually synonymous with "Son of God" [202]. It is the category of "sonship", however, with which Ritschl sees fit to best interpret the life and self-understanding of Jesus (as was shown above [203]). The juxtaposition of terms is thus not a way of interpreting Jesus' Messiahship either from the term itself, or by means of clear exposition of passages where the self-designation of Jesus as Messiah is to be found. Rather, it is an imposition of Ritschl's interpretation of Jesus through the category of "sonship" upon other evidence. For this reason, too, the Messiahship of Jesus should not be seen as central to Ritschl's picture of Jesus.

It is true that a definition of the term "Messiah" was given by Ritschl in E50 [204]. Yet the definition given is in terms of the founding of the Kingdom and of judgment.

Ritschl moves on to explore the former more fully as the key to Jesus' mission and purpose, but does not develop the latter to the same extent. For this reason, it cannot be left as Ritschl's last word on the subject or as evidence that he saw it as of the utmost significance.

The following passage from ICR provides a useful summary of Ritschl's understanding of Jesus as "prophet" and "Messiah":

> The historical connection of Christianity with the religion of the Old Testament...makes it natural that Jesus should in general represent himself as a prophet sent by God who was ordained in God's decree concerning the world and humankind. However, he sets himself above all the preceding prophets of the Old Testament by making himself known as the Son of God and the promised king of David's race (Christ the anointed), who need not first prepare the way for the kingdom of God but effects *the* work of God...The prophetic vocation of Jesus is not annulled by his claim to messianic dignity, but only modified by it, since he exercises his right as lord only through his morally effective teaching and by his readiness to engage in the action of a servant... [205]

In short, both terms - "prophet" and "Messiah" - are taken up into the picture of Jesus which Ritschl presents very much on the margins. They are insufficient to express fully who Jesus was and what his mission entailed; Jesus as Son, and as Founder of the Kingdom serve that function far better, in Ritschl's estimation. The terms should therefore be understood as useful, but necessary, background material in Ritschl's picture of Jesus. They are Jesus' own links with the context in which he found himself, and the past to which he related [206].

3.1.8   Ritschl's Picture of Jesus: Summary

A summary of the six aspects of Ritschl's picture of Jesus expounded above best takes the form of an assessment of which of the aspects presented, if any, are most important.

Of prime significance for Ritschl are undoubtedly the notions of the sonship of Jesus, and Jesus' role as founder of the Kingdom of God. It can safely be said that all other aspects of Ritschl's picture are subordinate to, and can be accommodated within, a framework in which these two aspects receive most attention. It should therefore come as no surprise that these two aspects of Ritschl's picture of Jesus are taken up by Ritschl in the articulation of his own theology [207].

Jesus' understanding of himself as Son of God is thus the foundation of his life's work. Because he enjoys this intimate relationship with God his Father, he can be obedient to the will of God. On this basis also he is able to carry through his specific task to found the Kingdom of God through his own words and actions. His role as teacher is to be understood within this general task. His Lordship is to be seen as the activity appropriate for one living with the goal of his own life attuned to God's will for the world: the Kingdom of God.

This summary sketch of Ritschl's picture is, it should be stressed, a sketch of a theological assessment of the life of Jesus. It is not itself a "Life". But as was stated in the introduction to this section, it should theoretically be possible at all points, given Ritschl's methodology in Christology, to draw a direct line between historical datum and the christological assertion being made in the theological assessment which Ritschl presents. To what extent Ritschl achieves this aim must be assessed in section III.2 below. At this stage it has been necessary only to expound what use Ritschl in practice makes of the Gospel material in producing a picture of Jesus to place at the centre of his theological system.

3.2. The Relationship Between Ritschl's Work on the Gospels and his Emerging Picture of Jesus

In the introduction to the previous section, it was noted that to attempt to abstract a "picture of Jesus" from Ritschl's work is to attempt something Ritschl himself not only does not do, but would not advise. Ritschl does not automatically assume that the attempt to piece together a "picture of Jesus" would fall foul of the same criticism he levels against contemporary attempts to write a "Life of Jesus", namely, that it substitutes a biography for a theological assessment of the life of Jesus. Yet there is in his approach an implicit reserve against doing what has just been undertaken. It was for this reason that the point was made on a number of occasions; Ritschl's "picture of Jesus" is not a historical "Life of Jesus". It is a theological assessment of the life of Jesus constructed, Ritschl maintains, in accordance with historical norms.

Whether the distinction here being made is simply too subtle to carry any weight (or whether it is simply a false distinction) remains to be seen. It is necessary to note, however, that Ritschl is attempting to create a theology located between a simplistic use of the New Testament (thus reading off from the texts without an awareness of a historical-critical approach) and one which deems all to have been said about Jesus when the historian has done her/his work. Ritschl is, in other words, attempting to interpret the New Testament with respect for its theological subject matter; God as revealed in the person of Jesus Christ.

In this context, the picture of Jesus which Ritschl seems to be using is of the utmost importance. Important also is how he reached his understanding of Jesus. Clarity in this particular aspect of the theological process is thus a central feature of this present study. In order for Ritschl's picture of Jesus to be properly understood, it is necessary to relate his picture to his ongoing work on the Gospels. Two preparatory remarks are, however, needed.

First: though Christology may be seen as the ultimate goal of Gospel study for Ritschl [208], it was not the sole purpose of his study of the Gospels. Ritschl understood that more basic work had to be undertaken as preparatory study for the interpretation of the Gospels before that which has been termed the "ultimate goal" could be reached. It is in this category that even the vitally significant essay on the Synoptic Gospels of 1851 should be placed. There exists therefore the possibility of tracing parallel development in Ritschl's study of the Gospels and his picture of Jesus.

Second: if, as is quite clearly the case, Ritschl's work on the Gospels was continuing and thus open to change, then it should surely also be assumed that his picture of Jesus was also liable to develop [209]. This ostensibly simple conclusion is more complex than first appears. For though development in both areas may be deemed inevitable, its implications are highly significant. At this point, the close link between Gospel study (the fruits, for example, of literary and historical work on the Gospels) and theological construction would be evident. For if conclusions in the realm of the theological assessment of Jesus' life and work are as susceptible to change as first appears, what can then be said for stability of thought through the Christian tradition, let alone the objectivity of the (historical) criteria by which Ritschl seeks to operate ?

Ritschl clearly operates with a "historical picture" [210]. This "historical picture" appears to be composed of readily available, reliable historical material from the Gospels. As a result, as we have seen, historical data provide norms in Christology, as Christology does in theology. This scenario in itself suggests that little development in a "picture of Jesus" would be possible. It will be a matter of becoming clear from the outset about the picture and then remaining true to that picture. The historian's contribution to the task of the theologian is thus indeed considerable and decisive.

However, observations can be brought to counter this apparent certainty in the realm of history, observations which then support the second remark: Ritschl's picture of Jesus *can* be seen to develop in relation to his ongoing work on the Gospels. The first observation has already been anticipated in our chronological study of Ritschl's New Testament work (II.1.5 above) and will be filled out below. The very fact that the Kingdom of God as a prominent concept appears relatively late on the scene in Ritschl's exposition of the teaching of Jesus (the 1857 edition of _Die Entstehung der altkatholischen Kirche_) shows at the very least a shifting of emphasis going on in Ritschl's presentation of Jesus.

It could, of course, be contended that such a change is one required by ongoing historical research. But in truth, though Ritschl seeks to adhere as closely as possible to objective historical study, as will become clear, developments in his picture are made not only on the basis of historical judgment alone.

Second, one can point to the discovery made above that Ritschl's picture of Jesus is not only not a "Life of Jesus", but it is also not simply a summary of historical data. As was shown, Ritschl's rejection of a "Life of Jesus" includes within it the rejection of the idea that a collection of historical data can serve as a satisfactory substitute for a theological assessment of Jesus' life. Ritschl thus paves the way for understanding the picture of Jesus with which the theologian works as itself part of the theological process, even if recognition of that fact is far from explicit [211]. The two preliminary remarks can thus be allowed to stand: i) Gospel study reaches its goal in helping in the creation of a Christology but is not itself swallowed up by that goal, there is thus in Gospel study a major part which stands apart alongside which the "quest for Jesus" undertaken with respect to the Gospels can be viewed; ii) the possibility for change in a theologian's picture of Jesus exists as soon as it is seen in relationship to continuing Gospel study. This in itself highlights that Gospel study is not just about undertaking historical research.

The mention of these two preliminary remarks requires, however, that the implications also be considered. They are as follows: a) The possibility of change in Ritschl's picture of Jesus, though it can be viewed more positively from a current standpoint, undoubtedly compromises the belief which Ritschl holds that his Christology is constructed in accordance with historical norms. Or, to express the matter more precisely, though it is now possible to point out that historical research is less objective, and more relative, than has often been perceived (not only because of the standpoint of the historian, but also because of the need perceived to be open to new sources), Ritschl leaves insufficient room for such relativity to play a role in his Christology [212]; b) some way must be found to express the built-in relativity and potentiality to change in the picture of Jesus, which Ritschl's procedure at one extreme allows (by his rejection of a "Life of Jesus") and at the other rejects (by his concentration upon the historical norm of Christology) [213]. The term chosen to express this state of affairs must also seek to do justice to the fact that the interpreter striving to become clear about Ritschl's picture of Jesus faces the task of having to snatch glimpses of the picture from various different contexts within the Ritschl corpus and, more significantly, from different stages in Ritschl's academic career.

The former implication is a major one and can only be properly affirmed on the basis of the more detailed and analytical critique of Ritschl's picture of Jesus to be undertaken below.

The second implication is no less major, though can be allowed to pass unexplored at this juncture, covered by a term which expresses the difficulty the interpreter must face.

I propose to use the term "an emerging picture of Jesus". This signifies two things. First, at a basic level, it acknowledges that Gospel study is continuing and has an effect upon what one is ultimately attempting to do on the basis of that study, namely, write a historical-critically responsible Christology. Second, it suggests that the task of constructing a picture of Jesus remains an ever incomplete task not simply on historical-critical grounds - i.e. because the material required for its compilation is inadequate - but because the relationship between constructing a picture of Jesus, understood as making a theological assessment of Jesus, is inevitably linked to the process of theological construction. As such it will remain incomplete.

The task to be undertaken in this section is thus an attempt to do justice to the many observations made of Ritschl's theological approach to the New Testament, from the perspective of the relationship between his work on the Gospels and his "emerging picture of Jesus". The following features of Ritschl's approach are thereby respected: the Gospels are more than purely historical documents (i.e. his respect for the theological dimension of the Gospels); his picture of Jesus is not a "Life of Jesus"; the construction of a picture of Jesus is a theological task; the task of the interpretation of the Gospels is both a historical and theological undertaking. On the basis of this clarification, a consideration of the relationship between his work on the Gospels and his emerging picture of Jesus can begin.

This part of the enquiry must make plain what has been implicit in other parts of the study undertaken thus far. Of particular importance is the study conducted into Ritschl's New Testament work. Ritschl's "emerging picture of Jesus" must now be located within the framework set up in that part of the enquiry, i.e. into the chronological account of Ritschl's development as a New Testament scholar (especially as a Gospel critic). Two aspects featured in the above enquiry, aspects figuring prominently in the summary of II.1.5, need highlighting at the outset of this parallel study. They are: i) Ritschl's change of mind on the Synoptic Problem; and ii) his increasing use of the Fourth Gospel from the 1850s to the 1870s. Before these aspects receive their full treatment and proper assessment it is appropriate first to look at the manner in which Ritschl warrants his picture of Jesus at the three key points in his development, namely 1850, 1857 and 1874. It comes as no surprise to find that the three dates can be said to represent three different foci in Ritschl's use of the Gospels, and, by extension, three different approaches to his construal of a picture of Jesus.

In 1850 in the aspects of the picture of Jesus presented in E50, Ritschl leans almost exclusively upon the Gospel of Matthew in reaching an understanding of Jesus' attitude to the Mosaic Law. Though an "argument from statistics" should not in every case be allowed to have the last say in such matters, in this case, the sheer weight of use of the Gospel, when taken alongside the structure and content of the chapter in question, speaks in support of the Matthean control of Ritschl's presentation. The fifty-one references to the first Gospel far outweigh the four references to the other three Gospels, the latter including three grouped together and mentioned purely to make a grammatical point [214].

Added to this, the prominence given to Mt 5.17 should be noted. The verse serves effectively as the superscript for the entire chapter and the chapter's purpose thus becomes but the unpacking of the meaning of the verse in question. Ritschl is in short, dependent almost entirely upon the Gospel of Matthew for what he presents about Jesus in 1850 [215].

By 1857, the situation is significantly different. Though Matthew is the Gospel which is cited most in the chapter on Jesus in E57 - in this respect mirroring the presentation of E50 - the emergent role played by the Gospel of Mark should not go unnoticed. It is at this point that the comments made above concerning the limitations of the statistical argument, which would determine the influence of a Gospel upon Ritschl's presentation solely in terms of explicit reference to a particular Gospel, are especially pertinent. For here, though the references to Matthew outnumber those to the Gospel of Mark by three to one, there is sufficient reason to suggest, on grounds of the structure and content of the chapter, that it is Mark, not Matthew, which is functioning normatively for Ritschl at this point [216].

The structure of the chapter suggests that this is indeed the case in the following way; after an introduction to the chapter clarifying his position on the Synoptic Problem, Ritschl declares that one must turn first to Mark to see what clues that Gospel provides concerning the matter in hand before turning to the Sermon on the Mount

(Ritschl's previous starting-point) [217]. Five pages dealing with central Marcan texts (1.44, 2.23-28, 7.1ff, 10.2-9, 12.28-34) then follow before the assessment of the Matthean material begins. The Matthean evidence is being "accommodated" within the normative framework provided by the Gospel of Mark. This remains the case despite the fact that ten pages are devoted to the Matthean evidence [218]. After consideration of each Gospel, it is the Marcan evidence which is called for as the yard-stick by which the evidence must ultimately be measured [219].

Jodock is in a sense right to point to the lack of "substantive difference" between the two versions of the chapter [220]. For at first sight, the Matthean evidence receives similar coverage in E57 to the first edition of 1850. Yet his reading of Ritschl must be qualified because he fails to perceive the elements in the content which are pointers - and no more at this stage - to a major shift under way in Ritschl's thinking. He also fails to see the significance of what may be termed the "insubstantive" differences between the two versions of the chapter in that he does not set the comparison he himself makes of Ritschl's works within a still broader canvas. The essential similarity of the two chapters is thus undoubtedly a product of the framework within which the chapter is placed. In each case, in other words, the field of vision is restricted to a study of Jesus' stance towards the Mosaic Law. The differences which are nevertheless present, however, must be pressed. The comparative lack of interest in the topic of the Messiahship of Jesus in the second edition may be cited [221]. A reduction of emphasis upon the person of Jesus in general can also be detected in the second edition [222]. Though this should not lead one to assume that the person of Jesus ceases to be significant for Ritschl, the matter may perhaps be expressed positively; what Jesus says and does becomes of immense significance. The observation just made accords with the main difference in the second edition, a difference best expressed through direct quotation. In E50 Ritschl states:

> ...die vollendete Gerechtigkeit, welche Jesus als Bedingung des Eintrittes ins
> himmlische Reich gegenüber den Pharisäern forderte, (wurde) durch ihn
> selbst wirklich dargestellt. Jenes Postulat wäre ohne Erfolg verhallt, und
> hätte keine Gemeinschaft bilden können, wenn nicht ein wirklicher Mittelpunkt
> für jenes Leben der vollendeten Gerechtigkeit in der Person Jesu dagewesen

wäre. [223]

Here it is necessary to note the emphasis upon the person of Jesus, together with the stress upon the "righteousness" (*Gerechtigkeit*) which Jesus embodies.

By contrast in E57 we read the following:

...überhaupt nicht die Gesetzgebung und die Auseinandersetzung mit dem mosaischen Gesetze, sondern die Gründung des Gottesreichs durch Darstellung seiner persönlichen Würde als Menschensohn und durch seine Erweckung des Glaubens an sich die erste und höchste Aufgabe Jesu war. [224]

In this quotation, the emphasis upon the person of Jesus is qualified by reference to his work. Above all, the focus is now placed upon the Kingdom of God.

The move from an emphasis upon righteousness to an emphasis upon the Kingdom of God is thus the third and most important difference between the two chapters. Such differences cannot be left unexplored and Jodock's analysis therefore falls short in failing to account for them. Though the immediate cause for this change of focus should by now be clear, it will be repeated below. More importantly at this stage, however, the full implications of the results of the shift of emphasis will be explored.

The more immediate task is to turn attention to 1874, and study the third focal point picked up from the earlier survey of Ritschl's New Testament work, as it pertains to the matter in hand, i.e. the relationship between Ritschl's study of the Gospels and his picture of Jesus.

Though the picture of Jesus offered by Ritschl in *R u V* is in many ways more complete, in some ways it is much more problematic than those offered only in part in Ritschl's earlier works. By 1874 Ritschl was much more confident about his procedure in writing a theology. He knew in general terms how he was to approach the task. And, as has been shown at numerous points throughout this study, he was quite clear about what use should be made of the Gospels as far as the construction of a picture of Jesus was concerned. It is thus not surprising that all the most important emphases with which Ritschl draws his picture of Jesus are to be found presented at some point in *R u V*. In this sense, then, it is the most complete presentation.

The problematic character of the presentation given by Ritschl derives in part from the work's overall purpose; $R \, u \, V$ is a theological construction planned and built on a grand scale. The picture of Jesus built into the superstructure is thus but a component part, if a highly significant one. The comments made earlier in this present study concerning the difficulty of isolating Ritschl's picture of Jesus thus reverberate at this point.

The problematic character of this later presentation derives in part, however, from a different source. It is a problematic presentation for the simple reason that it is more difficult to pinpoint than the limited part-pictures of 1850 and 1857. A number of consequences follow.

First, in contrast to the chapters on Jesus in E50 and E57 this later picture does not rely primarily on the evidence of a single Gospel. This implies that when it came to "filling out" his picture of Jesus from the narrow base upon which Ritschl began to piece together his portrayal - i.e. upon the base of an understanding of Jesus' attitude to the Mosaic Law - he could no longer rest on the Gospel of Mark.

Second, it may be suspected that Ritschl's approach may be one of harmonizing the four Gospel portrayals of Jesus.

Third, close scrutiny of the criteria which operate in Ritschl's use of a wider Gospel-base is called for, should Ritschl be adhering to the historical norm which he has built into his Christology.

The primary task, then, is to determine the nature of Ritschl's picture in $R \, u \, V$ as far as the Gospel warrants are concerned. The main contours of this part of the enquiry are provided in essence in the documentation for the exposition of Ritschl's picture of Jesus presented above (II.3.1.). In the evidence adduced for the exposition, it became apparent that with the possible exception of the category of "Jesus as Prophet and Messiah", the elements of Ritschl's picture of Jesus presented are all to be found in $R \, u \, V$ [225].

To that basic observation, however, must now be added three further considerations: i) the elements that can be said to have been added to "fill out" the 1857 understanding of Jesus; ii) the Gospel evidence upon which such a "filling out" process was based; and, iii) the difference, if any, between $R \, u \, V \, II$ and $R \, u \, V \, III$ and the significance of that difference.

i) In simplest terms the expansion of Ritschl's understanding of Jesus, as can be judged from a comparison of his 1857 portrayal and that built into _R u V_, is to be seen in the exploration of the Lordship and Obedience of Jesus. Neither of these receive treatment in the chapter on Jesus in either _E50_ or _E57_ [226]. Furthermore, though there is a starting-point for the perception of Jesus as "Son of God" in the earlier works, the extension of the understanding of Jesus' sense of Sonship is something which takes place after 1857 [227]. "Jesus as Teacher" and "Jesus as Founder of the Kingdom" are thus the two key aspects of Ritschl's picture of Jesus which remain at the heart of his picture from the earliest into the later works [228].

ii) The warrants for such expansion are found mainly, though not exclusively, in the Fourth Gospel. Ritschl thus makes numerous references and allusions to the Fourth Gospel in _R u V_, in the sixth chapter of _R u V III_ in particular [229]. But Ritschl also seems to be in the process of reappraising the Synoptic evidence. He thus picks up elements found in the Synoptic evidence which he had not stressed previously. The Sonship of Jesus as found, for example, in Mt 11.27 receives special emphasis [230]. Ritschl explores further the significance of Jesus' death, making considerable use of Mark 8.35ff and 10.45 [231].

iii) Is there a difference between _R u V II_ and _R u V III_ in the use of the Gospels ? In general terms there appears to be little difference. All _four_ Gospels are heavily used in _R u V II_, the only striking thing being perhaps Ritschl's use of Luke in some cases [232]. The only major difference between the use of the Gospels made by Ritschl here and the use made in 1857 is the appearance of the Fourth Gospel [233]. Luke drops out altogether in chapter six of _R u V III_, yet all other three Gospels are used, Matthew and John in particular [234].

But once more there is a great danger of reading too much into the statistical evidence alone. For it is clear that the allusions to the Fourth Gospel are as important as the explicit references [235]. The Fourth Gospel can be seen to have a much greater significance than statistics alone might suggest. Furthermore, the manner in which the Gospel of Mark is used, and not used, is quite striking. The emphasis culled from Mark (evident both in the _E57_ and in _R u V II_) upon Jesus as the founder of the

Kingdom of God is far less prominent in J & R III. Mark is taken up, rather, in the context of the exposition of the limited character of Jesus' own mission, the significance of his death and Jesus' understanding of the family [236].

The difference between the two volumes should, however, not be overstressed. It is necessary to pay attention once more to Ritschl's reminder that these two volumes were conceived as one. In this light, the apparent lack of emphasis upon the Kingdom of God in chapter six of R u V III from the perspective of the use of Mark's Gospel should not cause the reader to assume that Ritschl saw the Kingdom of God as any less significant either in Jesus' own teaching and actions, or in Ritschl's own theological system than other factors suggest. Such factors would be the prominence given to the Kingdom in R u V II and the clear importance of the concept of Kingdom stressed in the opening sections of R u V III [237]. On this basis, the relatively few references to Jesus as the Kingdom's founder are out of all proportion to the content of the references themselves [238].

It may be suggested, therefore, that the most complete and succinct summary of Ritschl's picture of Jesus is to be found in ICR, where, in effect, the more extensive presentation worked out in R u V is to be found in popular, abbreviated form. The frequent use of ICR in the exposition of Ritschl's picture of Jesus above is thus not without consequence [239].

To a preliminary consideration of the rationale behind a study of the relationship between Ritschl's work on the Gospels and his emerging picture of Jesus has now been added a study of three focal points in Ritschl's development as a New Testament scholar. At these three points - 1850, 1857, and 1874 - notice was taken of the main emphases of Ritschl's presentation of Jesus, and the Gospel warrants provided for those emphases were highlighted. It is now both possible and necessary to consider the study of these three focal points in relation to the two features of particular importance about Ritschl's work highlighted at the outset, namely, Ritschl's change of mind on the Synoptic Problem and his increasing use of the Fourth Gospel.

The first of these features, the change of mind Ritschl underwent on the Synoptic Problem, can be dealt with swiftly. It can be seen, and the evidence presented above documents this, that Ritschl's change of mind has a direct effect upon his use of the

Gospels and thus upon his picture of Jesus. The change of focus highlighted above - from righteousness to Kingdom of God - is directly attributable to the shift of attention brought on by Ritschl's shift of position on the Synoptic Problem; Mark, not Matthew, was to become normative for an understanding of Jesus.

The second feature has been documented, yet is not as easily explicable. Though the increased use of Mark is to be explained in terms of Ritschl's shift of position on the Synoptic Problem, the increased use by Ritschl of the Fourth Gospel is not as easily attributable to a single source. An appeal to Ritschl's interest in the New Testament canon - on the basis of which the need arises to do justice to all four Gospels - would be possible, yet would not explain Ritschl's persistent lack of interest in the Gospel of Luke.

Be that as it may, if the increased use by Ritschl of the Fourth Gospel cannot readily be accounted for, it must at the very least be carefully studied. For, given the historical constraints which Ritschl builds into his Christology, though the use of Mark, as opposed to Matthew, is defensible, the eager use made by Ritschl of the Fourth Gospel - less readily delivering historically reliable material about Jesus - is open to closer scrutiny. Even allowing for the fact that Ritschl is not seeking solely historical data, his use of the Fourth Gospel requires justification.

A main feature of the critique of Ritschl's picture of Jesus must therefore be the nature, legitimacy and adequacy of warrants drawn from the Fourth Gospel for particular aspects of the picture presented.

Some conclusions can nevertheless be drawn from the material presented in this section.

It is clear that the later, more complete, picture of Jesus which Ritschl presents, is based upon more than one Gospel. It is, however, not a simple harmonization of the four Gospel pictures under the heading of "historical Jesus", despite Ritschl's own concern to operate with an understanding of a "historical picture" of Christ. The evidence points to the observation that Ritschl is operating with a picture of Jesus derived primarily from Mark and John, supported with material from the other two Gospels (more so from Matthew), yet not controlled by the latter pair of Gospels. This conclusion can be drawn on the basis of the centrality of the Kingdom of God (derived from Mark) and of the Sonship of Jesus (derived from John), both of which were highlighted in the exposition of Ritschl's picture of Jesus presented above (II.3.1).

A second conclusion suggests itself; that the picture of Jesus with which Ritschl operates develops in accordance with the particular Gospel upon which he focuses at different stages in his theological development. This is ultimately not simply fickleness of his part - for the concentration on Matthew is by and large dispensed with after 1857 - but rather a process of being newly informed, of "folding in", we might say, new insights into the "dough" of his theology, an image which itself suggests development and growth.

Again, the *reason* for such a change of focus is not clear. But if, as the whole process of an "emerging" picture of Jesus suggests, the task of constructing a picture of Jesus for a Christology is concerned with the theological viewpoint of the theologian, then the self-involving character of christological language is merely being affirmed in practice [240]. The development of Ritschl's picture may thus be seen as much to be bound up with Ritschl's own development as with the contingent nature of his New Testament enquiry [241].

Summary Ritschl's picture of Jesus, expounded above in II.3.1 in a thematic fashion, has thus now been viewed from a different perspective. It has been located within Ritschl's own theological development and related to his continuing study and use of the Gospels. On the basis of this angle of enquiry it can be seen that the two primary emphases in Ritschl's picture of Jesus - Jesus as the "Founder of the Kingdom" and Jesus as the "Son of God" - are to be related to Ritschl's enagagement with two of the canonical Gospels in particular, namely Mark and John.

This observation can, however, be pressed further; these two emphases are to be related also to separate stages in Ritschl's own career as a theologian, stages corresponding to the finding of a satisfactory solution to the Synoptic Problem (in preparation for a revised edition of a history of earliest Christianity) and the writing of a large-scale theological work.

Ritschl thus takes up the findings of his Synoptic research (Mark as the first Gospel; Jesus as, above all, the Kingdom's founder) and seeks to complete his picture of Jesus by using primarily, though not exclusively, the one Gospel which presents

Jesus as the Kingdom's founder least of all (the Fourth Gospel).

The significance of these findings must be assessed. Such an assessment will, however, be possible only when the critique of Ritschl's picture of Jesus has been offered, and the analysis of his use of the Gospels to that end has been made (III.1-2).

3.3. The Relationship Between Ritschl's Work on the Gospels and his Theology as a Whole: the Importance of the "Picture of Jesus" Within Ritschl's System

3.3.1   Introduction

In accordance with the chiastic structure of the expository centre of this present study, it is necessary, finally, to relate Ritschl's picture of Jesus to his theology as a whole. This present section, though marginal to the study, is important in that its purpose is to demonstrate how Ritschl's theology as christocentric New Testament theology actually operates. It shows how Ritschl's picture of Jesus informs the content of his theological system. The particular - the discovery and presentation of the Jesus at the heart of the Gospels - is thus related to the more general; Ritschl's theology as a whole. This final piece of exposition takes the form of a study of six particular examples of where Ritschl's picture of Jesus relates to his theology. The examples are six themes common to each: Sonship, Vocation, Kingdom of God, Community, Love and Righteousness.

3.3.2   Sonship

The concept of "sonship" is a significant means by which Ritschl relates Jesus' relationship to God to that of the present-day believer. Here the focus is primarily on the individual believer, though as will become clear the social collective reference is not lost.

Jesus saw himself as enjoying a special relationship to God his Father. He sought to bring his immediate followers into the same relationship with God which he himself enjoyed.

Ritschl can thus write:

....Jesus was conscious of a new and hitherto unknown relation to God, and said so to his disciples; and his aim was to bring his disciples into the same attitude toward the world as his own, and to the same estimate of themselves...[242]

The way Ritschl continues this quotation is instructive, for it shows that though Ritschl talks here in terms of the immediate Twelve [243], by the reference to the work of the Kingdom of God - which it is "the disciples" responsibility to take up - Ritschl shows that his understanding of sonship goes far beyond the immediate Twelve. Ritschl continues:

that under these conditions he might enlist them in the world-wide mission of the Kingdom of God, which he knew to be not only his own business, but theirs.

The first followers of Jesus are therefore in this respect merely the prototypes of later Christians. The Kingdom of God, which it is Jesus' task as Son of God to found, is termed "the new community of the sons of God" [244].

There is, according to Ritschl, a "proof" of this sonship:

Practical proof of sonship with God in spiritual freedom and dominion over the world and labor for the kingdom of God fill out the Christian life which is a new creation of God, when compared with the sinful state which is presupposed in man. [245]

Ritschl does not, however, see the uniqueness of Jesus' sonship compromised through this correlation. Jesus can have no equal either in terms of the quality of his God-consciousness or his role with respect to the Kingdom of God [246]. In this way Ritschl seeks to resolve the tension which needs to be coped with in any Christian interpretation of Jesus, that is, to talk of Jesus as "Son of God" in a unique sense and yet relate his relationship to God to Christian experience.

3.3.3 Vocation

The concept of "vocation" (*Beruf*) is similarly a category with which Ritschl seeks to interpret the life of the individual believer. Again, Ritschl relates his understanding of Jesus' beliefs about his own identity and purpose to the life of the believer. The correlation is made quite explicitly:

> ...he (Jesus) rendered his vocational obedience not only for its own sake, but at the same time necessarily for the purpose of bringing mankind into the same relation toward God which he occupied, as their father. [247]

Once more, therefore, ideas are linked together. Vocation and sonship are linked, in that Jesus fulfilled his task (primarily to found the Kingdom of God) because he enjoyed the relationship to God of a Son to a Father. Believers may in turn be sons of God, in that they recognise the sonship of Jesus and share in it. They may thereby participate in the task of establishing the Kingdom of God [248]. A point worthy of note here, however, is the inevitability of the fact that Ritschl leans heavily upon the Fourth Gospel for his basic material, even if he is then in a position to explore other New Testament material in order to make the correlation [249].

3.3.4   Kingdom of God

It is widely held, and with some justification, that the Kingdom of God is crucial, if not indeed central, to Ritschl's reading of the Gospels and to his theology as a whole [250]. As noted earlier, Ritschl clearly perceived the role of the Kingdom of God as decisive for Jesus as portrayed in the Synoptic Gospels, in Mark in particular [251]. Ritschl developed that understanding, however, and made the Kingdom of God in turn a key aspect of his own theological system. The Kingdom of God became one of the two foci in his interpretation of Christianity as an ellipse rather than as a circle. A lengthy passage from J & R III can be quoted to express the matter in Ritschl's own words:

> Christ made the universal moral Kingdom of God his end, and thus he came to know and decide for that kind of redemption which he achieved through the maintenance of fidelity in his calling and of his blessed fellowship with God through suffering unto death. On the other hand, a correct spiritual interpretation of redemption and justification through Christ tends to keep more decisively to the front the truth that the Kingdom of God is the final end. Now theology, especially within the Evangelical Confessions, has laid very

unequal emphasis on these two principal characteristics of Christianity. It makes everything which concerns the redemptive character of Christianity an object of the most solicitous reflection. Accordingly it finds the central point of all Christian knowledge and practice in redemption through Christ, while injustice is done to the ethical interpretation of Christianity through the idea of the Kingdom of God. But Christianity, so to speak, resembles not a circle described from a single centre, but an ellipse which is determined by two foci. [252]

This is a telling passage. For it expounds succinctly not only Ritschl's understanding of the Kingdom of God in conceptual terms in the realm of the structure of Ritschl's work, but relates that understanding to the use he intends to make of his picture of Jesus in his Christology. His intention is to correct an imbalance in Christianity, evident throughout its history; Jesus' personal role in the effecting of redemption has become overstressed at cost to the perception and understanding of the Kingdom of God to which Jesus' own life had been dedicated and for which, Ritschl in effect claims, Jesus ultimately gave up his life.

The matter can be simplified in terms such as; Ritschl seeks a methodological shift away from the *person* of Jesus to his *work*. Naturally, from what has been seen, such an observation would be accurate in general terms. The danger is that Ritschl would be understood on the basis of Harnack's extension of Ritschl's ideas, should such a simplification of Ritschl's intent be allowed to stand unqualified [253]. It would therefore be more accurate to say that Ritschl calls for greater attention to the content of Jesus' life and actions *within* a proper understanding of the significance of his person. The interpreter may feel that Ritschl's construal of Christianity - when expressed in these terms - is inaccurate if a correlation between the life of Jesus and the structure of Christianity is being perceived by Ritschl at this point. That is to say, perhaps Christianity should be seen by Ritschl as two concentric circles, rather than an ellipse. The relationship between redemption and the Kingdom of God would then be better correlated to his understanding of Jesus [254]. It should, however, be admitted that Ritschl does not press the correlation at this point [255].

A comment on the importance of the Kingdom of God can also be made upon the basis of the above passage. Ritschl seems to suggest that the Kingdom of God, being the end, or purpose (*Zweck*), of Jesus conditions Jesus' understanding of redemption. Perhaps Ritschl is showing, even in his methodological reflection, a propensity to imbalance in the opposite direction to the Christian tradition he endeavours to correct. Clearly he seeks to maintain balance through his two foci model. But it is not altogether clear that he is not guilty of an opposite imbalance [256].

Ritschl certainly does not "sell out" in a reductionist fashion to an ethical interpretation of Christianity. What he is doing, and the passage cited above demonstrates this admirably, is summoning Christianity to greater ethical responsibility, recognising that the Kingdom of God in the teaching of Jesus is shot through with an ethical demand. He in no way separates this perception from his task of interpreting the Christian tradition within which he stands, recognising the concomitant importance of a theological interpretation of Jesus. He notes, in short, that Christology and ethics must be mutually supporting, interdependent disciplines.

As the goal of Jesus' and God's work [257], it is imperative that the Kingdom of God should be kept distinct conceptually from the Church, lest the Church feels it has a monopoly on the work of God. The Kingdom of God is thus rescued by Ritschl from its ecclesiastical captivity.

Methodologically, its importance should be stressed even though Ritschl casts his theological system in a Pauline mould. Though justification and reconciliation are prominent in Ritschl's theology, it is the Kingdom of God which heads the presentation of the system [258]. Its formal position represents the extent to which Ritschl seeks to trace his understanding of Christianity to Jesus in the Gospels; it is not a system which merely expounds Paul. Such a system would have no significant place for the Kingdom of God.

3.3.5 Community

The manner in which the Kingdom of God finds expression in Ritschl's theology is as "community". The religious and ethical concept of the symbol Kingdom of God is found in concrete application as an emphasis upon the role of the community both in the task of theological construction and in the carrying through of ethical demands.

On the first point, Ritschl is quite categorical:

We can discover the full compass of his (i.e. Jesus') historical actuality solely from the faith of the Christian community. Not even his purpose to found the community can be quite understood historically save by one who, as a member of it, subordinates himself to his person. [259]

It should be stressed that Ritschl is talking here not simply of standing within a particular theological tradition - though he is talking of that too [260]. He is talking far more in terms of a real, concrete believing community of people. That this is so is confirmed by the directness of the relationship Ritschl perceives between this emphasis upon community and the concreteness of the community of the "sons of God" created by Jesus in its first form as the Twelve [261]. As Jesus' own purpose to found the Kingdom of God called him directly to found a community (*Gemeinde*) [262], so the relationship to Jesus can only properly be appraised and understood from the standpoint of the community (more accurately perhaps *a* community) referring back to him.

There is, of course, a problem implicit in Ritschl's approach where the notion of the community of the Kingdom of God is viewed independently of the concept of the Church, as it is indeed Ritschl's own wish to do. The two concepts are to be kept distinct. Theoretically, however, one could force Ritschl to admit that the distinction is possible only for one standing inside the Church in the first place, that is, inside the community of believers able to perceive the work of the Kingdom of God and its relationship back to the work and message of Jesus.

As an ethical entity, however, the Kingdom of God is theoretically and practically existent, for Ritschl, in a community where God is made known as the God of Love [263]. What the distinction Church/Kingdom of God enables Ritschl to achieve is the effective suspension of the specific identification of the Kingdom of God, *because* it is "supernatural" and "supramundane" [264]. In this way, the incompleteness, but also the concreteness, of the Church is maintained. At the same time, the tension between the concrete presence and the "transcendent" presence of the Kingdom of God is upheld and used [265].

The community focus as part of this understanding is paramount, however. It is

Ritschl's way of resisting individualism, an individualism which he perceives as only damaging to the Church; there can be no such thing as a "private theology" [266]. Individualism had ultimately been the major fault of Schleiermacher's attempt to place theology on a new footing [267]. Ritschl seeks to prevent his succumbing to the opposite temptation - that is, falling into sheer institutionalism - by keeping Church and Kingdom of God apart.

3.3.6 Love

The life-style to be expected of one living within the Community of the Kingdom of God needs to be explored. Two ways in which Ritschl expresses such a life-style he derives directly from the Gospel tradition, and from the life-style of Jesus as there presented.

The first of these is "love". Love lies at the heart of Ritschl's understanding of God:

> In my work on justification I amplified the opinion that the assertion of the personal character (*Persönlichkeit*) of God can only be firmly established upon the substance of love and in the directing of the will (which is implied in that love) toward the kingdom of God; in other words, the world view of the Christian church is fully established upon the Son whom God loves eternally. Everything else that pertains to the concept of God must be demonstrated within this framework. [268]

Love is the highest good and as such is the core of the ethics of the Kingdom of God:

> The concept of God as love corresponds to that idea of humankind which sees humanity destined for the kingdom of God and for the activity directed toward this kingdom...The kingdom of God is the highest good only in the sense that it forms at the same time the ethical ideal for whose attainment the members of the community bind themselves to each other through a definite type of reciprocal action...The righteous conduct through which the members of Christ's community share in effecting the kingdom of God finds its universal law and its personal motive in love to God and to one's neighbor. [269]

It is significant that this idea first finds expression in Ritschl's work through his interpretation of Mk 12.28-34 in E57 [270]. As well as demonstrating the extent once more to which biblical study and theological interest interweave in Ritschl's work, it is pertinent to suggest the importance of the Marcan emphasis, as opposed to the general Gospel emphasis, at this point [271].

3.3.7   Righteousness

The sixth and final theme to be considered as an example of the way Ritschl's picture of Jesus informs and relates to his theology is that of "righteousness". If it is fair to say that the theme of love was taken up first by Ritschl in connection with his interpretation of the Gospel of Mark, then it is certainly true that it was his interpretation of Matthew which produced his emphasis upon righteousness as a means of expressing the life-style befitting a member of the community of the Kingdom of God. This contention is confirmed by the fact that the importance of the concept of righteousness is apparent first in E50. It remains evident in *R u V* despite the fact that Ritschl had moved position quite considerably on his understanding of Jesus between these two points in his career [272].

Righteousness is seen by Ritschl as the activity correlate to membership of the Kingdom [273]. Its meaning is simply this; to be ethically obedient to the will of God. For Ritschl:

> *Jesus hat in seinem Begriff von der Gerechtigkeit den ursprünglichen sittlichen Gehalt der Aufgabe erneuert, welche von den Propheten und Psalmisten in jenem Worte bezeichnet worden war.* [274]

He did this by embodying in his own words and actions the righteousness of God. In "actualizing" complete obedience as God's Son in the fulfilment of his task to found the Kingdom of God, Jesus makes himself known as "the complete revelation of God as love, grace and faithfulness" [275].

As a direct result of this inspection of the life of Jesus as presented in the Gospels, it is possible to see that the righteousness of God is not something demanded. The relationship between the participant in the Kingdom of God, the actions performed to the Kingdom's end and the manner in which God may be said to affect or effect those actions, under the rubric of righteousness, is more subtle. For righteousness is ultimately faithfulness, the faithfulness of God first and foremost, yet also the faithfulness as expressed by God's people [276]. Thus:

> ...in the New Testament...the righteousness of God is recognized as the
> criterion of the special actions by which the community of Christ is brought
> into existence and led on to perfection; such righteousness cannot therefore
> be distinguished from the grace of God. [277]

Righteousness is thus a concept which, like love, expresses something of the nature of God, is found embodied in Jesus, and describes an aspect of the life of the Christian [278].

3.3.8   Summary

This brief survey of six significant themes in Ritschl's theology has tried to show how Ritschl relates his picture of Jesus to his construal of the Christian faith in general.

It should be stressed immediately that not all of the major themes of Ritschl's theology can be highlighted in this way. The very fact that he chooses to frame his *magnum opus* in Pauline terminology is sufficient demonstration of this; there are other influences. But Ritschl attempts to correlate and mutually interpret concepts across the differing theologies in the New Testament, as for example in his attempt to correlate justification and the Kingdom of God in J & R III [279].

Such observations are not, of course, without importance. But the analysis of their implications lies beyond the scope of the present study. The point which this section set out to make is clear; Ritschl's picture of Jesus is important for his theology as a whole in that it provides him in a direct way with material for his own constructive task.

4. SUMMARY

The chapter just concluded has been essentially expository in character, seeking to clarify what Ritschl was attempting to do and say. The aim of the chapter was to expound Ritschl's picture of Jesus which, it was claimed, is the essence not only of his Gospel study but, in some sense, of his theological system as a whole. Before that could be done, clarification of that premiss was first necessary. It was necessary to begin with broad sweeps and general methodological questions in order to determine how Ritschl perceived the task of theology. That enquiry took place in II.1.1-2.

On that basis, it was possible to see quite clearly the methodological significance of the New Testament for Ritschl.

This was then highlighted in II.1.3. A further aspect of Ritschl's understanding of theology - its Christocentricity - was then provided (II.1.4) prior to a survey of Ritschl's work as a New Testament scholar, in II.1.5.

Through attention to the christocentric character of Ritschl's theology, and particularly to the manner in which Ritschl construed that Christocentricity, it became clear that Ritschl attached special significance to the Gospels in his theology. For that reason it was then necessary to clarify how Ritschl perceived the Gospels, before beginning the task of expounding how he used them. This task was undertaken in II.2.1-2.

A section linking that part of the enquiry to the exposition was then provided (II.2.3). It was seen that Ritschl's concerns fall into the nexus of questions related to "the problem of the historical Jesus". How Ritschl used the Gospels is seen above all in his work in the realm of Christology. It was seen as imperative to expound Ritschl's picture of Jesus as is evident from his major works, building into the presentation the acceptance that Ritschl does not present his material in a straightforward fashion, and that the material is thus drawn from different points in Ritschl's career and from works of different genres. The exposition of Ritschl's picture of Jesus formed the heart of the chapter, and was presented in II.3.1.

From that central point of exposition, the move was then made back to Ritschl's use of the Gospels in more general terms. The enquiry sought to determine what relationship, if any, existed between Ritschl's study of the Gospels and particular aspects of his picture of Jesus (II.3.2). It was suggested that Ritschl's picture undergoes development in accordance both with his own theological development and with his Gospel study.

Finally, in II.3.3, the attempt was made to return to the more wide-ranging considerations with which the chapter began. The links between the picture of Jesus expounded at the chapter's heart, and the theological system which Ritschl constructs, were drawn.

The investigation must now turn to its critical and its constructive tasks. In focussing once more directly upon Ritschl's picture of Jesus, questions must be posed concerning its adequacy and legitimacy in its own right, and its status as a part of a theology in the sense Ritschl describes. On the basis of this critique it will then be possible to assess whether Ritschl's approach has anything positive to offer the present task of the Christian theologian.

Notes to Chapter II

1. Ritschl bibliography under entries for 1857, 1872, 1889 and 1902.
2. ibid. under entry for 1886.
3. See e.g. Dunn 1977 p342 and p416 n3.
4. E.g. Gunton 1983 p26ff esp.; also Pannenberg 1968 p45 and pp208ff and Calvert 1983 p89.
5. See Ritschl bibliography under 1881.
6. Ibid. under 1872. Gunton 1983 also lists J & R I in his bibliography (p213) but does not appear to refer to it explicitly in the text.
7. This does not appear to be a fault only of those who mention Ritschl in passing. Richmond 1978 is by no means exempt from this same criticism, being essentially an exposition of Ritschl's theology on the basis of Ritschl 1902 and 1881. Though he does refer to other works (e.g. to J & R I on p121 nn49 and 51, p216 n58 and p218 n132; and to ICR and others in the introductory survey p26), these references are peripheral to the main intention and approach of the work as a whole. Weyer-Menkhoff 1988 is a notable exception in giving attention to all of Ritschl's main works and more.
8. See Ritschl bibliography under entries for 1878, 1881 and 1889. The *Geschichte des Pietismus* was published in Bonn, the three volumes appearing in 1880, 1884 and 1886 respectively. *Schleiermachers Reden über die Religion und ihre Nachwirkungen auf die evangelische Kirche Deutschlands* was published in Bonn in 1874. Ritschl's essay *Über das Gewissen* appeared in 1876, and can be found in the second volume of the collected essays (*Gesammelte Aufsätze* Freiburg i.B. and Leipzig 1896). Other important works include *Fides implicita* (Bonn 1890) and the three-part *Geschichtliche Studien zur christlichen Lehre von Gott*, published originally in J.D.T. 1865 (part 1) and 1868 (parts 2 and 3)

and available in the second volume of the collected essays.

9. Others writing on Ritschl specifically naturally make use of the work (e.g. Hefner, Lotz, Busse, Mueller, Schäfer and Weyer- Menkhoff).

10. The work is still in print (de Gruyter, Berlin). The introduction to the work is available in E.T. (Hefner 1972).

11. E.g. Ulrich Zwingli (J.D.T. 1872), *Die Entstehung der lutherischen Kirche* (Z.K.G. 1876) and *Über die beiden Principien des Protestantismus* (Z.K.G. 1876). There is as yet, to my knowledge, no adequate assessment of Ritschl's work on Pietism, though some attention has been given to his work on Luther (Lotz 1974) and his historical work generally (Hefner 1964 and 1966 ch.2).

12. Ritschl-specialists apart, Hans Hübner is a notable exception (Hübner 1983 p303f). Hefner's failure to make fullest use of *R u V II* is surprising despite the reasons given (see Hefner 1966 p12f).

13. See bibliography under entry for 1851.

14. Ibid. under entries for 1861 and 1862.

15. See details in bibliography under appended entry for 1877-8 (Unpublished work).

16. See e.g. esp. Ritschl 1887 and ICR §3 p221f. See also Lotz (1974) p16ff.

17. As e.g. by such recipients of Ritschl's theology as M.Reischle, W.Herrmann and J.Kaftan.

18. As e.g. by W.Rauschenbusch (see e.g. W.Rauschenbusch: Selected Writings, Paulist Press, New York 1984 p71f).

19. E.g. - and influentially - by J.Macquarrie (1963) p76f. Wrzecionko has, however, provided the necessary qualifier to all attempts to label Ritschl a "Kantian" too easily (see Draper 1984 p7f).

20. Merk 1972.

21. See below III.3.

22. Kraus 1970 p255 and below II.1.3.

23. Draper 1984 p47.

24. Draper 1984 p52ff and 50ff. Cf. J.L.Houlden (1985) p122 for a modern English perception of the difficulty of discipline-definition, with respect to "New Testament theology" (ultimately Ritschl's own difficulty also).

25. B.Weiss 1882 p1.

26. ibid. p2.

27. ibid. pp2 and 20.

28. ibid. p20. Though it must be admitted that an essential inner unity is perceived within the New Testament as the basis of biblical dogmatics (p20f).

29. Kähler 1897 p199.

30. Morgan 1973 pp11 and 68-116. It should be recognized that to move beyond the canon in order to construct a "New Testament theology" is in one sense logically impossible. Hence Wrede's *"sogenannte"* New Testament theology.

31. I & R II p23 (see n45 for trans.). Cf also BT §1. There would thus appear to be more of Gabler's definition of "biblical theology" in Ritschl's thinking than Draper allows (Draper 1984 p53). See I & R III p14f and O.Ritschl (1893) p229.

32. I & R III p15.

33. ibid p1.

34. ibid p14.

35. ICR §3 p222 (Ritschl's emphasis). The German text reads: *"(es) gilt als Grundsatz der evangelischen Kirche, daß man die christliche Lehre allein aus der heiligen Schrift schöpfe." (Unterricht* 1966 ed. edited by G.Ruhbach: Mohn, Gütersloh; p13). See also I & R III p194 and *R u V II* p9 and p12.

36. Though Hefner draws attention to the fact that ICR proved to be by no means as "popular" as Ritschl had hoped: Hefner 1972 p220.

37. *R u V II* p20 (see n44 for trans.).

38. "Holy Scripture: the exclusive source for the theological understanding of Christian revelation"; Schäfer 1968 pp193-196 esp.193.

39. ibid. p193.

40. *R u V II* pp23-5; i.e. Ritschl sees the need for a way of sorting out the New Testament's diversity; he seeks, in short, a criterion for such selectivity.

41. ibid. p2ff esp.p4.

42. There is much more to be said on this matter. Further clarification of Ritschl's position must draw upon his emphasis on the communal character of theology (see e.g. *R u V II* p23, O.Ritschl 1893 p230). Here, the purpose has been solely to draw attention to it, and to establish that Ritschl's understanding of the discipline "biblical theology" is not as uniform as first appears. See further *R u V II* p12 and p16 and IV.2 below.

43. He thus builds directly on Baur yet sees the danger of the implications of Baur's position. A central problem proves to be the question of Christian theology and the New Testament canon, a point at which the inherent difficulty of the very

term "New Testament theology" emerges in its clearest form (cf n30 above).

44. "Holy Scripture, the NT especially, proves itself as the source for positive theology through interpretation" _R u V II_ p20 (my translation and emphasis).

45. "...biblical theology, especially that of the NT, is not a system or series of theological propositions...rather, it presents a set of religious trains of thought." ibid. p23 (my translation and emphasis).

46. "...theology is called, for the purpose of guiding education in the Church, to gain directly an authentic awareness of the Christian religion and revelation; this can only be drawn from records which derive from the time of the Church's founding epoch, and from no others." ibid. p13 (my translation)

47. "...theology, whose task it is to present the Christian religion as found in the original sources, is directed only to the New Testament writings." ibid. p16 (my translation; see further ICR §3).

48. As e.g. by Kraus (1970) p255.

49. As the development of New Testament study has clearly shown, this was an unwise move (cf Draper 1984 50f, 91-97 but esp. p205ff). For a persistent statement of one aspect of the importance of looking beyond the biblical canon for material relevant to the task of the interpretation of the New Testament, see Vermes 1983 esp. chs. 5, 6, 8 and 9.

50. See immediately below

51. "For Christianity's body of ideas can only be drawn directly from the New Testament. The failure to distinguish between the Testaments when using Scripture is inadmissible, because even concepts and sentences which sound the same in two respective places are elements in differing contexts, and also because the religion of Israel is, despite its close relationship to Christianity, nevertheless a different religion." (Ritschl in Schäfer 1968 p193; my translation).

52. ibid.

53. ibid.

54. F.L.Cross (ed.): The Oxford Dictionary of the Christian Church (London 1958) article: "Christocentric" p278; also J.K.Riches (1972) esp. p223. See further Draper (1984) p140 and my forthcoming article "Christocentricity and Community: Ritschl's quest for norms for a biblical theology" in Darrell Jodock ed. Community, Science and Theology: Albrecht Ritschl's Significance for Twentieth-Century Theology (Augsburg Fortress: Minneapolis).

55. This appears to be suggested in Cross (op.cit.). This is at least the case in the more specific first definition given (in connection with which Ritschl is specifically mentioned): "Christocentric theology bases itself on a literal interpretation of Mt 11.27, to the exclusion of the passages in Scripture which

seem to refer to or imply a revelation in nature, and thus precludes the possibility of natural theology altogether."

56. By the term "earthly Jesus" is meant "Jesus as he was", as a historical figure who lived at a particular point in human history regardless of the question whether or not details of his life are recoverable. That Ritschl moves on under the assumption that details are available raises further issues and discloses the nature of the "problem of the historical Jesus". For discussion of sonship and the founding of the Kingdom see below II.3.1.2 and III.2.5.

57. Ritschl 1871 p161f and _R u V II_ p21f.

58. Ritschl 1861 makes a distinction between the _"historische"_ or _"geschichtliche"_ _"Christus"_ and the _"ideelle Christus"_. The use of the term "historical Jesus" is thus a more contemporary construal of the distinction - even disregarding the problems of the term "historical Jesus" itself. That Ritschl was not wholly consistent with his use of the terms "Jesus" and "Christ" when referring to Jesus has, however, been observed; see e.g. Menke 1903 p19f.

59. J & R III p406.

60. ibid. p432 (cf also p431 and p468).

61. This point has been made most recently by Calvert 1983.

62. As will become clear at many points below throughout this study, Ritschl's approach can be built upon precisely because it does not remain ultimately tied to the historical norm, i.e. Ritschl sees Christology as something more than the sum of its historical parts. It is therefore in the realm of the reception of the religious ideas which are related to the historical data about Jesus that the discussion of the adequacy of Ritschl's "picture of Jesus" takes place.

63. Ritschl assumes there _is_ such material available. Ultimately, however, his case does not rest totally on this material.

64. Cf above n56. If the earthly Jesus is of direct relevance to Christianity, then the fruits of historical research cannot but be of interest to the Christian theologian. This is a recognition which New Testament interpreters have come to with some difficulty. For Ritschl it is an assumption which requires no examination.

65. Otto Ritschl 1893 and 1896. Hefner 1972 pp3-16; Richmond 1978 pp18-28.

66. There is reason to feel that Otto Ritschl's portrait of his father is less analytical and critical than it might have been. McCulloh (1973 p9f) draws upon material collected and published by E.Ehrenfeuchter in _Jahrbuch der Gesellschaft für niedersächsische Kirchengeschichte_ 60, 1962 pp 146-150.

67. See, for example, the entry on Ritschl in F.L.Cross (ed.): The Oxford Dictionary of the Christian Church (O.U.P. London 1958) p1168, where the suggestion seems to be that once Ritschl began to lecture on "systematic theology" his

Tübingen background (and concomitant interest in the New Testament and early Christianity's history) were simply jettisoned.

68. Otto Ritschl 1893 p449, 1896 p534f.

69. Cf. Otto Ritschl 1893 p105.

70. Baur had already produced such works as *Die Christuspartei in der korinthischen Gemeinde, der Gegensatz des petrinischen und paulinischen Christenthums in der ältesten Kirche, der Apostel Petrus in Rom* (T.Z.T. 1831), *Die sogenannten Pastoralbriefe des Apostels Paulus aufs neue kritisch untersucht* (Tübingen and Stuttgart 1835), *Die christliche Gnosis* (Tübingen 1835) and *Die christliche Lehre von der Versöhnung in ihrer geschichtlichen Entwicklung von der ältesten Zeit bis auf die neueste* (Tübingen 1838).

71. Ritschl encountered Baur's work on Gnosticism, and the doctrines of reconciliation and the trinity in particular; see O.Ritschl 1893 p69ff.

72. ibid p77.

73. For a discussion of Ritschl's "break" with Baur see esp. Jodock 1969.

74. See, e.g., the final paragraph of Ritschl 1861 (p459) and Hefner 1972 (p24).

75. Ritschl's relationship to the Tübingen School is an object of study in itself, and is made yet more complex by the question of his personal relationship to Baur. See, however, Jodock 1969 and Harris 1975 ch.7.

76. Ritschl 1847.

77. Ritschl 1851 p43; cf O.Ritschl 1893 p180.

78. Ritschl 1846 p176.

79. ibid. p172 (see below II.2.2)

80. ibid. p174f and p193ff.

81. Ritschl consistently pays relatively little attention to the third Gospel throughout his career. It is most prominent in §§ 5, 6 and 28 of *R u V II*, yet §§ 7, 11 and 13 do not mention it. It is referred to 5 times (the same as the Fourth Gospel) in the opening chapter of E57. The Gospel of Luke loses out on both counts in the Griesbach hypothesis/Marcan priority debate. The generally late date given to Luke in this period (that Baur picked up Ritschl's thesis about Marcion's Gospel and the Gospel of Luke should be noted), not unrelated to its unPauline character, explains the background of modern German reception of Luke. In the Bultmann school, the "historicization of the kerygma" has been seen as negative (cf. Bultmann 1955b p116ff, Conzelmann 1960 and 1969 pp149-152).

82. Hefner draws attention to the fact that Baur and Ritschl represent two essentially distinct models for construing the development of early Christianity (which may be termed the thesis-antithesis-synthesis model and the kernel/husk model);

Hefner 1962 p262f, 1966 pp14-21, 26-30 and 43f. See also W.G.Kümmel 1973 p162f.

83. Reservations may, in other words, be expressed about Ritschl's attempt to detach Paul from the Paulinists/Gentiles and Peter from the Petrine/Jewish Christian party. Though he succeeds in pointing out the greater complexity of earliest Christianity than Baur had allowed, the manner in which he finds his way through the complexity may ultimately be shown to be too neat. For Ritschl renders Peter and Paul "orthodox" in an anachronistic fashion.

84. Dunn's use of Ritschl (1977 p342) marks a major, welcome rediscovery of Ritschl's work at this point.

85. Below II.1.5 and II.3.2. It is worth noting that Ritschl's own move from seeing the question of obedience to the Mosiac Law as a major issue for Jesus to one where other aspects of the Jewish tradition in which he stood - sonship and Kingdom of God - are seen as central is in some ways reflected in recent work on the Gospels (e.g. pre-eminently Sanders 1985).

86. Ritschl 1851.

87. The Tübingen School was not uniform in its thinking on this question, though Ritschl stepped noticeably out of line through his shift of position (i.e. Matthean priority was commonly supported, but in different ways e.g. by Baur and Hilgenfeld; see Ritschl 1851 pp2-25, esp p2ff and Harris 1975 esp.pp 209-13, 226-229 and 232-7). In taking up the argument for Marcan priority, Ritschl adopted a simplified form of Ewald's thesis: 1851 p25ff.

88. Its importance is perceived by Farmer (1961 p35 n46; 1976 p29). Farmer does, of course, have a particular point to make, one which the present writer would not share, yet his contribution is valid nevertheless. Richmond (1978) does not begin his consideration of Ritschl's work till 1857. Hefner (1966) and Lotz (1974) make no mention of the 1851 essay; even allowing for the limitation demanded by their particular interests, the omission is somewhat puzzling.

89. Tuckett 1983 esp. pp5-12. Farmer noted the dogmatic consequences, however (see previous note and Ch. I n9). The two arguments are ultimately not mutually exclusive.

90. There are over sixty references to the Gospel of Matthew, of which a third are to the passage Mt 5.17-20.

91. One might even say the "kirchliche Verantwortlichkeit" (ecclesiastical responsibility) of such enquiry, given Ritschl's procedure. Mueller draws attention to Ritschl's perception of the need to be a Christian theologian within the believing community (1969 p30; cf.e.g. J & R III p2 and p4). See also a related though not wholly similar section in Draper 1984 p58ff. Schäfer (1968 pp166-170) relates this perception of Ritschl's to the latter's tendency ultimately

to skirt round the problem of the existence of different religions and simplify the theological task through his concern to include theological commitment on his agenda.

92. Jodock 1969 p170.

93. Cf O.Ritschl 1893 p439. Some of this work Ritschl was able to include in E57 (e.g. the 1855 essay on the Essenes published in T.J. that year).

94. Ritschl 1859.

95. The use of Mt 10.34-39 (Ritschl 1859 p15) and Mk 3.28ff should be noted, however. These references apart, the Gospel of John is the only Gospel to be used.

96. O.Ritschl 1893 p369.

97. The work on Hebrews appeared in T.S.K. in 1866. The work on the death of Jesus appeared in two parts in J.D.T. in 1863, much of its material being worked into *R u V II*. A major example of Ritschl's work in the history of dogma in this period is the three-part *"Geschichtliche Studien zur christlichen Lehre von Gott"* (J.D.T. 1865-68). The question of method in the history of dogma was dealt with in an essay in 1871 (in J.D.T.).

98. Ritschl 1861 p434f.

99. ibid p437f. The tension between the "realism" and "idealism" of Baur's Christology - producing the problem of the concreteness of the life of Jesus within a theology structured along Hegelian lines - is discussed in Hodgson 1966 (esp. pp100-121) and in compact form by Morgan (1985 esp. pp278-82).

100. ibid. pp434 and 437 (cf p447). There is the attendant problem of the fluent and imprecise use of *"geschichtlich"* (435, 443, 447 and 448) and *"historisch"* in a seeming identical sense. See also above n58.

101. When expressed in such terms, the matter seems obvious and Baur's error therefore quite plain. Yet clearly both are operating in the area of both history and theology, seeking to construct historical theologies, both concluding that a New Testament theology ought to be sought. The precise nature of the difference between the two men is more subtle than such a brief treatment suggests. See esp. Jodock (1969).

102. See discussions in O.Ritschl (1893 pp393-9) and Jodock (1969 pp257-269). Both are ultimately favourable towards Ritschl, the former predictably so. But even O.Ritschl recognizes that his father was under pressure and made mistakes (1893 p399), a prime example being picked up by the anonymous writer's response to Ritschl's 1861 essay (see next note): Ritschl quoted Hegel when he thought he was quoting Baur.

103. The anonymous writer of the original article to which Ritschl offered his 1861 response proved to be Eduard Zeller. Zeller retorted with *"Die historische Kritik und das Wunder"* (1861), and then later with *"Zur Würdigung der Ritschl'schen 'Erläuterungen' "* (1862). Ritschl became embroiled in a philosophical-epistemological debate about miracles, a realm in which, it may be felt, he was not properly equipped to argue.

104. The questions of a *New Testament* theology (as problematic for someone following a rigid Tübingen approach), the problem of the canon *per se* and the whole issue of the theological relevance of historical enquiry into the life of Jesus would all have been areas of interest derivable from the initial exchange.

105. The problems of Ritschl's epistemology are widely known and often cited (e.g. Orr 1898 p64; Garvie 1918 p819; Mueller 1969 p43). Aside from the question whether the wholesale rejection of Ritschl's approach can be legitimated by reference to such a deficiency in Ritschl's thought (as attempted e.g. by Orr), the recognition of Ritschl's limitation as a philosopher can nevertheless be made (cf Draper, using Wrzecionko, 1984 p7f).

106. *R u V II* pIII (*Aus der Vorrede zur ersten Auflage*).

107. Troeltsch 1977 p63f, esp. p64.

108. ibid. p5.

109. See esp. nn30 and 43 above.

110. On Ritschl's rejection of "Lives of Jesus" see esp. opening pages of II.3.1. On the question of the diversity of the New Testament see esp. III.3.. The term "Canonical Jesus" is my coinage and will be explored with respect to Kähler's position below (III.3). On Ritschl, rather than Kähler, as a way forward in Christology, see IV.3-5.

111. i.e. though a theological understanding of Jesus, it must be controlled nevertheless by a historical norm.

112. The precise meaning of the term "normativity of Jesus" must be explored (which "Jesus" ? in what sense "normative" ?). The former question is the main focus of this study. See III.5 for a summary of Ritschl's actual answer to this question.

113. Below esp. II.2.3., II.3.2. and II.3.3.

114. In *R u V II* this is especially the case in §§ 6, 13 and 28.

115. In the 7 paragraphs of the sixth chapter of *J & R III* there are only 20 explicit citations from the Fourth Gospel. There are, however, other more general references to the Gospel (e.g. p436ff, p443, p450 and esp.p453). The extent to which Ritschl's picture of Jesus is at this point largely determined by his use of the Fourth Gospel is spelled out by McCulloh: "What we find is that Ritschl reads directly from the Gospel narratives an account of the decisions of the mind

of Christ in accord with Ritschl's own notion of the vocation of Christ as the founder of the Kingdom of God which ignores the different tendencies of the individual Gospel traditions and harmonizes them to present a picture of Christ similar to the Johannine Gospel" (1973 p48 n1). That there is more to this problem than McCulloh allows, and that McCulloh rests too heavily, like many interpreters of Ritschl before and after him, upon J & R III, must be demonstrated.

116. *R u V II* p27f n1.

117. ibid §§ 5 and 6, in which there are 65 references to Mt, 49 to Mark and 33 to Luke in the space of 14 pages of text.

118. The third reprint of J & R III was identical to the second. Fabricius (1909) explores the development of Ritschl's theology through scrutiny of the alterations. His study concentrates on J & R III, however, and is as such incomplete. A more detailed comparison of the different editions of *R u V II*, as requested by Hübner (above n12), would be most welcome.

119. Picked up first of all by W.Herrmann, then later by e.g. J.Kaftan, A.Harnack, M.Reischle and - critically - by E.Troeltsch. "Ritschlianism" and "the Ritschl school" were the pace-setters in the closing decades of the 19th Century in German theology. See e.g. Mildenberger (1981) esp p127ff; and the comments made by Gerrish (1984) p5f.

120. E.g. an 1875 essay on the Fourth Gospel, an 1883 essay on the Kingdom of God and *Die Entstehung der lutherischen Kirche* (1876).

121. *Theologie und Metaphysik* (1881); ICR; *Geschichte des Pietismus* (Vol.1 1880; Vol.2 1884; Vol.3 1886).

122. Ritschl 1846 pp193ff. and below II.2.2.

123. Lecture-notes for the 1867-8 series are also available (and would be of more direct use in helping to fill in the detail about Ritschl's developing thought in the period 1857-74). They are sadly almost illegible. But from what one can tell, there appear to be few differences, though closer scrutiny would be necessary to establish this.

124. "...that they were not intended to be historical documents at all (lit: not intended to supply historical records). As collections of traditions about the life of Jesus, they were subordinate to the dogmatic tendencies of particular parties." Ritschl 1846 p172 (my translation).

125. For even Baur accepts much of what the Gospels present - Matthew in particular - as historically reliable. The notion of Evangelists (or their communities) "creating" material only gained widespread popularity and credibility with Bultmann.

126. E50 p27 re. Mt 5.17.

127. ibid. p37.

128. It should again be stressed that the selection of material does not yet mean alteration (and thus the use of material as suggested by redaction criticism). However much Baur's *Tendenzkritik* may be seen as a precursor of redaction criticism, Baur was not himself a redaction critic.

129. Ritschl 1851 p39.

130. ibid. "The Gospel (i.e. Mark) admittedly lacks a dogmatic characteristic of the kind unmistakeably displayed by Matthew and Luke. But when it is recalled to what extent, in Matthew and Luke, the dogmatic tendencies contribute to the obscuration and abridgement of the historical picture of Christ, the alleged dogmatic indifference (of Mark) can only be deemed a sign of greater historical worth, rather than a sign of its secondary character." (my translation)

131. E.g. Mt 5.17-20 is still used extensively in E57. See also, however, the use of Mt 17.24-7 (p31), 10.5,6 (p34) and 7.21-3 (p35).

132. E57 p43f n2 (cf a similar case on p29 n2).

133. BT contain the order Mk - Mt/Lke - Jn in terms of worth for the exposition of religious ideas (BT p107).

134. Esp. recently McGrath (1986) p58 and p66 n21 (cf also above n115).

135. Ritschl seems keen to respect the "Johannine" element in the Fourth Gospel (e.g. his reference to the "Johannine speeches of Jesus" in *R u V II* p99). The value of the Fourth Gospel relative to the Synoptic Gospels (see above n133) is one which Ritschl maintained (E57 p28 and pp48f n1; also *R u V II* pp26-7 n1). For a more detailed discussion of the nature of that relativity see further below III.1.1-2.

136. E.g. *R u V II* p100 and J & R III p387 and 476. See esp. below II.3.1. "Jesus the Son".

137. An issue which receives attention in the wake of work undertaken by C.H.Dodd (1963), O. Cullmann (1975) and, recently, J.A.T.Robinson (in The Priority of John London 1985). See also Carson 1981.

138. E.g. Ritschl 1871 p161 and *R u V II* p21f.

139. Ritschl may not have been the first to make this observation, yet he is to be respected for seeking to work out its implications.

140. Though the existence of diverse communities is recognized, it is not by any means clear that Ritschl is in a position to work through all the logical steps which should accompany the recognition. That is to say, Ritschl still appears to assume an essential harmony of an original "apostolic community" (cf *R u V II* p22).

141. The expression is mine. For further discussion of the problem of the diversity of the New Testament and Ritschl's response to it, see III.4.

142. A complex theological point could be raised at this juncture concerning the religious believer's "encounter" with Jesus from the standpoint of faith. Such complexity is not in view here. The point made here is more simple: the reader confronts the words of the Evangelists in the text of the Gospels. It is, in other words, taken for granted that the Evangelists desire their hearers/readers ultimately to "encounter Jesus" in a religious sense through their words.

143. Ritschl appears to make a distinction tending in this direction in *R u V II* p22.

144. i.e. Paul shows a distinct lack of interest in historical details about Jesus' life.

145. See below II.3.1.

146. Schweitzer 1968. On the modern reception of Schweitzer: J.M. Robinson 1959 ch.2. and Meyer 1979 (pp25-59, esp. p43f). I agree wholeheartedly with Colin Brown Jesus in European Protestant Thought 1778-1860 (Baker Book House 1988) p.xvi that Schweitzer's account has severe limitations (see C.Marsh 1989).

147. If it was felt on the basis of the previous section that Jesus' teaching and not self-understanding (if such a sharp distinction can be made) was Ritschl's sole interest, consider Ritschl's concern for the "attitude" of Jesus (*Verhalten*) and the "person" of Jesus in e.g. E50 pp 41, 43 and 45, and E57 p46.

148. "Picture of Jesus" is the most appropriate term in that it retains a degree of ambiguity. It does not need to be, though it may be, a "historical picture" in the sense that it can consist only of historically verifiable data. It could also mean a "theological interpretation".

149. More precisely, he rejected the idea of writing a Life as if it were automatically of theological relevance (J & R III p3). Whether Ritschl would have claimed that there was, in theory, sufficient material for the writing of a Life (or at least for the writing of a continuous account of the last three years of Jesus' life) remains unclear.

150. The reason for this is clear: Ritschl rejected "Lives of Jesus" as theologically irresponsible. Ritschl's nearest equivalent to a systematic presentation of aspects of his "picture of Jesus" is to be found in B.T. §16.

151. Though it is accepted that such aspects are "built in" in different ways and to different ends i.e. the earlier pictures of 1850 and 1857 find their place in histories of earliest Christianity, and the later picture(s) of 1874 are incorporated into a biblical, systematic theology.

152. Draper (1984 p58) notes the near identity of "Church theology" (*kirchliche*

Theologie) and the "history of dogma" (*Dogmengeschichte*) for Ritschl. This observation can perhaps be extended in order that Ritschl's Church History may also be seen under the same rubric. The theological importance of Church History thus becomes apparent.

153. See below III.2.

154. Toulmin's terminology (in the discipline of theology as taken up by Kelsey) has become standard usage in the field of argument (S.Toulmin <u>The Uses of Argument</u> (C.U.P. Cambridge 1963). The term "warrant" is here used to denote historical data used by Ritschl to support his christological assertions.

155. <u>ICR</u> §2 p221. Ritschl does explore "Son of God" as a title (e.g. <u>B.T.</u> p159f) but this aspect of his exposition does not control his understanding of the "sonship" of Jesus.

156. ibid §12 p225.

157. "The entire self-presentation of Jesus according to the sources is misconstrued if it is denied that Jesus calls God his Father in the same sense as he denotes himself the Son of Man." <u>R u V II</u> p49 (my translation).

158. <u>J & R III</u> p386; cf.<u>B.T.</u> p134.

159. ibid. p387 n1 (cf also <u>ICR</u> §§ 47 and 48; <u>B.T.</u> p171).

160. <u>ICR</u> §22 p229f (cf also §44 and <u>J & R III</u> p413 and p465).

161. <u>J & R III</u> p482 (cf also <u>ICR</u> §22)

162. ibid. p449 (cf. <u>B.T.</u> p172).

163. ibid. p475f.

164. Particularly in <u>J & R III</u>; see e.g. pp 387, 404, 436f, 439, 443, 449f, 453, 461 and 476f.. But note also <u>R u V II</u> esp. pp36ff, 97ff and p244. Ritschl is also able to draw on Synoptic material, however: e.g. <u>R u V II</u> p96ff, <u>J & R III</u> p454; <u>ICR</u> nn1 and 29; <u>BT</u> p145f.

165. <u>E57</u> p35.

166. "...it was Jesus' concern to bring up a particular circle of people (in)to the Kingdom of God through the exertion of regular influence upon them." <u>R u V II</u> p31 (my translation) (cf also ibid. 31f and <u>J & R III</u> p386).

167. "It is therefore just as incorrect to maintain that Jesus did away with the ceremonial law and affirmed the moral law as it is to consider Jesus primarily as a law-giver." (<u>E57</u> p46 my translation).

168. <u>J & R III</u> p413; see section p413ff in general, esp. p415.

169. "Jesus knows that as Messiah he brings into being the reign of God through his distinctive work. Because of this, the realization of that reign as a kingdom of

106

obedient subjects depends for him upon his creating a community fit for the moral task of the divine Kingdom. Members of the community are fit for their task if they recognize in their master the Son of God and the bearer of God's reign." *R u V II* p3lf.(my translation).

170. Below 3.1.6.

171. J & R III p386.

172. ibid p387.

173. e.g. Foerster and Quell 1958; Cullmann 1959 (ch.7 pp195- 237); Hahn 1969 (ch.2 pp68-135).

174. J & R III p401.

175. J & R III p468.

176. ICR §13 p225f.

177. J & R III p406 and p446.

178. ICR §47 p241.

179. ibid, §50 p242.

180. J & R III p463.

181. ibid. p446 (cf p447f). Ritschl's discussion at this point about what the Kingdom of God would look like in actual practice is surely one of the reasons for his critics' claim that he is a captive of his bourgeois culture (Barth, Walther, Niebuhr) and that he had misunderstood what the Kingdom of God is about.

182. J & R III p480 (cf. also ICR §§41-2).

183. J & R III p477.

184. ibid. p444

185. "Jesus foresees that even in death he gives up his life solely to his Father, and that in his voluntary death he not only retains the particular suitability of his life for God, but even renders himself more suitable. This being the case, his life cannot be compared with the lives of other human beings, whose designation as servants of God is confronted by the destiny of death which broods over them." *R u V II* p84 (my translation). A full discussion of Ritschl's handling of the topic of the death of Jesus would require a separate treatment, particularly his dependence upon Mk 10.45 and 8.35ff in *R u V II* pp80-8. It need only be stated at this point that for Ritschl Jesus foresaw his own death and saw it as of particular significance, a "fact" which Ritschl interprets as Jesus' fulfilment of his vocation.

186. Below II.3.2. See e.g. Perrin 1963; Perrin 1976 p66 and Chilton 1984 pp4-7.

187. E57 p33.

188. "The summary of the original proclamation of Jesus links the generally applicable summons to a change of mind to the promise of the imminently approaching revelation of God's reign (Mk 1.15 cf 6.12; Lke 13.3, 15.7). This demand is only fully understood when it is recognized that Jesus imparts in differing degrees of clarity to opponents and doubters alike that the distinctive action he undertakes in accordance with his own vocation itself brings God's reign into being. His healing of the demonically sick - through which the power of the devil is restricted - enables God's reign to enter human life (Mt 12.28). In bringing the message of the Kingdom of God to the poor and release to the captives, and in enabling the blind to see, he proves himself to be the bearer of the reign of God. (Lke 4.17-21; Mt 11.2-6). *R u V II* p30 (my translation).

189. E57 p33.

190. ibid.

191. ibid. p46.

192. Though it must be admitted that it would fit in well with the ambiguity inherent in Ritschl's use of the word "founder" with respect to Jesus (see further below III.2.3).

193. See n166 above.

194. *R u V II* p30 (and p32).

195. See above n169.

196. Throughout §§ 5 and 6 in *R u V II*.

197. I have so far resisted using a term such as "mature" picture of Jesus, or "later" or "developed" picture. The reason for this is simply because it is a major feature of the study to disclose the interrelationship of Gospel study and theological development. Caution must thus also be exercised about referring to *the* picture of Jesus which Ritschl presents. It is precisely the theological responsibility which Ritschl persistently maintains which renders his picture both not readily definable *and* susceptible to a charge of subjectivism. Nevertheless it is clear that his use of Mark after 1851 is a turning-point in his construal of the Gospel material with respect to the question of working out a picture of Jesus.

198. Jesus' Messiahship is prominent in B.T., where it is interpreted in the light of the Davidic tradition (B.T. p157f). It is still understood within the framework of his work as the Kingdom's founder, however (B.T. p125).

199. See e.g. E50 p48.

200. *R u V II* p27f, p29; B.T. p116, 118f, 137 and 144ff.; J & R III p427 and p441; ICR § 20 p229; n56 p271.

201. i.e. as part of the *munus triplex*, subjected to reassessment by Ritschl in § 46 of J & R III. See recently McCulloh 1973 for a discussion of this aspect of Ritschl's work.

202. E57 p32f.

203. See 3.1.2. above. The obedience displayed by Jesus depends upon this relationship. These considerations consume Ritschl's interest in the "Messiahship" of Jesus.

204. E50 p49.

205. ICR § 20 p229. Allowance can be made for Ritschl's error (or at least confusion) with regard to the narrow Old Testament background at this point. "The religion of the Old Testament" is, of course, best understood more widely than as the religious ideas simply found in the texts.

206. Kingdom and Sonship relate also to Judaism's past as Jesus receives its tradition. These are, however, the two which Jesus, in Ritschl's interpretation, may be said to have developed. For an interesting, if overdramatized, treatment of the question of Jesus' development of the understanding of the Kingdom of God, Riches 1980 chs.4 and 5 (and more generally in Harvey ed.1985 pp37-60).

207. See below II.3.3.1 and II.3.3.3..

208. See above II.2.3.

209. The potentiality for change should not necessarily lead to the assumption that change has occurred, of course. As will become clear below, however, significant development *is* to be discerned.

210. A term Ritschl does use himself (e.g. E50 p51; see also J & R III p460 and the use of the phrase *"Geschichtsdarstellung"* in *R u V II* p100).

211. It must be admitted that Ritschl cannot be presented too much as a "man before his time", as one who anticipated the subtle distinctions demanded by the understanding of the theological significance of interest in the "historical Jesus". Yet the manner in which he works and the conclusions he reaches certainly do provoke further fruitful discoveries. See below Ch.III.3 and 4. and ch.IV esp. 2-4.

212. Barnett 1976 esp. ch.3 pp139-241.

213. This is, it should be stressed, not a simple matter of distinguishing between what Ritschl sought in principle and achieved in practice, even though such an observation would not be wholly inappropriate. For as will become clear below (III.4), Ritschl seeks both respect for the role of diverse communities (but without perceiving the full implications of that respect) *and* a firm historical norm (which he maintains can be found and function more objectively than is

the case).

214. There are 51 references to Matthew in E50 on pp27-47. The four references to the other three Gospels include on p30 a reference to Mk 9.37, Lke 10.20 and Jn 12.44 on grammatical grounds. The only other reference to a non-Matthean Gospel is to Lke 16.17 (p28).

215. Cf. above II.1.5.2, where a similar dependence upon the Gospel of Matthew was mentioned (cf Ritschl 1846 pp172-202: Ritschl recognizes fully the dogmatic tendency of the first Gospel, yet believes its portrayal of Jesus to be the most reliable as an account of details of Jesus' life).

216. There are 65 references to the Gospel of Matthew in E57 (see above n90) and 19 references to Mark.

217. E57 p28.

218. The coverage of Matthean material in E57 is, however, slight when compared with E50 (pp 35-45 in E57 and pp27-43 in E50).

219. E57 p45.

220. cf n.92 above.

221. See esp. E50 pp47-51; but also discussion of Messiahship above in II.3.1.7.

222. This is an awkward claim to make and it is difficult to document. One may point to a reduction in the number of references to the *"Person Jesu"* in the later edition. But E50 p48 would seem to suggest that Jesus' teaching, not person, was important from the start. More appropriate, therefore, would be the claim that Ritschl has revised his understanding of the way in which the significance of the person of Jesus is to be understood and expressed. The revision in Ritschl's understanding of the main thrust of Jesus' teaching (see below n228) is thus directly related to Ritschl's understanding of the manner in which Jesus' person is significant.

223. "...the perfect righteousness which Jesus demanded over against the Pharisees as a condition of entry into the heavenly Kingdom was presented as a reality by Jesus himself. Such a postulate would have come to nothing, and could not have created a community, had there been no focal point for that life of perfect righteousness in the person of Jesus." (E50 p45 my translation).

224. "In no way was law-giving and confrontation with the Mosaic Law the main task of Jesus. Rather, Jesus' first and highest task was the founding of the Kingdom of God through the presentation of his personal worth as Son of Man and through the awakening of faith in him." (E57 p46 my translation).

225. Though stress upon the "titles" of "Messiah" and "prophet" may not be prominent (except in the discussion of the *munus triplex* in J & R III § 46), the importance of the "prophetic tradition" in Ritschl's understanding of Jesus

should be mentioned (e.g. *R u V II* § 5; cf. above n200).

226. Though discussion of the Lordship of Jesus does feature in Ritschl's chapter on Paul (E57 p80f.).

227. See e.g. E50 p46, though Ritschl uses a strange - indeed erroneous - argument in this context.

228. The Mosaic Law ceases to be of central significance for Ritschl, even though - depite Ritschl's recognition that Jesus was no law-giver - the opening chapter of both E50 and E57 is entitled *"Christus und das mosaische Gesetz"*. In J & R, the question of the Mosaic Law seems to have disappeared from view.

229. See above n164.

230. J & R III pp 451 and 454; *R u V II* p96; also B.T. p146ff., 157 and 164.

231. Cf esp. *R u V II* §§ 7 and 11 (e.g. pp42, 83 and 87f).

232. It can safely be said that Ritschl's use of Luke is never a constitutive use, i.e. his position is reached essentially with reference to Matthew and Mark (and later, John) with support from the Lucan evidence where appropriate (see above n81).

233. Below III.1.2.

234. There are 15 explicit references to Matthew, 9 to Mark and over 20 to John in ch.6 of J & R III.

235. Above n115.

236. J & R III pp 452, 457 and 458.

237. *R u V II* § 5 and J & R III esp. § 2 (but see also §§ 6, 34-6, 38-9 and 53). See above n106 for Ritschl's comments on the relationship between Vols. 2 and 3 of *R u V*.

238. J & R III pp 450f, 453, 468f and 482f.

239. See the use of ICR in e.g. nn155, 159-161, 164, 176, 178-9, 182, and 196 above.

240. J & R III § 44; see esp. 392 and 398. Also ICR § 22.

241. There are subtle distinctions to be made here. The point is being made, without being properly developed (see further below IV.5), that Ritschl's own development as a Christian and as a theologian has a role to play in the use made of the Gospels and the picture of Jesus being "worked with" at various stages in his career. That is not to say that "what Ritschl happened to be working on at the time" produced the picture of Jesus. Nor is it to say that his picture of Jesus simply collates Ritschl's own theology at any particular point in his own development, though both of these rather negative construals of the aspect being considered here may have something to contribute to the enquiry. Rather, the

complexity of the theological process - the interplay between tradition and lived history; the necessary existential dimension to theology; the self-involving character of theological language - is being respected and found at work at the heart of Ritschl's academic work and personal development. In this regard, the intriguing autobiographical sketch penned by John Macquarrie entitled "Pilgrimage in Theology" which suggests that a Christian theologian is constantly engaged in the quest for an adequate Christology - an expression of the fact that the riches of Christ are "unsearchable" - is worthy of mention (1986 ch.1 p9). The following comments are also not without relevance here: "A complete and finished christology, consisting of one single reading of all the (biblical and/or dogmatic) material having to do with Jesus of Nazareth, is a dead-end street, in my opinion. Indeed it is not Christian." (Segundo 1986 p39).

242. J & R III p386.

243. See also ICR §5 n7 p265.

244. ibid § 20 p229.

245. ibid. § 47 p240.

246. ibid. § 12 and esp. § 22. (see also above n160).

247. ibid § 42 p238 (cf. also J & R III pp 449, 476 and è68).

248. The suggestion seems to be that believers are sons of God by recognising Jesus as their father (cf John 17.20-26; ICR § 42 n112 p277). This is surely also an expression of Ritschl's reserve in claiming that believers enjoy a direct relationship with God.

249. See e.g. the use of Jn 4.34, 15.11 and 17.4,13 in J & R III p449 (cf also pp463 and 476).

250. In this way, the "Christocentricity" of Ritschl's theology can be explored further. "The movement Ritschl began" (Chilton 1984 p26) thus shows itself to be the relating of the preaching of Jesus to systematic theology at this decisive point: the meaning and relevance of the concept of the Kingdom of God (ibid p5f).

251. Above II.3.1.6.

252. J & R III p10f.

253. Such that the person of Jesus would be of relatively little significance. See however n244 above. A fruitful parallel to this discussion is that of Sykes' attempt to clarify Harnack's position with respect to Jesus (Sykes 1984 ch.6 esp. p134f). It is telling that Sykes salvages the deep concern shown by Harnack, the Ritschlian, for the person of Jesus, in the face of a common assumption - shown by Sykes to be a misconception - that Harnack was concerned solely with Jesus' teaching.

254. Clearly both presentations are imperfect. Ritschl's ellipse runs the risk of suggesting that there are *two* centres to Christianity. The revised image of the two concentric circles provides the reminder that it is God - and God alone - who stands at the heart of both Church and Kingdom, but suggests also that being in the Church inevitably means being in the Kingdom, a suggestion which Ritschl himself sought to avoid.

255. The distinction drawn by Ritschl between the Kingdom of God and the Church is pertinent here (J & R III § 35).

256. The model of two concentric circles would correct this.

257. e.g. ICR § 22.

258. See e.g. the content and strategic position in *R u V II* and *R u V III* respectively of § 5 and §§ 2 and 6.

259. J & R III p3. The full significance of the term "historical actuality" ("*geschichtliche Wirklichkeit*") will become clear below, once the inherent ambiguity entailed in Ritschl's encounter with the "historical Jesus" is explored (III.2. and III.3.).

260. See e.g. *R u V II* p23ff.

261. See above II.3.3.1.

262. As Ritschl himself expresses it : "...*die Herrschaft Gottes (hat) durch Jesus eine Gemeinde gefunden...*" ("the reign of God founded a community through Jesus') (*R u V II* p30.

263. ICR §§ 5 and 6 p222f.

264. ibid. § 8 p223.

265. The term "transcendent" is of course problematic and inadequate. But the attempt is here being made to show what Ritschl wishes to stress through his emphasis upon Kingdom and community. The community of the Kingdom of God includes and transcends concrete manifestations. The Church's incompleteness may, in fact, point to a future manifestation of the Kingdom of God (though Ritschl is unspecific). This is, in any case, Ritschl's way of construing the Kingdom's future sense (cf. Perrin 1963 and 1967, though see Chilton 1984 p20f esp. p21; also Metzler's "proleptic ethics": Metzler 1971 esp. ch.5.). His hermeneutic is thus not one which interprets the future sense of the Kingdom by deleting it. That there is a weakness, however, in Ritschl's construal of the Kingdom need not be doubted (below III.2.3).

266. E.g. *R u V II* p7f; J & R III p20ff, p23.

267. Seen by Ritschl as a fault in Schleiermacher's understanding of Christianity (J & R I pp440-452 esp. 443f and 445ff). Despite reservations, Ritschl is, of

course, in general warmly welcoming of Schleiermacher's undertaking (see e.g. *R u V II* p2ff). For varying opinions on the nature and success of Ritschl's relationship to Schleiermacher see Graby 1966, Ryan 1966 and Barnett 1976 ch.3. See Barnett's critque of Ryan in Barnett 1976 n2 p272f.

268. Ritschl 1881 p162 (cf ICR § 13f; J & R III §§ 34 and 39).

269. ICR §13 p226 (also § 5 p222 and § 6 p222f).

270. E57 p32f.

271. Given, that is, how the material is handled by other Evangelists, there being no direct parallel to the content of Mk 12.34a. The development of Ritschl's understanding of love as an aspect of Christian living did take place, however, under Johannine influence (see e.g. ICR §§ 12-14, esp. nn 29-32 p268f.).

272. See e.g. E50 p30f and p45; also *R u V II* §31. The question to what extent Ritschl really set aside his earlier stress on Matthew, which cannot properly be gone into here, does arise. Negative criticism of Ritschl would be compelled to conclude that Ritschl simply picked and chose what suited him from the Gospel tradition. The path chosen here suggests that Ritschl's change of mind on the Synoptic Problem enabled him to make a significant shift from a Matthean Jesus to a Marcan, though he was able to keep Matthean elements where these squared up with the picture of Jesus emerging under Marcan control.

273. *R u V II* p274.

274. "In his grasp of the meaning of righteousness, Jesus restored the original ethical content of the task denoted by the word as used by the Prophets and Psalmist(s)." (ibid p277 my translation).

275. ICR § 22 p229f; quote from p230.

276. ibid § 16 p226f.

277. ibid p227.

278. Righteousness may also be seen as a bridge-concept for Ritschl, relating his use of the Gospels to his reading of Paul (see e.g. *R u V II* § 32 p292f). Ritschl also explores links with Peter and John; ibid p279f.

279. § 6. On the question of diversity, see below III.4.

Chapter III

Ritschl's Picture of Jesus:
a Critique

1. RITSCHL'S USE OF THE GOSPELS:
PRELIMINARY CRITICAL COMMENTS

It is both more appropriate and more pertinent to comment on Ritschl's use of the
Gospels when viewed in practice - that is, within the study of Ritschl's picture of Jesus
to be conducted below. Some critical comments of a preliminary nature are, however,
necessary. By drawing together, and adding to, observations already made in the
course of this study so far it is possible to construct a general framework within which
Ritschl's use of the Gospels can be assessed. The comments are presented in two
sections. First, Ritschl's attitude to the Synoptic Gospels will be dealt with. Then,
his stance toward the Fourth Gospel will be considered.

1.1. The Synoptic Gospels

First, the manner in which Ritschl "reads off" historical material from Mark requires
further exploration. In this, the 1851 essay on the Synoptics should receive special
attention. In this essay the alleged "neutrality" of Mark, which Ritschl allows to
remain "alleged", nevertheless seems to become important to the drift of his
argument. This is significant. For this neutralizing tendency of the Gospel of Mark
- which F.C.Baur had assumed was a hallmark of the Gospel's lateness [1] - was used
by Ritschl to enable him to reach the opposite conclusion. For Ritschl, Mark revealed
itself to be as yet uncoloured by a dogmatic concern. Furthermore, because - and
despite the fact that - Baur and Ritschl both shared the common ground of
Tendenzkritik, they were of the opinion that the earthly Jesus could be discerned with

some ease in the Gospels. The matter of finding a solution to the Synoptic Problem thus automatically became a matter of determining where the most historically reliable material about Jesus was to be found [2].

The issue of the acceptance of Mark's essential historical reliability was, however, taken one step further by Ritschl. For Ritschl built further upon the consequences of his reaching a solution to the Synoptic Problem. The argument for Marcan priority, in other words, gave Ritschl a historical framework for the life of Jesus. Ritschl thus attached significance to (by accepting as historical) Mark's outline of the life of Jesus.

It is now clear, of course, that the question of the historicity of material in the Gospels is not to be answered by sweeping reference to the overall reliability of one or other of the Gospels. It is, rather, to be answered by reference - on the basis of detailed analysis utilizing stringent criteria of authenticity [3] - to individual pericopae. This observation has been commonplace in New Testament study at least since K.L.Schmidt. One might almost say it has been a commonplace observation since D.F.Strauss, who may perhaps be cited as the first truly radical Gospel critic. Yet the systematic analysis of individual pericopae needed to be tied to the abandonment of reliance upon the historicity of the Marcan framework to be fully effective. It was this abandonment which Schmidt called for in spectacular fashion [4]. For as long as the Marcan framework remained intact alongside the argument for Marcan priority, then assumptions about the historicity of material in Mark could continue unchecked.

Ritschl is open to criticism on both counts in his use of the Gospel of Mark; his acceptance of the Gospel of Mark as essentially historical in both detail and framework. This observation has inevitable consequences for the historically-controlled model for Christology which Ritschl sought to create.

For, quite clearly, if the basis upon which Ritschl built has been shown not to be historical (or at least not in the sense in which Ritschl understood it), then a major problem emerges. This observation must thus figure prominently in the discussion of Ritschl's picture of Jesus to follow.

Attention should also be given to Ritschl's use of the Gospel of Matthew. Ritschl operated with the same premiss in his investigations into the Synoptic Problem in

1850 as he did in 1851 and 1857. On concluding that Matthew was the first Gospel to be written - as he did in the earlier years of his career - he accepted the portrayal of Jesus in the Gospel to be historically authentic [5]. It is important, therefore, to assess what the significance of Ritschl's change of mind, and the resulting shift in his picture of Jesus, had on his use of the Gospel of Matthew. For the claim made in 1850 - "*Allein das Matthäusevangelium bietet gar keine Lehre von der Person des Gottmenschen und von dem Glauben an ihn dar...*" [6] - could not be given up without major repercussions. As soon as Jesus' unwilling acceptance of Messianic status and the call for silence about his identity as found in Mark became for Ritschl fixed historical points, such that Matthew seems far too explicit by comparison, a major revision in his thinking was under way. Mark was seen now to offer the essential "kernel of the Gospel (hi)story" [7]. Matthew could thus only be viewed in the light of Mark [8].

The present-day reader of the Gospels can, however, be nothing but struck by how much of the Gospel of Matthew Ritschl can nevertheless accept as authentic, even *after* viewing the Gospel in the light of Mark. Such passages as Mt 17:24-27, 10.6, 7:21-23, as well as 5.17-20 and other excerpts from the Sermon on the Mount, to name but the most obvious examples, are taken up by Ritschl in this way [9]. As a prime expression of this tendency, as has already been observed, Ritschl maintains his interest in the concept of "righteousness", derived from his study of the first Gospel, and sees it as Jesus' own means of articulating the manner of existence lived by participants in the Kingdom of God [10]. Ritschl's uncritical attitude towards the Gospel of Mark is thus matched by a seemingly equally uncritical use of Matthew. Whether the extent of Ritschl's use of much Matthean material as historically authentic is justified must therefore feature as a background consideration in the study of his picture of Jesus to follow. Once more, also, the implications for the christological model with which he operates must be drawn out.

1.2. The Fourth Gospel

There has been cause at a number of points in the discussion so far to draw attention to Ritschl's use of the Fourth Gospel. In particular, the observation of Ritschl's extensive use of the Fourth Gospel in *R u V* needs to be stressed. The heart of the issue of Ritschl's use of the Fourth Gospel may be expressed in these terms; Ritschl himself claims that his Christology is constructed in accordance with a strict historical norm - no christological assertion should be permitted which cannot be warranted by reference to the life of the earthly Jesus. Ritschl's early work seems to indicate that he regarded the most reliable historical material about Jesus to be found in the Synoptic Gospels, especially Mark. How is it therefore possible for Ritschl to make considerable use of the Fourth Gospel in his later work ? (Has Ritschl's verdict on the Fourth Gospel changed in the meantime ? Does Ritschl not adhere to his own christological method ?)

This central question concerning Ritschl's use of the Fourth Gospel, and the questions which derive from it, are vital to our enquiry. For, as some recent studies seem to suggest, Ritschl's uncritical use of the Fourth Gospel is his "Achilles heel" as far as his use of the Gospels in Christology is concerned [11].

There can be little doubt that in *R u V* Ritschl is prepared to attach some weight to the Fourth Gospel as a reliable historical account of Jesus and his ministry. Examples of this practice can easily be cited.

Ritschl refers, for example, to "the undeniable features of Jesus' presentation of himself, especially in the Fourth Gospel" [12]. Here it is clear that Ritschl is talking about reliable historical material and, in so doing, bringing the Fourth Gospel alongside the other three. More striking are the specific appeals to Johannine material as historical data when Ritschl seeks support for his case for Jesus as the Obedient One, the one who uniquely fulfils his vocation [13]. Here Ritschl draws in particular upon Jn 4.34, 17.4, 15.11, 17.13 and 10.18. Furthermore, even particular sayings and actions of Jesus as recorded in the Fourth Gospel are perceived to be authentic. Ritschl uses Jn 16.33 in this way, for example, and also 15.10f, as evidence for the, according to Ritschl, essentially accurate presentation of Jesus' prayer-life [14].

There can equally be little doubt, however, that Ritschl remained keenly aware in this later stage of his career of the historical-critical problems presented by the Fourth Gospel. Thus, though less negative from the first about the Fourth Gospel than

118

his Tübingen colleagues - pre-eminently Baur - he was nevertheless ready to concentrate on the Synoptic Gospels rather than the Fourth Gospel for the main contours of the picture of Jesus with which he operated [15]. There are, in other words, signs that Ritschl imbibed much of what Strauss and Baur had concluded about the Fourth Gospel.

First, Ritschl quite clearly allows in a number of instances for the possibility that the words of Jesus as presented in the Gospel are in fact the words of the Evangelist [16]. As a result, second, the question of the authenticity of material is raised at the level of the content of the material in general rather than specific terms [17]. Consideration is also given to the fact that some aspects of the Johannine presentation may themselves be "religious judgments" rather than simple historical data [18]. It is, therefore, not the Fourth Gospel - which shows traces of "reliable recollection" - but the other New Testament Gospels which, for Ritschl, prove more reliable in terms of hard evidence for historical detail about the life of Jesus. For in them the "authentic picture" of Jesus can be seen to be a "historical representation" (*Geschichtsdarstellung*) [19].

Nevertheless an explanation is required of why Ritschl can use the Fourth Gospel later in his career in the way he does in *R u V* if he could not do so earlier, if the perception of the Fourth Gospel which Ritschl held remained wholly consistent. There are at least four possible explanations of why Ritschl felt able to begin using the Fourth Gospel in his later work. The attempt will now be made to probe these four possibilities in the hope that some light will thereby be shed on the nature of Ritschl's use and the resulting content of his picture of Jesus.

First, one can argue that there was a greater gulf between *R u V II* and *J & R III* than Ritschl himself wished to admit. On the basis of this gulf it would be possible to perceive two very different tasks going on in Ritschl's presentation, such that the second (biblical) volume proves to be less intrinsic to Ritschl's resulting constructive proposals than seems initially the case. On this view, *R u V III* is seen to be based rather on an interpretation of Jesus akin to and derived from the Fourth Gospel than from all four, or the Synoptic, Gospels. The position so described represents a common assumption made about Ritschl's work, even if not one which is always explicitly expressed. As soon as Ritschl is presented as depending unduly on John, then this assumption lurks somewhere in the background [20]. It is, however, an assumption tied together with the failure to respect the actual *content* of *R u V II*. That this very failure has had a detrimental effect upon the understanding of Ritschl's theology as biblical theology is a basic contention of this present study. Such a suggestion also fails to respect Ritschl's own declared intent to bind together the contents of *R u V II* and *R u V III*. For both these reasons, therefore, the suggestion is to be rejected.

A second explanation is that Ritschl clearly had different aims in his later writings from his aims in 1850 and 1857, when putting together his material for *Die Entstehung der altkatholischen Kirche*. The difference is that in the earlier period he wrote a history and in the later period a theology. On this basis the earlier writings could, in any case, not make as great a use of the Fourth Gospel as the later work.

There is undoubtedly an element of truth in this suggestion. But the terms in which it is expressed fall far short of the clarity required to be helpful. For it is precisely in the gaining of clarity on *how* the historical work takes its place in the theological task as Ritschl sees it that must figure as a, if not the, key aspect in an enquiry into Ritschl's theological method. Thus, though it is true to point to the different intention of Ritschl in the two periods in question, it is not true to make so sharp a distinction as the above suggestion demands. For, as stated earlier, there is a clear sense in which the earlier "historical" work is seen by Ritschl as of direct theological significance [21]. Furthermore, Ritschl's historical norm for Christology, as defined in *R u V III*, spells out the theological significance just referred to. Such a simplified distinction will therefore not suffice as an explanation. One could also argue that Ritschl's own norm should cause him to take up only Synoptic material. As it stands, therefore, this second suggested explanation is also to be rejected.

A third possible explanation relates to the second and refines it. It could be argued that Ritschl's earlier work was restricted by the narrowness of its historical brief. In other words, though historically accurate, the picture(s) of Jesus presented in E50 and E57 were not, and did not purport to be complete pictures. There lay implicit the possibility that there was more historical material available about Jesus which did not deal with the question of the Mosaic Law (and that some, or much, of this was in the Fourth Gospel). Ritschl's true thinking about the Fourth Gospel did not therefore have the chance to emerge.

Again, as an explanation this suggestion is inadequate. There is ample, if not extensive, evidence to demonstrate that Ritschl put the Fourth Gospel in a different category in 1850 and 1857 [22]. Ritschl does not use the Fourth Gospel in the early period because he does not perceive a preoccupation in the Fourth Gospel with the question of the Law, for which reason - Ritschl presupposing that the Law was significant for Jesus - the Fourth Gospel shows itself to be less reliable. This is a historical judgment. But it is difficult to conclude from this that Ritschl believes at this stage that the Fourth Gospel provides as reliable historical data as the Synoptics on other aspects of Jesus' life and work.

The suggestion thus needs supplementing even if there may, again, be an element of truth in the perception that the restricted brief of the chapter on Jesus in E50 and E57 has a significant role to play.

A fourth suggestion is that Ritschl uses the Fourth Gospel in his later work for the simple reason that he comes to respect more the New Testament canon and thus feels compelled to do justice to the Fourth Gospel. This view has, of course, found favour with Ritschl's more negative critics [23]. Once more there is some truth in the suggestion: in R u V, as seen earlier in this present study, Ritschl gives expression in his most lucid form to the theological significance of the canon of the New Testament [24].

This will, however, not suffice as a complete explanation unless it be held simultaneously that Ritschl, as well as positively perceiving the significance of the canon, totally fails in his attempt to build his Christology in accordance with a historical norm. In other words, though Ritschl begins to use the Fourth Gospel more, if he is at all heeding the historical norm in Christology, there is in his method at least some check on the uncontrolled acceptance of all that the Fourth Gospel presents about Jesus. The question therefore arises; how consistent is Ritschl's use of historical-criticism within his theology ?

The suggestion to be favoured is thus one which takes on the kernel of truth preserved by each of the final three suggestions, giving greater respect in each case - pending the further enquiry to be conducted below - to Ritschl's historical criterion in Christology and the potential consistency of its use. There is indeed a hiatus between the intention behind the earlier work (especially E50 and E57) and the later work, as represented above all by *R u V*, with respect to the picture of Jesus which Ritschl creates and with which he works.

1857 was, however, a bridge year in this respect. As shown above, the move to Marcan priority had the effect of impressing upon Ritschl the restricted character of the subject-matter of his chapter on Jesus in E50. E57 did not prove to be the place where Ritschl displayed fully the inevitable next step in his thinking, even though the seeds are there for a radical shift in his thinking about Jesus, caused by his perception of the Kingdom's centrality for Jesus himself. The shift had to come at some time, however. I suggest that it came between 1857 and 1874, finding its fruition in *R u V*.

But by this time a number of other interests had coincided. Ritschl's large-scale theological work was presented in its first form. In this work, though christocentrically conceived, there were Pauline elements which also had to be accommodated. As part of the work, indeed, the canon of the New Testament had to be respected. Fundamental as far as the christological basis - and thus Ritschl's picture of Jesus - are concerned, however, was the *historical* conclusion which Ritschl has clearly reached in the meantime, namely, that the Mosaic Law was not as crucial for Jesus as he had first thought. He had signalled in 1857 the move from his earlier position but not effected it. By 1874, the shift was complete. On this basis, therefore - for the understanding of the Kingdom of God needed to be filled out - the Gospel of John was open for reassessment.

Ritschl never fails to respect the fact that the Kingdom of God is far from prominent in the Fourth Gospel. He does see, however, that there are links between Mark and John (e.g. Love as the essence of the Kingdom of God) and Matthew and John (e.g. Sonship as best expressing Jesus' relationship to God). The near absence of the Kingdom of God in the Fourth Gospel thus proves less of a problem for Ritschl than the near absence of the question of the Mosaic Law [25]. The reason for Ritschl's later use of the Fourth Gospel can therefore be seen, I contend, to be Ritschl's shift of position on his historical perception of Jesus, and the resulting theological conclusions Ritschl draws from that shift.

Given the attendant complexity of this increased use of the Fourth Gospel it remains clear nevertheless that the manner in which Ritschl uses the Gospel must be left open to the closest possible scrutiny. For if Ritschl is building historical considerations in a fundamental way into his Christology, then the present-day reader, reared on an approach to the Fourth Gospel which demands great suspicion as to its historical reliability, must test Ritschl's method all the more if the Gospel is used at times in the same manner as the Synoptic Gospels [26]. If, at the same time, theological considerations are being permitted to play an explicit role from other angles (e.g. via a respect for the canon or through the religious tradition within which the theology is being constructed) then it is not only possible that the use of the Fourth Gospel by Ritschl signals a weakening of the criterion built into Ritschl's Christology but also that interpreters of Ritschl may have misread him because of the coincidence of interests.

Ultimately, then, the matter is one of assessing to what extent Ritschl points the way toward redaction criticism (and thus treats the Gospels as all theological in their use of history) or to what extent back to pre-criticism (and thus lets go of what he had learned from Baur). Only on the basis of such an assessment will it be possible to see how his use of the Gospels is at all relevant to current discussion of the role of the Gospels in Christian theology.

2. RITSCHL'S PICTURE OF JESUS: A DETAILED STUDY

2.1 Introduction

It is now necessary to turn to a detailed study of Ritschl's picture of Jesus. Some preliminary comments are required. First, it should be recalled that Ritschl's picture is not a "Life of Jesus". Yet it is undoubtedly presented as a "historical picture". For, apart from Ritschl's own use of the expression "historical picture", it is clear that the historical norm which Ritschl builds into his Christology demands that considerations about detail of the life of the earthly Jesus should not only figure prominently but also function normatively [27]. The extent to which and the legitimacy with which Ritschl builds upon the historical data is our prime concern. The tension between historical and theological concerns at this point lies at the heart of the enquiry. It should therefore be observed at the outset what are the possible consequences of the study.

It may be possible to see that Ritschl overstates the potential breadth of the historical base. What Ritschl takes to be historical data may be shown to be less secure than he himself believed. As a result, Ritschl's historical criterion, if not his Christology, will have to be questioned. Correlated to this will be a process of questioning with regard to his use and understanding of the Gospels. If Ritschl has overstated the case with regard to available historical material about Jesus, then has he also misunderstood the nature of the Gospels as literary texts ? But even if neither of these points is valid, the question whether Ritschl's christological method contains a kernel of truth must be posed. In short, the question to what extent historical enquiry, in its relation to the interpretation of the Gospels and the construction of a picture of Jesus, has a bearing on theological construction in the realm of Christology must be posed.

Ritschl's approach may, in other words, be salvaged intact. If so, the implications - drawing parallels with some present attempts to construct a relevant Christology - must be drawn. His approach may have to be abandoned, in which case the inadequacy of similar current attempts would need to be disclosed. Alternatively, his approach may be salvaged in heavily modified form. In this case, the terms of the recovery of Ritschl's approach would need to be spelled out.

What follows is thus first and foremost a historical-critical enquiry, an enquiry which is aware that in itself it should be inadequate to assess fully Ritschl's picture (his picture being a theological assessment) yet adequate enough to determine the essential correctness or incorrectness of Ritschl's picture (i.e. the extent to which theological assessment is continuous with historical knowledge) [28].

The six aspects of Ritschl's picture of Jesus expounded in the previous chapter

will be dealt with in ascending order of difficulty as far as the historical-critical angle
of approach is concerned; Jesus as Teacher, as Founder of the Kingdom of God, as
Messiah and Prophet, as Son, as Lord and as Obedient One.

2.2 Jesus the Teacher

A recent writer has remarked "...that Jesus was first and foremost a teacher...is seldom
explicitly stated (i.e. in the Gospels). One discerns it simply by reading books about
Jesus." [29] It is our purpose to examine this contention and then relate it to Ritschl's
own conclusions.

Clearly, by the very fact that there has been so much reference to the message
(*Botschaft*), preaching (*Predigt*), proclamation (*Verkündigung*) or - simply - teaching
(*Lehren*) of Jesus throughout the recent history of Gospel study, it has been felt that
Jesus functioned as a teacher and can be shown to have been such. Thus, in this
understanding of Jesus, J.Weiss, Harnack, Bultmann, Dodd, T.W.Manson, Perrin,
Hengel and Meyer - for example - are in basic agreement [30]. They may not be -
indeed are not - at one as to the precise content of that teaching; but the fact that Jesus
was a teacher is for all of them beyond doubt.

Considerations of the reliability of the Gospel material in giving access to Jesus
and his teaching have inevitably been intertwined with reflections on the manner of
his teaching. Thus, at one extreme, Bultmann is willing to admit a creative role to the
communities in which sayings of Jesus were preserved and by whom they were used
in new situations [31]. At the other extreme is the view popularized by Riesenfeld
and Gerhardsson, contending that Jesus modelled his teaching-methods on those of
a rabbi, thus guaranteeing for the Gospels a high degree of reliability as records of the
teaching of Jesus. Having been taught to remember his words, the disciples would
easily be able to preserve and pass on his teaching [32].

Greater complexity is introduced into the discussion when the topic of the genre
of Gospel is allowed to play a role. The question, for example, of whether the Gospel
of Mark represents Jesus as a teacher of wisdom in the mould of the teacher in
Graeco-Roman literature picks up a theme which emerged from the history-of-religions

school, was taken up by Bultmann, and even now finds consistent application [33]. The matter of how much, and more especially which parts, of the teaching of Jesus can be accepted as authentic is not, however, one that can be gone into in detail here. For sure, Riesenfeld and Gerhardsson overstepped the bounds of probability and Bultmann was perhaps too ready to admit too high a degree of creativity to the early communities [34], but the question of what constituted the teaching of Jesus is not answered by such critical observations. A briefly argued and documented case for the fact that Jesus was indeed a teacher must therefore suffice. Aspects which are pertinent to Ritschl's own presentation can then be highlighted.

Support for the fact that Jesus was recognized as a teacher in his own day can be found in Mk 10.17 parr., 12.14 parr., 12.19 parr., 14.14 parr., and probably also Mk 5.35 par.Lke 8.49, Mk 9.17 par.Lke 9.38 [35]. No individual case can conclusively be held to be a correct record of a particular event. Yet as a cumulative argument, these separate pieces of evidence prove fairly conclusive. That Jesus was a teacher tells us comparatively little, however. Far more significant is the content of his teaching. Few would wish now to claim that the Sermon on the Mount represents authentic teaching of Jesus, let alone that it was somehow delivered in the form in which we find it [36]. Isolation of distinct Matthean traits and wording throughout Mt 5-7, a procedure provoked in particular by the emergence of redaction criticism, has shown to what extent the Sermon on the Mount is a Matthean creation, even if it does incorporate some material deriving from Jesus. The manner in which the Sermon must be broken up in order to determine such authentic material (e.g. "Q" passages such as Mt 5.44-48 par., 6.22f par., 6.25-33/4 par., 7.1-5 and 7-ll par.) from Matthean additions is thus indicative and paradigmatic of the way the search for the teaching of Jesus must proceed.

On similar grounds, the recognition that Jesus told parables is of itself insufficient a reason for considering a passage to be authentic Jesus-material. As is now well-known, a parable must be subjected to detailed critique before one can say with any degree of certainty that it derives from Jesus. And even then there is the problem of determining its meaning [37].

Yet there is little doubt that Jesus used parables as a form of teaching. The cumulative case again wins the day even if there are in individual cases many layers of interpretation, re-interpretation, even allegorization to cut through and if, on the other hand, there is a tendency to be over-confident in the degree to which it is possible to "get back to Jesus" as far as the precise form of the original parable is concerned [38]. But there seems little point spending too long on the question whether Jesus spoke in parables at all.

A third and most crucial aspect of Jesus' teaching concerns the content most directly. Meyer states, "No account of the aims of Jesus could claim plausibility if it failed to accord with the central theme of his proclamation and teaching, the reign of God." [39] In this respect, current thinking moves as near towards consensus as it is ever likely to; Jesus was first and foremost concerned with the Kingdom of God and that central concern affected his teaching directly. This aspect of the mission of Jesus will be dealt with further below under the heading of "Jesus as Founder of the Kingdom of God". At this juncture it is necessary to note only the importance of the Kingdom, accepting that there is a problem of being clear about sayings (and their meaning) and actions [40]. To be clear about the fact that the Kingdom was central to Jesus' self-understanding and mission does not yet tell the interpreter precisely how that Kingdom was conceived, either by Jesus or his followers.

Turning now directly to Ritschl's own understanding of Jesus as teacher, it is evident that for Ritschl the link between the Kingdom of God and the teaching of Jesus is decisive. The centrality of the Kingdom for Jesus is not, however, tied by Ritschl solely to the words of Jesus, but is related to his actions too. Furthermore, Ritschl extrapolates from his reading of the Gospels an understanding of the Kingdom of God which is directly related to Jesus' teaching activity [41]. It is this conclusion which renders aspects of Ritschl's reading of the Gospel tradition problematic. For it appears to be intrinsically bound up with an acceptance of the historical reliability of the Marcan framework. That is to say; Ritschl is right to focus on the Kingdom of God as central to Jesus' message. His construal of the relationship between Jesus and the disciples is, however, if not incorrect, at very least questionable in that it reads too much too readily from the Marcan portrayal.

The "gradual development" of the disciples' discovery of Jesus' identity, linked with the emerging "community of disciples" - constitutive of Ritschl's understanding of the concept of the Kingdom and his reading of the history of earliest Christianity - is, in other words, too easily derived from and substantiated by reference to the Gospel of Mark. The Marcan framework is paramount.

The same element of gradual development is found also in Ritschl's reading of relevant parables [42]. Though the view which suggests that Ritschl is here guilty of forcing the Gospel material into some sort of mould of 19th Century bourgeois cultural developmentalism can be shown to be too simple, if not simply wrong [43], it is clear that a reading of Mark too much at face value has left an indelible impression upon Ritschl's interpretation of Jesus as teacher.

Within this understanding of the nature and content of the teaching of Jesus derived from Mark are inserted other elements. It is at this point that Ritschl's use of Matthew is pertinent. Again, the ease with which Ritschl uses material uncritically must be mentioned. For Ritschl's stress upon the "new righteousness", as the life-style appropriate for people of the Kingdom of God, cannot but be affected by the process of dismantling the Sermon on the Mount referred to above, as a result of which much of this emphasis is revealed as Matthean. For this reason, there are problems for Ritschl's understanding of Jesus as teacher at this point too.

Above all, the question of how much Jesus taught about himself must be raised. Ritschl's historical criterion demands a direct link between christological assertion and historical data. A crucial issue will thus inevitably be that of the extent to which Jesus could perceive, and teach about, his identity in the terms in which Ritschl's picture of Jesus suggests, i.e. under the specific headings considered below. Redaction Criticism in particular demands that the question be posed how much of the Christology - implicit or explicit - to be found in the Gospels is from Jesus. Not only that, a more subtle approach to the study of New Testament than that preferred by Ritschl might ask to what extent Jesus would need to *teach* about himself in the terms which Ritschl often seems to demand. Without losing the historical criterion to which Ritschl attaches such importance, it is possible to say that Jesus taught nothing about himself other than that he heralded the Kingdom, yet that Lordship, Sonship and Messiahship were all appropriate and correct understandings of Jesus. Such understandings would, however, derive from observation of the actions of Jesus [44].

In summary, then, the problematic aspects of Ritschl's understanding of Jesus as teacher are primarily bound up with his understanding of the Kingdom of God and are in turn directly related to the uncritical tendencies in his use of the Synoptic Gospels. The fact *that* Ritschl drew attention to the Kingdom of God as a key concept in the teaching of Jesus can only receive support [45]. But the difficulties evident in Ritschl's reading of the Gospels means that his understanding of Jesus as teacher is too problematic to be very helpful. Admittedly, though not treading the path of Riesenfeld and Gerhardsson, he does conceive of the Jesus-disciple relationship in very specific terms. But the limitations of what the Gospels provide, and Ritschl's tendency to overuse Mark cause his contribution to be questionable. But though the role of Jesus as teacher was a key issue for Ritschl, he was not guilty of suggesting that Jesus was first and foremost a teacher. In this regard, therefore, Ritschl has escaped Sanders' criticism. Ritschl considered Jesus to be more than a teacher. It is necessary to examine whether this was a correct assessment and whether Ritschl was accurate in his identification of that "something more".

2.3 Jesus the Founder of the Kingdom of God

Ritschl perceived the importance of the concept of the Kingdom of God for Jesus. In this respect he correctly evaluated the Synoptic portrayal over and above that found in the Fourth Gospel. This enquiry must, however, concern itself with the meaning of the concept "Kingdom of God" for Ritschl and also with the use and understanding of the term "founder" and terms related to it.

As was shown above, Ritschl does not make the mistake of confining his understanding of Jesus as teacher purely to the words of Jesus. It is also in his filling out of the notion of Jesus as the bringer or founder of the Kingdom of God that Ritschl expands his interpretation of Jesus' actions. It is here where problems occur. Furthermore, because the Kingdom of God is so central in Ritschl's own theology (belonging thus to both the descriptive and interpretative tasks of biblical theology), an additional twist to the problem arises. In the same way that the interpreter of the

Fourth Gospel has difficulty distinguishing the words of John from those of Jesus, so the interpreter of Ritschl has difficulty seeing where Jesus' use of the term Kingdom of God (according to Ritschl) ends and Ritschl's own use of the term begins.

The interpreter is helped to some extent, of course, by the structure of Ritschl's works [46]. But given the methodology with which Ritschl operates, not only should the distinction be more clear than it sometimes is, but also the link - that is, between (descriptive) biblical theology and (biblical, historically-controlled) systematic theology - should be evident. That there is a problem, in particular in J & R III, where the notion of Jesus as the Kingdom's founder is taken up into Ritschl's creative contribution to theology, highlights the fact that Ritschl fails to make the distinction and link explicit.

Before a study of Ritschl's own understanding of the meaning of the terms in question is embarked upon, it is necessary to present some of the major findings of New Testament study since Ritschl on this question. It is somewhat ironical that the scholar who first provoked interest in the Kingdom of God as a topic for New Testament study (as opposed to philosophical ethics or systematic theology) should come under attack from his own son-in-law on this same question, and that the latter's interpretation should come to be not only prominent but normative in discussion about the Kingdom of God from that point on. Challenges have been made, and these are looked at briefly below. Nevertheless, it is now expected that a modern scholar come to terms with Johannes Weiss's Jesus' Proclamation of the Kingdom of God and not read a page of Ritschl. Weiss is thus to be regarded as the starting-point of modern discussion about the Kingdom of God as far as Jesus' understanding as found in the Gospels is concerned.

Surveying the scene since Weiss, it soon becomes clear that the question of eschatology has been uppermost in discussion about the meaning of the Kingdom [47]. Given the nature of Weiss' own contribution - focussing as he did upon the eschatological dimension to the Kingdom not as one element in the understanding of it but as the determinative background to it - this was inevitable [48]. Even in the work of C.H.Dodd, who above all swam against the tide of eschatology in this century, the question of the eschatological coinage of the mission and self-understanding had not only to be posed but also dealt with. It is he, therefore, who, when pressing the present dimension of the Kingdom, is nevertheless compelled to do so with respect to the question of eschatology. Dodd thus demythologizes the eschatological references in Jesus' teaching by interpreting them as "realized eschatology" [49]. Such "Q" passages as Lke 10.23f, 11.20 and 11.31f thus become crucial for the discussion [50]. But if Dodd was taken to task "for offering a portrait of Jesus which does not take adequate account of the world in which he lived" [51], then it is evident there is a task of interpretation which involves the comprehension of what have become known as the "present" and "future" dimensions of Jesus' proclamation of the Kingdom of God. That is to say, even if one feels compelled to delete either one dimension or the other, an account of reasons and justification for such an act must be provided, for *both* are to be found in the Gospel tradition and are thus as such presented to the reader by the early Church (or at the very least by the communities lying behind the Synoptic Gospels) even if not by Jesus himself [52]. The importance of such verses as Mk 9.1 parr. [53], Mk 10.23-7 parr. and Lke 11.2, 13.28f and 22.30 (3 "Q" passages) has to be reckoned with. In all of these cases, the Kingdom is quite clearly intended in a future sense. More could be added where this *may* be the case [54]. One thing is clear; the solution is unlikely to be a simple "either/or", such that from Jesus derive all the present references and from the earliest communities the future references (or vice versa). This much can be stated beyond doubt; the early Church placed its understanding, in part at least, in an eschatological context (cf. Lke 19.11-27). The very preservation of words of Jesus and the existence of communities which asked pressing (religious or moral) questions provoking responses based on words of Jesus bear witness, however, to a tendency in conflict with such eschatological traits. Indeed, it may be argued that the "future references" in the Lucan parable just referred to have, in fact, already been uprooted from their eschatological soil; perhaps teleology has replaced eschatology [55].

Be that as it may, teleology certainly pervades Ritschl's own interpretation of the Kingdom of God and his reading of the Gospel tradition. Such an understanding is able to keep future references to the Kingdom in harness, whilst one focuses simultaneously almost exclusively on the Kingdom's present dimension. The future emerges from the present which has a distinct goal (teleology); the future does not effect a sharp break with the present, causing a disjuncture (eschatology). This is evident in Ritschl's exposition of Jesus' realization of the Kingdom in his own actions. Here, Mt 12.28, Lke 4.17-21 and Mt 11.2-6 are adduced in support of the interpretation [56].

This point, that Jesus' actions are appealed to in support of the interpretation, is important. For it is, ironically, on this ground that Sanders' critique of so much study of Jesus in the form of a revised form of Weiss' picture of Jesus - itself based on a methodology which favours action-centred interpretation [57] - may be open to question.

Questions must, of course, once more be posed about Ritschl's use of sources. For it is far from clear whether the appeal being made here is to Jesus or to an Evangelist. The passage Lke 4.17-21 may be taken as an example. In drawing upon such a passage, a passage in which the Kingdom of God is not mentioned, Ritschl in effect makes a step quite commonly made, even though he makes it for the wrong reason. Though assuming that this is a passage recording an event in the life of Jesus (which it may well be, though it cannot be proved to be so), he may equally be seen to be accepting the narrative as a correct summary of the life of Jesus. Such a summary, though coined - even invented - in its present form by the Evangelist is thus "historical" in a sense in which Ritschl may not explicitly use the word, but in a sense adequate for the purposes of his interpretation.

Yet Ritschl's procedure here is worth careful note. First, an assumption is made about the link between the activity of Jesus and the presence of the Kingdom. Second, an assumption is made that the Evangelist was right to sketch Jesus' activity in this way by reference to the Isaiah passage. Third, it is assumed that the Evangelist correctly assessed the intention of Jesus by making the link. Even more problematically than in the other two cases, in other words, Ritschl here relies, in fact, upon the words of the Evangelist rather than upon words of Jesus.

There is nevertheless a sense in which Ritschl is resting upon the actions of the earthly Jesus, even if they are interpreted actions. As Stanton has indicated, it is important to note what may be called the "incidental elements" in the Gospel tradition, which prove to be important in filling in more than simply the background to Jesus' life [58]. Jesus' tendency to mingle with women, children, and tax-collectors may seem a trivial observation; yet it ties in with this central passage from Luke. In this way, therefore, Ritschl's interpretation may be seen to be dependent upon the actions, if not the words, of Jesus. It must be admitted, however, that the link is much more indirect, and includes much more inference, than Ritschl's own method suggests.

In one very significant respect Ritschl has quite clearly attempted too much in his interpretation of the Kingdom of God. In a similar fashion to his overuse of the Gospel of Mark in filling out the detail of Jesus as teacher, he has overused Mark once more. As a result, he is too specific about the nature of Jesus' activity with respect to the Kingdom. Just as he reads too much into the role of Jesus as the educator of his disciples in a close relationship, so he interprets the Twelve too closely as already the first community of the Kingdom. As this perception is dependent upon the relationship between Jesus and the Twelve derived from Mark, it is thus dependent ultimately on the Marcan framework and is as such an illegitimate argument [59]. For though the appeal to the Luke passage above may be seen as legitimate (supported by a cumulative appeal to other, separate elements in the Gospel tradition which present the actions of Jesus), the appeal to Mark in this way cannot be permitted because of the questionable character of the Marcan framework, which ensuing study has disclosed to be a literary construction [60].

It is now necessary to consider the term "founder" itself. Ultimately the word is unproblematic, as long as it is clear in what context Ritschl uses the word. For there are two distinct contexts in which the word appears. First, there is the understanding of Jesus as "founder" (*Stifter*) worked out in the context of biblical theology's descriptive task [61]. Here, allowing for the required revision of the term Kingdom of God along the lines suggested above, it is clear that Ritschl's understanding is that the presence of Jesus (that is, the earthly Jesus) and the proclamation and presence of the Kingdom belong together [62]. The second context renders the word "founder" more fluid in meaning. That is to say, from the perspective of the Christian community (be it early community or present community) the role of Jesus as "founder" takes on a different nuance. Ritschl relates the "founded" community to the one to whom that community refers for its existence (as the explanation of why it is there at all and as the source if its power [63]) in a very direct way. Jesus is thus the founder of the community of the Kingdom of God in this broader sense [64]. At this stage, however, despite a conscious attempt on Ritschl's part to distinguish Church and Kingdom, it is not altogether clear that such a distinction can be maintained [65]. Furthermore, Ritschl talks in terms of Jesus as the "Founder of Christianity" [66]. There is at this point no doubt that we are far removed from the primary context in which Jesus is referred to by Ritschl as "founder", that is, as the founder of the Kingdom of God in the first sense outlined above. Such ambiguity, though problematic, need not detract from the legitimacy and essential accuracy of Ritschl's basic perception that (the earthly) Jesus and the Kingdom's presence and proclamation belong together. Awareness of the fluidity of the term and the concomitant difficulties is, however, clearly required.

In summary, then, it can be said that Ritschl's focus upon the present dimension of the Kingdom of God and the way in which he expounds that focus with respect to Jesus' activity as recorded in Lke 4.17-21, Mt 11.2-6 and 12.28 can be supported. His exposition of the Kingdom of God as community on the basis of the Marcan understanding of the Twelve must, however, be open to question. In this way Ritschl again reveals his overuse of Mark. Perhaps not unrelated to this wrong emphasis, though distinct from it, is Ritschl's weakness in interpreting the so-called "future sayings", expressed by the apparent collapse of eschatology into teleology in his Kingdom-interpretation [67]. In this latter respect in particular, Ritschl's understanding of the Kingdom of God may be seen to be deficient. Ritschl's understanding of Jesus as "founder" of the Kingdom of God preserves an important insight - namely that the actions of Jesus are determinative for a Christian understanding of the Kingdom of God, but his use of the term "founder" in at least two distinct senses calls for caution on the part of his interpreters.

134

2.4 Jesus as Prophet and Messiah

Ritschl places no great stress on these two titles of Jesus. Yet they merit consideration, for both have been prominent in discussion about Jesus' understanding of himself throughout this century.

As far as Ritschl's own understanding of this issue is concerned, a point of clarification is first needed; though the title "Messiah" seems to have been of little importance for Ritschl, there is no escaping the fact that he appears to lay great store by what may be termed Jesus' "messianic consciousness". By "messianic consciousness" is meant Jesus' own awareness of his role as divine Son and Founder of the Kingdom in the manner already expounded [68]. This aspect of Ritschl's thinking should thus be examined as such, especially as it is in this form - primarily because of the work of Holtzmann and of those reacting against him - that the discussion took shape at the turn of the century [69].

It would not be accurate to talk of scholarly consensus on the question of Messiahship. As will become clear below, one may perhaps talk at most of consensus on the difficulty of determining a specific, pre-conceived definition of Messiahship. As a result, Messiahship is a discussion topic with respect to Jesus in view of the fact that the vagueness, or lack of specificity, of the concept allows Jesus' life to be viewed in terms of it. On this basis, one appropriate angle of approach is to see more precisely what is here being referred to by the reference to "Messianic consciousness" as far as Ritschl is concerned.

It should be said at the outset that in not focussing upon the title "Messiah" in any sort of depth, Ritschl reveals the extent to which his mentioning of *"Jesu(s) als des Messias"* refers only to a general perception or impression of "Messiahship"/ "Messianic consciousness" [70]. For this very reason he escapes much of the more critical enquiry into the Gospels on this question and anticipates some of the most recent comment. For some recent voices have responded to the issue posed in sharpest form by Holtzmann at one extreme and Bultmann at the other by pointing to the complexity of the problem of Messiahship/Messianic expectation/eschatological hope.

Holtzmann had been quite clear that Jesus gradually realized he was the Messiah [71]. Bultmann was equally clear that Jesus' life and work was not messianic and that thus he could not have thought himself to be Messiah [72]. More recent scholarship has been more cautious, however. Leivestad's comments can with some justification be considered typical of the current state of the debate:

> In großen und ganzen scheint die Lage im Judentum zur Zeit Jesus die gewesen zu sein, daß der Messias das gemeinsame, sammelnde Symbol des von Gott versprochenen Heils war, ohne daß man sich besonders konkrete Anschauungen über seine persöhnliche Art und Weise macht. Alle Juden konnten in diesem Symbol ihre höchsten Ideale und Hoffnungen verdichten. Der Messias war sozusagen mehr eine formale als eine materiale Kategorie. [73]

The term "Messiah" is seen, in short, to be a sort of terminological basket into which Jews at the time of Jesus could throw all of their eschatological eggs; their eschatological hopes were thus found united by reference to this particular figure, even if these hopes were themselves in content quite different.

Rowland echoes these sentiments, whilst accepting that "some groups in Judaism looked forward to the coming of some kind of messianic agent, usually human" inspite of the diffuseness and diversity of expectation [74]. Rowland then goes on to dwell on the question which has featured in much twentieth-century discussion of Jesus' Messiahship, namely whether it is a matter of Jesus accepting one "type" of Messiahship whilst rejecting another. Into the latter category falls the understanding of of the term "Messiah" as "Son of David" in the sense of a warrior-king [75]. Holtzmann had seen Jesus accepting Messiahship in terms of suffering, a view repeated often in New Testament scholarship since his day [76]. Rowland himself ultimately concludes that if there is to be any talk of Jesus' seeing himself as Messiah, then it is as "the agent of the good news of the Kingdom of God". Intriguingly, Rowland substantiates his case by appeal to some of the same passages upon which Ritschl himself draws in his exposition of Jesus' activity as the Kingdom's Founder, namely Lke 4.16f and Mt 11.2ff [77].

This much, then, is apparent; the question of Messiahship can only be raised in terms of its clearest and most literal meaning - Did Jesus consider himself to be "anointed by God" for a specific purpose? If he did, did he demonstrate that awareness by words or actions? Ritschl's answer, like that of the recent voices mentioned, is affirmative in the first case. In the second case he points to both words and actions, though makes no claim to Jesus having used the term "Messiah" of himself; messianic consciousness was, in other words, expressed in different terms. In short, affirmative responses to the above questions do not fill in precise details about the nature of that Messiahship. Such details must be provided through other channels.

, It should be stressed that only a framework for understanding Jesus is set up by reference to his Messiahship. The term "Messiah" therefore functions as a "formal category" in the manner suggested by Leivestad.

In one respect, however, Ritschl's understanding of the Messiahship of Jesus may not be affirmed. Here it is again necessary to draw attention to Ritschl's over-dependence upon the Gospel of Mark. For Ritschl talks in terms of the gradual self-revelation of his identity by Jesus [78]. Ritschl seems to assume that Jesus was always aware of his own identity. This may itself be questioned, though is not the direct point at issue here. The revelation of that identity - of the "messianic consciousness" of Jesus - is seen as a gradual process. The reliability of the Marcan presentation, a *"wohlgeordnete und in sich übereinstimmende Darstellung des eigentlichen Kernes der evangelischen Geschichte"* [79], is the foundation for this conviction. Abandonment of the Marcan framework thus brings into question also the assumption being made by Ritschl, that is whether Jesus was at all times fully aware of his own identity.

If Ritschl had been accurate in his identification of the realm in which Jesus' Messiahship is best understood [80], he had erred in making too great a claim for the New Testament critic's ability to perceive the manner in which that Messiahship was made evident in terms of a chronological and consistent strategy.

Turning to Jesus as "prophet", it is striking how prominent renewed exploration of this aspect of Jesus' life and work has been in recent treatment of the person of Jesus [81]. Its sheer topicality should not be allowed to belie its significance, however. For quite clearly, respect for the Jewish prophetic tradition is essential for an understanding of the background and context of Jesus [82].

References to Jesus as Prophet (be they self-references or references to Jesus on the lips of others) are not numerous in the Gospel tradition. One can refer to Mk 6.4 parr. plus perhaps Lke 13.33 for self-references and to Mk 8.28 parr., plus perhaps Mt 21.11 and 21.46 for references on the lips of others. But it should be recalled that the issue is by no means settled on the basis of such references [83]. Again Rowland is helpful here, filling in detail of prophetic traits in Jesus' origins, self-understanding and activity. Thus, Jesus' baptism and his spirit-possession, his Kingdom-proclamation, his message of judgment, his recognized authority, and his role as God's emissary (later developed in the Fourth Gospel) are all indicators, maintains Rowland, that Jesus was regarded as a Prophet and that the prophetic category is indeed a good angle of approach to the understanding of Jesus [84].

Cullmann takes "Jesus the Prophet" as the starting-point of his enquiry into New Testament Christology [85]. It is noticeable, however, how swiftly he seeks to move on to the question of the uniqueness and particularity of Jesus' prophetic status [86]. Though there is, especially for a Christian scholar - though also because of the content of the Gospels themselves - a degree of inevitability about the posing of such a question, there is nevertheless considerable exegetical and historical-critical work to be undertaken first. Such work would have to consider in particular the lack of uniformity in the understandings of John the Baptist and the relationship between the Baptist and Jesus himself. For it is clear that John the Baptist himself stands firmly within the prophetic tradition, yet the precise nature of Jesus' continuity with John is by no means so clear [87]. Cullmann himself fails to offer this work.

The details of that continuity need not, however, be gone into here. It will suffice for the present study to note the rough consensus of the importance of the prophetic tradition, and the fact that Jesus stood within it. There is no need necessarily to express the uniqueness of Jesus in these terms.

Ritschl was undoubtedly correct in locating Jesus firmly in the prophetic tradition in his attempt to find antecedents for Jesus' proclamation of the Kingdom of God. That he does not concentrate too heavily upon the title "prophet" or press the singularity of Jesus' prophetic status too far means he does not make Cullmann's mistake.

Ultimately, however, Ritschl's argument points to essential agreement with Cullmann in one very significant respect; the term "prophet" is simply not big enough to encompass the work of Jesus. Jesus is, for Ritschl, more than a prophet. For Ritschl Jesus is also unique. In expressing that uniqueness in terms different from that of the role of prophet he does not stretch the available evidence in this particular area.

The uniqueness of Jesus was thus expressed by Ritschl under other headings. One, the Founder of the Kingdom, has already been considered. It is to others that we must now turn.

2.5 Jesus the Son

The importance of "sonship" in Ritschl's picture of Jesus has already been established. Familiarity with modern discussion of the question of Jesus' sonship, however, soon shows that both Ritschl's construal of Jesus' sonship and his use of Gospel warrants for that construal are open to critical questioning. The very fact that Ritschl makes no distinction between the terms "Son" and "Son of God" suggests that his reading of the Gospel material will be deficient when viewed in the light of a century's further study. His use of the Fourth Gospel in gaining clarity on this aspect of his picture of Jesus must figure in particular as a necessary line of enquiry for the critic of Ritschl's position.

To begin with it is necessary to consider the Synoptic base for a discussion of Jesus' sonship in order to determine what current scholarship regards as the historical basis for such a discussion. A number of texts should be considered: Mk 1.11 parr., 8.38 parr., 9.7 parr., 11.25 par. Mt 6.14, 12.1-12 parr., 13.32 par.Mt 24.36, 14.36 parr., and four pairs of sayings from the "Q" material: Mt 5.38 par Lke 6.36, Mt 6.32 par. Lke 12.30, Mt 7.11 par Lke 11.13 and Mt 11.25ff par Lke 10.21f.

What is striking in these references is that the focus is much more on the fatherhood of God than the sonship of Jesus. This feature demonstrates the sparsity of material dealing with Jesus' sonship. It also provides a framework for understanding at least the Synoptists' perception of the nature of Jesus' sonship.

Dealing with the texts cited, it soon becomes clear that a number can be discounted as far as the question of their value as historical material in a discussion about the divine sonship of Jesus is concerned. Mk 1.11 and 9.7 are similar in content and find a similar place in their respective narratives, which are of the same form. Even allowing for differences in the historicity of the two events referred to, the sayings which are of relevance to our discussion can be nothing but interpretative [88].

Mk 12.1-12 also has little to offer such an enquiry. As we have it, the parable is clearly to be understood allegorically. It is difficult, if not impossible, to determine at what stage the allegorizing was first present. Perhaps it *was* an allegory from the start [89]. But even if one were to make the considerable assumptions required to construe it as evidence for Jesus' sense of divine sonship - i) that it derives from Jesus, ii) that he referred to himself - it can hardly be considered firm evidence for the enquiry [90].

Of the four other pieces of Marcan evidence, one - Mk 13.32 - can be dealt with relatively easily. This passage confronts the reader with both the sonship of Jesus and the fatherhood of God in their most refined form in the Gospel. Inevitably there are arguments in abundance for and against the authenticity of this quite remarkable saying [91]. But one thing is clear; that authenticity is so hard to establish in the face of potentially conclusive evidence to the contrary, renders the saying wholly unsuitable as a positive piece of evidence for Jesus' consciousness of divine sonship.

Three Marcan texts remain, all of which deal with God as Father rather than Jesus as Son.

Mk 8.38 presents quite peculiar problems. Here alone (allowing for parallels) in the Synoptic tradition is the notion of the fatherhood of God linked with the term "Son of Man". This feature alone may lead one to assume that the reference to the fatherhood of God is secondary [92]. The suggestion that Lke 12.8 preserves the oldest form of the saying is quite persuasive and would support this view [93]. But in some ways such a solution is the easy one. The problem of a Jesus/Son of Man distinction admittedly remains. But recent linguistic considerations of the phrase ο υιοϳ του

140

ανθρωπου render even that difficulty less problematic than it used to be [94]. Ironically, those same linguistic considerations permit an understanding of Mk 8.38 as deriving from Jesus himself, and as supporting his use of the term "Father" for God [95].

Much would be entailed in the support for such authenticity, however, not least of which is the assumption that Jesus could conceive of himself in the role of such an eschatological figure. It is thus safer to assume that the notion of fatherhood did indeed enter the tradition at a late stage. The titular use of "Son of Man" is thus then presupposed, as is the identification of that figure with Jesus himself. The "υιοʃ" element is thus explored as a motif characterising the relationship between Jesus and God, leaving open the possibility that exploration and expression of that relationship in such terms was authorized by Jesus, by being a practice of Jesus himself. But for evidence that this was so for Jesus it is necessary to look elsewhere. A slender thread of evidence can be found in the Synoptic tradition, namely in Mk 14.36. As a preparatory consideration, however, it is worth looking first at Mk 11.25.

The Matthean ring of this saying has led some to question its authenticity, particularly in view of the proven addition of Mk 11.26 [96]. But given that addition - based on manuscript evidence [97] - we probably have an indication of the genuineness of Mk 11.25. But it has to be admitted that the saying does not tell us much that is new. That is to say, on the basis of this saying alone, there is no room for the assumption that Jesus moved beyond the Judaism of his time in calling God "your Father" [98].

Novelty appears in the reference to God found in Mk 14.36. Though hotly debated in recent years, it nevertheless seems clear that at this point Jesus is portrayed in a manner quite new. *If* something characteristic of Jesus is captured here then Jesus broached new territory [99]. For from what the modern enquirer can gather, "abba" was rare as an address for God in Judaism at the time of Jesus. Jeremias' overstatement claims that Jesus' use is unique in prayer [100]. Casey has since cited evidence to qualify Jeremias at this point [101]. Yet even so, the novelty, if not the uniqueness, of the calling of God "abba" is established. It is an "address of daring intimacy" [102]; "it would seem disrespectful to use it of God" [103]. Vermes' claim to the contrary - given the sparseness of the evidence - is unconvincing [104].

How much is to be built upon this slender thread of evidence ? Dunn has clearly overreached himself in referring to Jesus' "regular use of 'abba'" as a reference for God [105]. But there is a case to be made for the view that some simple form of reference for God lies behind the Lucan form of the "Lord's Prayer", the Matthean form representing a "liturgical elaboration" [106]. Yet it has to be admitted that the evidence found here in Mk 14.36 is the only firm evidence that exists on the basis of the Marcan passages considered for Jesus' awareness of some special relationship between himself and God.

Turning to Matthew and Luke, it seems at first glance as though the material dealing with the question of the sonship of Jesus and the fatherhood of God is quite extensive. The fatherhood of God is more prominent a motif. This is particularly the case in Matthew. The motif of sonship is, however, still less frequent once titular occurrences are removed. In Matthew, as a result, the baptism and transfiguration narratives apart, we are left with Mt 11.27 and 24.36 (the latter being almost identical to Mk 13.32). In Luke both the sonship of Jesus and the fatherhood of God are less prominent than in Matthew. There is the remarkable story of Jesus' boyhood (2:41-51), the christological overtones of which are not to be denied. Yet this is surely a later development along similar lines - if in a different form - to the theological interpretation of the life of Jesus found in the Fourth Gospel [107].

But despite the prominent position of this narrative the motif of sonship/ fatherhood is not one taken up to a consistent degree in the Gospel as a whole. Baptism and transfiguration stories again apart, the fatherhood of God appears in only 11 places in Luke [108] and the bare ascription "Son" but once (10.22).

Closer scrutiny discloses a very slender base of material indeed. Matthew's notorious expansion of the motif of the fatherhood of God must be stressed [109]. Luke 22.29 is fascinating but problematic given the Matthean form. In short, much material seemingly pertinent to the enquiry clearly stems from the post-Easter situation [110].

Of the four passages worthy of consideration common to both Gospels the three found in the Sermon on the Mount in Matthew and scattered throughout the Gospel of Luke (Mt 5.48 = Lke 6.36; Mt 6.32 = Lke 12.30; Mt 7.11 = Lke 11.13) can be treated together. All portray Jesus calling God "Father" [111]. All three sayings do not portray Jesus going beyond Judaism. Jesus is not to be seen here making any self-claims. We cannot be sure that "abba" lies behind the material before us. And on this basis the sayings are far from remarkable. Though there is no need to dispute the potential authenticity of a basic saying at the root of each, this material offers the enquiry little [112].

By the standards of the Synoptic Gospels, the content of Mt 11.25ff = Lke 10.21f (identical in Matthew and Luke save for minor details) is, however, quite astonishing. Bultmann sees a clear distinction between Mt 11.25f and 11.27, such that 11.25f is perceived as Jewish (an originally Aramaic saying which may even derive from Jesus himself) whereas 11.27 is a "Hellenistic Revelation saying" [113]. Opposition to Bultmann derives from the perception that his religio-historical categories are simply too neat and the renewed observation of the Semitic character of so much of the Gospel material [114]. The section Mt 11.25ff is thus seen to belong in the realm of Jewish Wisdom material [115].

Some of the argumentation offering an alternative to Bultmann is, however, rather poor. Marshall, for example, feels able to move swiftly from the unity of the section via a reminder of its Semitic character to an ascription of the saying to Jesus, supported in the knowledge that Jesus called God "abba" [116]. Three things must be said in response: i) it is a giant leap from the Marcan evidence that Jesus called God "abba" via the assumption that "abba" always lies behind the Greek πατερ in words attributed to Jesus, to an argument for the authenticity of a saying of Jesus; ii) Semitisms point only to the milieu of a saying; Jewish Wisdom sayings could have been put into the mouth of Jesus; iii) the argument of "Semitic flavour" is not automatically weightier than the observation of a "Hellenistic parallel". The term "Greek-speaking Judaism" covers a plethora of conceptual and linguistic possibilities. Such considerations do not conclusively counter Marshall's position any more than they reinstate Bultmann's. Yet they do show conclusively that this pair of sayings cannot be counted firm evidence in a historical-critical enquiry into the divine sonship of Jesus.

This conclusion is of the utmost importance given the weight attached to the saying by Ritschl himself [117]. That a critical reading of the Synoptic tradition does not permit the use of Mt 11.25ff in the way Ritschl's procedure requires, places a question-mark against both his use of the material and his eventual conclusions. This is especially the case given the overall conclusion of the enquiry thus far: Mk 14.36 stands alone as evidence for an understanding of God peculiar to Jesus; evidence for Jesus understanding himself as a unique Son of God is wholly lacking.

Detailed study of passages from the Fourth Gospel is not necessary to demonstrate the centrality of the motifs of sonship and fatherhood in the Gospel; the point is already well-established [118]. The Fourth Gospel presents an understanding of the relationship between Jesus and God as that of a unique Son to a Father in a sustained fashion. Though this manner of expression, as was seen above, may well have already been present in the Synoptic tradition, it was clearly in no way central to it. Indeed it was seen that such elements as are found in the Synoptic tradition are at the very least problematic given their context within the overall presentations of the first three Evangelists. It is thus highly likely that the Fourth Gospel's presentation of Jesus incorporates a creative development of the motif of sonship as part of an interpretative procedure.

On historical-critical grounds, therefore, the taking up of the motif of the divine sonship of Jesus is problematic. If one takes up the Fourth Gospel's portrayal as an essential component in an interpretation of Jesus as divine Son, one needs to be aware to what extent the portrayal found there is different from that found in the Synoptic Gospels and aware also of the fact that it cannot readily receive unquestionable historical support [119]. The way in which Ritschl takes up the Fourth Gospel in his own exposition of Jesus as divine Son thus renders his picture of Jesus open to question. More precisely it renders his picture of Jesus open to question as a *historical* picture gleaned from the Gospels on the basis of historical-critical enquiry.

The reader is thus urged to reconsider Ritschl's picture of Jesus, recognising that on the grounds of purely historical- criticism, his picture is inadequate at this point.

At this point it is necessary to remind ourselves of the method ostensibly at work in Ritschl's Christology; Ritschl sought to set up a historical criterion in his

Christology. He also knew that Christology did not consist simply in "getting back to Jesus" in the sense of writing his life-story. It is also necessary, however, to draw upon some related discoveries already made, especially with respect to the notion of the Messiahship of Jesus. What has become clear in this enquiry into the notion of Jesus as "Son of God" is that the firm evidence for the notion as deriving from Jesus himself is not great. The possibility is by no means excluded; it is simply only a possibility and no more. In this sense, then, the historical data which Ritschl's norm for Christology requires are not to hand.

This does not demolish his interpretation of Jesus as "Son of God". Though it is clear Ritschl draws ultimately only upon the Evangelists' viewpoints, and not necessarily on the words of Jesus, the question of truth being posed is not yet answered. That is to say, it may yet be true that Jesus is "Son of God" in the sense in which Ritschl understands and interprets that idea even if firm evidence is not to hand. It is at this point that the parallel with the Messiahship, and particularly the manner in which the term is dealt with, is pertinent. That is to say; important above all was whether Jesus demonstrated prophetic traits and, furthermore, whether he conceived of himself as anointed by God for a special purpose. The evidence seems to suggest that he did. Thus, similarly, the issue of sonship should be decided, given Ritschl's exploration of the notion of sonship, by the answer to the question whether Jesus displayed his consciousness of an intimate relationship to God. As with any discussion of a christological title, the discussion cannot be allowed to collapse into a discussion of a single term [120].

On this basis, therefore, it remains possible that Ritschl's interpretation may be saying something important. Yet it should be stressed that the interpreter has left the realm of firm historical verifiability and entered the realm of interpretation based on inference, where one is handling less than conclusive evidence. Nevertheless, the possibility remains that the contention being made - Jesus did believe himself to have a special relationship with God - could be refuted by fresh evidence. But as it stands the interpretation is consistent with the evidence.

This is indeed how Ritschl's understanding of the sonship of Jesus must be considered. For only this approach does justice to his positive findings (that is, the fact that he has perceived an element which is of clear importance within the Gospel tradition) and the fact that he respects the hiatus between historical enquiry and the theological assessment of the life of Jesus required by the nature of that life itself. That these conclusions have a detrimental effect upon Ritschl's construal of christological method is clear. The full effect must be assessed in due course in this study. For the time being it is necessary to note only that the root of that critique lies implicit in Ritschl's own work, pointing to a tension in his own approach. This tension, as has become clear, manifests itself in Ritschl's practical exposition and pre-eminently at the point of greatest importance, that is, in his exposition of a picture of Jesus.

In summary, then, Ritschl's understanding of Jesus as Son can receive support in its intention to express Jesus' consciousness of a close relationship to God. It cannot, however, be supported in the terms in which Ritschl himself chooses to express the relationship, that is, on the basis of firm evidence that Jesus himself used the term "Son" of himself and "Father" of God in a unique way. The clearest Synoptic evidence for the possibility that Jesus called God "abba" in a novel, if not unique, way is Mk 14.36. This is the closest evidence to that which Ritschl seeks and which his case requires to be supportable on the terms of his historical norm for Christology. But this evidence cannot be allowed to carry the weight Ritschl's argument demands.

Ritschl's interpretation can thus only be received on different terms, at which point his dependence upon the theology of the Evangelists and his more general appeal to Jesus' activity play a part.

2.6 Jesus the Lord

Ritschl's handling of the question of the Lordship of Jesus can be seen to be unsatisfactory as a historical-critical enquiry when viewed in the light of a century of further New Testament study. His discussion fails to come to terms with the historical background to the question of the Lordship of Jesus through a thorough study of the term κυριοϛ as used in the Gospel tradition. Such is a pre-requisite in the post-Bousset age [121]. That Ritschl fails to provide such a study is thus certainly a weakness. Whether Ritschl compensates for this deficiency through theological insight - be it in terms of content or methodology - must be determined.

For the purposes of our enquiry the preliminary historical-critical considerations cannot be left aside. What follows is an assessment of the Synoptic Gospels' contribution to the question of the Lordship of Jesus, approached through a study of the use of the term κυριος by the first three Evangelists.

It is immediately apparent that the matter is more complex than the question of sonship for two simple reasons: i) the fact that, at one extreme, the word κυριος can stand for the Aramaic word "*mari*" and yet even then not disclose in what sense the Aramaic might have been intended or understood, renders the issue highly problematic; ii) the fact that, at the other extreme, the word κυριος was a title used of God in the New Testament on the basis of its use in this way in the LXX only compounds the problem. The multiple layers of meaning of the term κυριος in the Synoptic Gospels should, however, first be displayed. Eight layers may be discerned: i) a general sense as "owner" (e.g. Mk 12.9) or "master" (e.g. Mk 13.35); ii) of Jesus = "sir" (e.g. Mk 7.28 par. Mt 15.27); iii) by Jesus, of the Son of Man (e.g. Mk 2.28 parrs.); iv) by Jesus (perhaps) of himself (e.g. Mk 11.3 parr. would seem to be the clearest possible case); v) of Jesus by others in a lofty sense (cf. e.g. Mk 10.51 with parallels in Mt 9.28 and Lke 18.41); vi) of Jesus in an "absolute" sense, i.e. as "ο κυριος" (especially in Luke's Gospel); vii) of God in biblical quotations (e.g. in Mk 12.29, 30 and 36) [122]; viii) more generally as a reference to God (e.g. Lke 1.6, 9, 11) [123].

The flexibility and fluidity in meaning between layers ii) and vi) in particular should be stressed. Clearly, ii) and v) may be indistinguishable; iii) and iv) raise difficulties and draw on conclusions reached in other realms of Gospel study (i.e. the Son of Man question; the degree to which Jesus spoke explicitly about his own identity). That the expression of Jesus' relationship in terms of his "divinity" is located in the fluidity between meanings vi) to viii) is clear too.

Above all else, however, we are left with a question about the Aramaic of Jesus' own speech, or those of his contemporaries. That is to say, no matter how much reference may be made to "Greek-speaking Palestine" in the first century, and the early influence of the LXX or the Greek language upon the development of Christian thinking, there is no escaping the primacy of Aramaic, and without recourse to it - and even then we are sure only of reaching the milieu of Jesus - there can be no satisfactory conclusions [124]. Though at first glance a pessimistic conclusion, on closer scrutiny a number of things become clear.

First, to present the matter in such blunt terms is, expressed more positively, only a different way of saying what has been concluded by a number of New Testament scholars of late, namely that the problems posed by New Testament Christology are not to be answered by simple recourse to study of supposed christological titles. The New Testament scholar is thereby freed from a narrow historical-critical enquiry along such lines, and must be so freed if (s)he is to come to terms with the Christology of the New Testament [125].

It is, however, also clear that a second consideration lies implicit in the first; rather than seek other ways of answering such a problem of New Testament Christology through historical-critical channels, it is seen to be necessary to make the enquiry more explicitly theological in order to do justice to the demands of Christology itself. Neither the reductionist scholar who begins with the Evangelists and seeks to strip away the layers of tradition on the assumption that "oldest is best" nor the historian of religion tracing the development of the tradition from Jesus to credal formulation under the assumption of legitimacy thus come to terms with such demands. In truth, elements of both procedures must be employed, though not in the manner just outlined.

Ritschl himself comes close to offering a model for a more adequate way of exploring the notion of the Lordship of Jesus. In starting quite consciously from the standpoint of the community which worships Jesus as its Lord, yet endeavouring to be controlled by the demand for a historical warrant which seeks to discover in what way Jesus' Lordship was evident in his own life, Ritschl offers in this case a sufficiently flexible and a sufficiently theological model for understanding the Lordship of Jesus [126]. Here, in other words, he builds into his understanding of Christology the theological dimension in a more explicit way. The strain placed upon his historical norm in general has proved too great, yet the inconsistency in Ritschl's application of the norm is due simply to his attempt to interpret the Gospels more on their own terms, i.e. as theological works.

In other words, because the findings of the historical-critical enquiry permit, but do not require, Ritschl's interpretation of the Lordship of Jesus and because Ritschl *in fact* says more than a mere historical-critical reading of the Gospel allows, he enables the Lordship of Jesus to function appropriately as a category of New Testament Christology.

In interpreting Jesus' Lordship primarily as moral Lordship and relating it further to Jesus' task of founding the Kingdom of God, the Lordship of Jesus is worked out by Ritschl in the context of the understanding of Jesus' activity in and for the Kingdom of God, activity which by its very nature - he and none other being the founder of the Kingdom - sets him apart [127]. Ritschl's appeal to the Synoptic tradition on these grounds could even now be made. For despite the obscurities of the discussion of the meaning of κυριο∫ in the Gospel tradition one thing is certainly clear; people came to Jesus and respected his teaching [128]. If reserve can be expressed at the use of the term "moral superiority" - a reserve not shown by Ritschl himself - there is nevertheless little doubt that Jesus acted in a very special way and related that action to the Kingdom of God.

It should be stressed that this is by no means yet wholly satisfactory as Christology. In other words, this construal does not necessarily link Jesus' uniquely to God [129]. McKinney's suggestion that Ritschl's Christology is "exemplarist" may seem quite pertinent at this point [130]. The Lordship of Jesus in the community could be construed in no loftier terms than that of the "model of behaviour" for the community. Yet Ritschl has at least sought to forge the link and to answer the question on both historical and theological planes.

Where Ritschl is clearly deficient is in his conviction that what he is doing is wholly determined by his historical enquiry. For his construal of the Lordship of Jesus already again includes his particular interpretation of the Kingdom of God as community derived from the Gospel of Mark [131]. He is thus already in part dependent upon the theology of one of the Evangelists. Though he is undoubtedly setting up a framework in which historical and theological planes receive due attention (and consciously does so), he misunderstands the manner in which this must happen in believing the overlap to be almost entire.

A further problem is his use of the Fourth Gospel. Though clearly the understanding of the Lordship of Jesus is in many respects akin to that found in the Synoptics, what Ritschl lifts from the Fourth Gospel is the notion of Jesus' "Lordship over the world" [132]. This is, however, a further step over and above the interpretation of the Lordship of Jesus in terms of activity in and for the Kingdom (which may not necessarily be viewed in the "world-dominating" terms suggested in the Fourth Gospel and taken up by Ritschl).

It is clear from this discussion of Ritschl's understanding of the Lordship of Jesus that under the impression that he is gaining access to a picture of the historical Jesus not in and for its own sake but for the purposes of locating a norm for the construction of a Christian theology, Ritschl does two things:

i) he assumes too much of his sources and too easily mistakes the Gospel-pictures for accurate narrative of the details of Jesus' life, with the result that his historical criterion is a restriction out of all proportion to its function as a norm [133];

ii) the historical assumptions made presuppose an essential harmony between the Gospels which the critical reader cannot allow, with the result that Ritschl is guilty of making the attempt to harmonize the presentations of each Evangelist.

Under the heading "Lordship", then, Ritschl makes most explicit the manner in which his picture of Jesus operates. Eschewing study of the title κυριοϛ, his use of the term "Lord" seeks rather to encapsulate the manner in which "Lordship" is evident in the life of Jesus. Over and above this, however, his own theological interest relates directly to the interests of the Evangelists themselves in posing the question how Jesus remains Lord of the Christian community. In this fashion, the theological responsibility of the interpreter of the Gospels - a role which Ritschl takes seriously - becomes clear, and the ambiguity of the phrase "the community" is evident. For Jesus' Lordship of the community is a category which relates Ritschl's own situation to that of the Evangelists he seeks to interpret. At the same time it masks his own concern to distinguish historical data about the earthly Jesus from interpretation for the purposes of his own criterion.

150

2.7 Jesus the Obedient One

We must turn finally to Ritschl's understanding of Jesus as "the Obedient One". This category of christological affirmation presents the most difficulties as far as a historical-critical approach to Christology is concerned. Ritschl's dependence upon the Fourth Gospel and the tentativeness of the link to the earthly Jesus are most evident. The following critique must therefore demonstrate this and suggest reasons for Ritschl's misunderstandings as well as offer a corrective of his reading of the Gospel evidence.

It is clear that Ritschl is engaged in the attempt to express the nearness of Jesus to God in terms readily comprehensible to his contemporaries. In a context in which neo-Kantian concern for the role of the human will in religion was uppermost, Ritschl's effort is understandable [134]. Seen in such terms, however, it is equally clear that Ritschl is thereby providing the answer to a theological question. Furthermore, - and in part because of the nature of the question just described - it is a question which is not readily answerable by historical appeal. For unlike all aspects of Ritschl's picture of Jesus dealt with so far, this aspect does not have a dimension to it which could be interpretable on a superficial historical level [135]. Ritschl's essential problem is thus that he construes the issue in a historical way and demands, on the basis of his historical criterion, an historical answer which he deems can only be found from the Gospels.

On this basis it is inevitable that Ritschl make considerable use of the Fourth Gospel, for there is so little material for him to use in the Synoptic Gospels. Ritschl's methodology thus makes demands on him once more which his sources are not equipped to deal with. As soon as the step is made to "read the mind of Jesus" then a step is being made to the realm of interpretation of the life of Jesus, the realm in which theological questions are being posed and answered. That such questions inevitably include reference to the life of Jesus is clear. For questions posed about the intention of Jesus (what Jesus thought he was doing) of necessity incorporate consideration of what he actually did. And one's answer to the question what Jesus was "really up to" is a vital element in the task of Christology; *was* this man truly of

God ?

It is thus apparent, too, that to do justice to the demands of Christology it is not true to say that one may not delve into the mind of Jesus [136]. It is true, rather, that some sort of conclusion about what Jesus thought he was doing is essential to the christological task [137]. That Ritschl's recourse to the Gospels takes place at the level of theology once more, however, and does not take the form of historical appeal can be seen in anticipation and will be demonstrated once more below. Ritschl thus fulfils one side of his endeavour once again; to do justice to Jesus and the Gospel tradition. But once more he fails to adhere strictly to his historical norm.

The notion of "vocation" (*Beruf*) is alien to the Synoptic Gospels. The nearest point of access to be gained is via a consideration of the notion of Jesus' fulfillment of God's will. Yet even here the evidence is not great. There are many references to the will of God the Father in Matthew's Gospel (e.g. 7.21, 12.50 - altering Mk 3.35?, 18.14). Outside of Matthew, however, there are few references to the idea. In Mark there is but one reference to the "will of God" (Mk 3.35) in a passage which may well, in any case, be a Marcan construct [138]. There is in this context no hint of a reference to an understanding of the fulfillment of the will of God peculiar to Jesus himself. Beyond this, the passage Mk 14.36 also deserves consideration. The falseness of the setting at this point has already been referred to above and on this basis cannot be allowed to stand as a record of a particular prayer. As recording something characteristic of Jesus, however, the same argument as for the word "abba" may apply.

The major problem with this particular line of argument is that in this case there is no back-up evidence in anything like the same quantity as for "abba". Unlike the question of Jesus' use of "abba", there are no other related passages where the existence of the idea may be discerned behind the words found in the text. The clause γενηθητω το θελημα σου (Mt 6.10) is missing from the Lucan version of the "Lord's Prayer" (Lke 11.2f). This leaves the passion narrative text (Mk 14.36 = Lke 22.42 = Mt 26.39) as the sole clear Synoptic passage where the issue is highlighted. This does not, of course, answer the question of Jesus' obedience to God's will. The matter of truth being touched upon is not to be answered by the historian dealing with the few scraps from the Gospels which (s)he is given to chew upon. These scraps are far from irrelevant. But they do not determine all.

The Fourth Gospel is on the surface a more fruitful quarry for relevant material. The motif of Jesus carrying out the will of God finds expression in his fulfilling of the will of the one who sent him (Jn 4.34, 5.30. 6.38,39) who is the Father (6.40). As such, therefore, the interlocking motifs of the Fourth Gospel become apparent. It also becomes apparent, however, to what extent and in what way the Fourth Evangelist offers an interpretation of the life of Jesus. The very fact that the Fourth Gospel has so few links with the Synoptic portrayals at this point, when it has already become clear that the question being posed highlights the theological dimension to an enquiry into New Testament Christology, demonstrates the theological coinage in which the Fourth Gospel is minted.

Ritschl is able to fuse the two presentations in his construal of the sonship of Jesus [139]. Finding the obedience motif and the Father/Son motif already linked in the Fourth Gospel, and supported by the strong conviction that the sonship motif is not an interpretative model but an expression of Jesus' own self-understanding (evidenced in the Synoptics) he can more easily draw conclusions on the basis of the Fourth Gospel and conclude further that they may with justification come under the rubric of his historical criterion. Again, therefore, Ritschl is guilty of harmonization of theological pictures under the misapprehension that he is at root dealing with historical portrayals.

What is surprising is that Ritschl does not follow up one of his own insights at this point. In claiming that one who truly loves God does not declare the fact, Ritschl stumbles across what may serve as a valid - if complicating - factor in such discussions about Christology [140]. By analogy it may be possible to say that one who is truly obedient to the will of God will not go around declaring the fact [141]. The moment one therefore understands the actions of another to be the works of one acting under the guidance of God, one is drawing inferences from the actions in question and making an interpretation of what the person does and says. Such a theological issue is at stake in Christology, in the theologian's use of the Gospels, and in the recognition of the limitations of the historian's enquiry into the Gospel texts.

There is, however, one more aspect of Ritschl's reading of the obedience of Jesus which deserves consideration, one which draws more on the Synoptic Gospels and on the face of it gives greater credibility to this particular aspect of Ritschl's overall picture. That is Ritschl's linking of the understanding of Jesus as the Obedient One with a reading of Jesus' perception of his own death.

It was in the first volume of J & R that Ritschl undertook much of the spadework for his understanding of the death of Jesus. In dialogue with the history of Christian tradition he constructed a framework for interpreting the doctrine of the atonement which already implicitly places the focus on Jesus' self-understanding rather than well-worked out later Christian interpretations of that death [142]. For our enquiry, Ritschl's use of the Gospel evidence for a perception of Jesus' own understanding of his death is important. It soon becomes apparent that Ritschl's uncritical stance towards the material before him again causes him to make statements and reach conclusions which cannot be held to be tenable on the same basis as Ritschl himself made them.

From a current perspective, Ritschl's dealings with the question of the death of Jesus seem deficient in three main areas: i) his use of the Gospels is such that he readily accepts as authentic what are now clearly seen to be problem passages [143]; ii) above all, he fails to deal with the question of the Son of Man and its significance for the complete perception of Jesus' understanding of his own suffering and death [144]; iii) in more general terms, he fails to relate what he perceives to be Jesus' self-understanding vis-a-vis his death to any other aspect than that of his vocation; the Johannine viewpoint therefore dominates. In taking up passages such as Mk 8.35-7 and Mk 10.45 and accepting them as essential for grasping Jesus' understanding of his own death, Ritschl goes against what would now be seen as acceptable in the historical-critical study of the Gospels. If, in other words, there is to be found in the Gospels material pertinent to the question of Jesus' *own* understanding of his death then it must be found elsewhere.

On this basis, the question of the Son of Man becomes of paramount importance, given that it is through this medium - the expression of Jesus' mission and self-understanding in terms of this baffling title "Son of Man" - that the Evangelists (esp. Synoptists) choose to make sense of Jesus' sufferings and death [145]. It is simply astonishing that Ritschl fails to deal with the Passion predictions in the Synoptic tradition [146]. Even then, of course, it would be possible to argue one is working only with material at the level of Marcan interpretation [147]. Furthermore, given Ritschl's rather free use of material as authentic the lack of attention paid to such texts is all the more surprising.

Ritschl's perception of Jesus' understanding of his own death is thus ultimately stifled by being considered primarily under the rubric of vocation. In current research, Jesus' anticipation and acceptance of his own death would be seen only in part - and a much minor part than Ritschl would wish - in terms of Jesus' obedience to vocation. Though such might feature largely as part of the explicitly *interpretative* treatment of Jesus' death, it is now clear that it simply will not do to attempt to comprehend the death of Jesus, or his own anticipation of his death, independent of the circumstances in which he lived his life [148].

Interpreting Jesus' death requires a wider task than the assembling of evidence based on the study of a handful of key sayings. It is an enquiry which must take on the study of Jesus' behaviour and its implications as a whole. It must also work out the possibilities of tracing roots of atoning significance in Jesus' own self-understanding [149]. Though Hengel's own enquiry in this respect strikes the reader ultimately as suspect in that it too easily finds too much of later interpretation already implicit in Jesus' own self-understanding (thus overstretching also the bounds of probability about the authenticity of some of the material used) it is surely a correct approach to broaden the base of the background against which Jesus is viewed [150]. Even if the threads of evidence linking Jesus' self-understanding to such a Jewish background as Second Isaiah *are* indeed "meagre", then the notion of Jesus as perceiving some particular significance in his own death is not seen as wholly out of the question [151]. The question ultimately focuses upon whether the interpretation of Jesus' premature and violent death began in some sense with Jesus, *given* the fact that Jesus saw his own death as imminent.

In conclusion, then, Ritschl's discussion of the death of Jesus can be seen to be accommodated into his picture of Jesus in this way in order once more to link historical knowledge with christological affirmation. Ritschl does not force the atonement upon the Gospel evidence in an "orthodox" way [152]. But the lingering conviction of the importance of the death of Jesus, when tied to the historical criterion with which he operates, demands that he be able to point out quite directly where the link is to be found. That he chooses to make this link at a point where the historical warrant for the particular aspect of Jesus in question is quite weak is detrimental to the case being made for the historical authenticity of the link. Even if there is substance to the claim that Jesus anticipated his own death (a distinct possibility) and began to interpret his own death, this is still a far cry from the claim for the historicity of Jesus interpeting his own death in terms of divine vocation.

The vocation of Jesus seems therefore very much part of a theological interpretation of Jesus. It is thus clear that we are here at the point where Ritschl has stretched the available evidence to the limit - to breaking point, in fact - and has furthermore made too great an appeal on historical grounds to the Fourth Gospel. It is for this reason the most difficult of the categories of Ritschl's picture of Jesus to consider from a historical perspective. There is not - and could not be - much material to go on. The question of the mind and intention of Jesus thus shows itself already to be a christological question even if it is in a sense "historical" also [153]. Ritschl was right to probe in practice the relationship between christological questions and historical answers. What Ritschl's exposition of Jesus as the Obedient One lacks is the full awareness of the extent to which the issue goes beyond the bounds of the historian's task in the way Ritschl conceives that task. Though the historian, too, depends at points on inferences, Ritschl has allowed for that aspect too little in his exposition and thus failed to see how much, once more, he is reliant on the Evangelists' own theologically interpreted history.

2.8 Summary

What has been attempted is a historical-critical critque of Ritschl's picture of Jesus.

In the course of the critique it has been possible to determine where Ritschl's picture is in part untenable as a "historical" picture, and where his use of the Gospel evidence shows itself to be deficient on the terms he himself outlined. These findings will be be summarized below. It has, however, also been stressed that Ritschl's picture of Jesus was not intended to be a Life of Jesus as a substitute for a theological interpretation of Jesus. Positively expressed, Ritschl was attempting to construct an interpretation of Jesus from the standpoint of the Christian community, controlled not by orthodoxy but by an appeal to history, that is, "Jesus as he actually was".

For this reason, it is clear why the historical-critical approach to the critique adopted, though helpful in offering a partial corrective to some of the content of Ritschl's picture proves ultimately inadequate to assess the picture of Jesus in its entirety. The possibility of construing a theological interpretation of Jesus was more difficult than Ritschl supposed. This is clear from the way New Testament criticism demands that his use of the Gospels be reappraised. That the whole of Ritschl's undertaking thereby collapses is, however, far from clear. In respecting the fact that Ritschl cannot be met solely in terms of a historical-critical critique there is reason to suppose that Ritschl's approach may yet have a valid contribution to make to present concerns. In practice Ritschl does not adhere to his historical criterion as rigidly as he himself believes. The reason for this is easy to pinpoint. The way in which he uses the Gospel material - at times taking as authentic what a modern critic could not accept with the same degree of certainty - enables him to assume a broader "historical" base for his criterion than is in fact possible. Though a role is played by the canonicity of the four Gospels in this process, it is not simply a matter of canonicity guaranteeing authenticity. The fact that Ritschl allows a historical approach to the Gospels to play its part prevents such simple biblicism entering his theology [154].

Again, though there is also a role played by the canonicity of the four documents in question in the process by which Ritschl reaches the picture of Jesus with which he operates it is not simply a matter of distilling a single historical picture from the four which functions normatively. Under the assumption with which Ritschl works - that after undertaking a historical-critical task, the interpreter has access to "Jesus as he was" - he naturally feels safe in assuming that the picture he works with is indeed historical (indeed must be, by the very demands of his own methodology). But the fact that he is embarrassed by certain aspects of the Gospel tradition, yet feels able to make theological judgments under a historical criterion, suggests an awareness that he is dealing with not simply a multifaceted picture but many pictures [155].

From a more advantageous perspective and with greater sensitivity to the degree of difference between these four pictures, the modern reader would wish to press that difference. (S)he would also wish to press Ritschl to give it greater play in his thinking. That he does not do so can be explained in terms of the time at which he wrote and the context in which he wrote, which, above all, saw him posing the question of the theological significance of the New Testament canon.

The full implications of these considerations must be looked at below [156]. For the time being, a summary of the limitations of Ritschl's picture of Jesus when viewed from a historical- critical perspective must be presented.

Of the first five aspects considered (Jesus as Teacher, Founder of the Kingdom of God, Prophet and Messiah, Son and Lord) it was seen that all may justifiably be viewed even now as reflecting aspects of Jesus for which there is, in varying degrees, historically reliable material in the Synoptic Gospels to support. In all but the first case, however, the evidence is by no means of the type or quantity to support what Ritschl makes of each aspect. Thus, though undoubtedly correct in the direction of its emphasis, Ritschl's understanding of Jesus as Founder of the Kingdom of God must be heavily qualified by a correction of his understanding of the Kingdom concept itself and his concomitant over-dependence upon the Marcan framework. Though supportable in the sense that Jesus undoubtedly fitted into the Jewish prophetic tradition, and accepting the essential unclarity of "messianic expectation" generally in first-century Palestine, Ritschl's reading of Jesus as Messiah and Prophet must be corrected in the degree to which Ritschl feels able to assume in some detail and with considerable certainty a specific awareness of Messiahship on the part of Jesus. Though there are faint traces of a quite novel understanding of an intimate relationship between Jesus and God, as so understood by Jesus himself - a tradition much expanded by the Evangelists, in particular Matthew and John, - and expressed in terms of sonship, it is neither as expansive as Ritschl would have us believe, nor as closely related to other key aspects of Jesus' ministry as Ritschl's picture suggests. Finally, though there may well be a root understanding of the "Lordship of Jesus" standing in close connection to the respect people showed Jesus for his ability as a teacher, this is not to be seen as identical to the sense in which the term κυριoʃ came to be used of Jesus, even though there may be a very direct line of continuity from one to the other.

In each case, therefore, Ritschl is found to be expanding on the permissible cases of historical appeal by appealing to aspects of the Gospel tradition where one can only talk in terms of the theologies of the Evangelists. Though already anticipated by Ritschl's own methodology (the community standpoint), the hiatus at this point in the methodology is not perceived by Ritschl himself.

The discrepancy is most apparent in Ritschl's exposition of the vocation of Jesus (Jesus as the Obedient One), where the historical base has disappeared almost totally, and the degree of dependence upon the interpretative tradition is at its clearest. Though an attempt is made to refer to the Gospel (especially Synoptic) tradition at a significant point - via an understanding of the death of Jesus - the attempt proves ultimately unsuccessful.

It is thus clear that some appraisal of the wider task which Ritschl is undertaking needs to be offered. This can be done by calling the picture of Jesus with which Ritschl works "the Canonical Jesus".

3. RITSCHL AND THE PROBLEM OF THE "CANONICAL JESUS"

In the light of Brevard Childs' attempt at a theological harmonization of the four Gospel portrayals of Jesus, the theme of the "Canonical Jesus" is quite topical. Indeed, Ritschl's approach is in some respects so similar to Childs' undertaking, that a critique of Ritschl functions also as a critique of Childs. For in the methods of each theologian lies the attempt to harmonize conflicting theologies whilst respecting historical differences [157].

Ritschl's interest in creating a picture of Jesus is, in practice, as we have noted, not simply a question of the distilling of a "historical picture" from the four Gospels which can then function normatively for a theology. This discovery now requires full explanation and qualification. For whilst the theological dimension of his picture of

Jesus has been stressed consistently, the interest in historical data - as finding clearest expression in Ritschl's historical norm - and its precise relationship to Ritschl's picture has been insufficiently explored. Furthermore, the question of the ambiguity of the term "historical" as it appears in such terms as "the historical Jesus" and "historical picture" must yet be directly addressed. Still further, the relationship between these considerations and the question of Ritschl's interest in the theological role played by the New Testament canon must be explored in order to determine the nature of the link between them.

First, then, it is necessary to be clear about what Ritschl takes his task to be. It has been made plain throughout this study that there exists a tension between Ritschl's concern for historical material about Jesus in the Gospels - and its importance for Christology - and the conviction that a "Life of Jesus" cannot serve as an adequate assessment of Jesus' life. The manner in which that tension finds expression in practice became clear in the study of Ritschl's picture of Jesus. It became evident that despite Ritschl's attempt to construct a Christology controlled by a historical norm he has, by the standards of current application of the historical-critical method, failed to achieve his goal. His picture of Jesus does not thereby collapse, precisely because what Ritschl in fact produces is a theological picture, which he hopes is consistent with what can be known historically. What he has not achieved, however, is the closeness of the relationship between christological assertion and historical warrant which he so keenly sought and felt to be necessary to guarantee the "correctness" of his picture [158].

The consequences are significant. Either the method employed is valid and Ritschl's picture is untenable, or the picture may yet be true, in which case the method used must be rejected. In the former case, the result can only be a minimalist position in Christology, which would allow very little to be said because of the slender nature of the historical base permitted by New Testament historians. In the second case, Ritschl is worth attention, recognising that the question of norms for appraising his (indeed, any) picture arises anew once the historical norm which he himself tried to build into his Christology has been dispensed with.

As will be clear, this study suggests the latter option on the grounds that even though not defensible for the reasons Ritschl himself gives, there are aspects to Ritschl's picture of Jesus which seem, on the basis of the Gospel evidence, to have preserved some valid aspect of Jesus' life, ministry and self-understanding, even if that evidence is slender and already itself interpretative [159].

This leads to the second consideration, namely the inherent ambiguity of the term "historical" in this area of enquiry. A distinction must be made between the use of the word "historical" in the expression "Ritschl's historical norm for Christology" and the same term in the expression "historical picture", when the latter is applied to Ritschl's own picture of Jesus. In clarifying the distinction, it becomes clear that the latter position remains defensible in a way that the former does not.

The former expression - "Ritschl's historical norm for Christology" - entails a reference to the earthly Jesus to which Ritschl felt he had direct access via the Gospel texts and to whom Ritschl made his appeal in attempting to create a picture of Jesus. This Jesus - Jesus as he really was - could do nothing but guarantee the correctness of Ritschl's picture.

The latter expression - "historical picture" - was a term which Ritschl himself used. It is precisely in this term that the ambiguity becomes apparent, however. For though Ritschl in his own mind makes appeal to the "earthly Jesus", the word "picture" makes it clear - and the study conducted above has borne witness to this fact - that Ritschl's appeal is, rather, to the Gospel picture [160]. The term "historical" may yet be appropriate, however. For though the meaning of the term is, in this second case, more akin to "history-like", to use Frei's oft-quoted term, there is no escaping the fact that the Gospels attempt to interpret the historical figure of Jesus [161]. Though also saying something about themselves, the Evangelists nevertheless seek to present an authentic interpretation of Jesus' life, an interpretation consistent with what was known of his life. Thus, though dependent in part on inference and assumption, and though involving an imaginative, creative component, there is a distinct sense in which the accounts remain "historical". This ambiguity bedevils discussion of the "historical Jesus" because one cannot always be clear in which sense the term "historical" is being used. The simplest solution is thus to admit that there is a real sense in which the Gospels preserve at least four "historical Jesuses", those presented by the Evangelists themselves [162].

But if this is the case, there is a real problem as far as Ritschl's own approach is concerned. His understanding of history fails to make this necessary distinction. Yet at this point it is necessary, as a third aspect to the question, to introduce Ritschl's emphasis upon the canon of the New Testament. For if Ritschl has left room for his basic methodological premiss in Christology to be shown to be false by, in fact, entrusting the Evangelists with correctly assessing Jesus, then this move requires the canon as a safety-net. Even though - as the present-day interpreter can now see - Ritschl deceives himself into thinking that the norm operating in his picture of Jesus is a historical one (i.e. the earthly Jesus behind the Gospels), it can be shown that Ritschl is equally concerned to perceive the theological importance of the four canonical Gospels for the construction of a picture of Jesus. It is thus *these* four pictures which must be interpreted, and these four pictures whose essential unity needs to be teased out, yet whose character as religious writings and not historical documents must be respected [163].

This assumption of essential unity, when supported by a general assumption of the essential unity of Christology in the New Testament [164], inevitably leads to a kind of harmonization of the Gospels' pictures. It is not, however, a simple fusion of the four pictures.

Working on the assumption that the earthly Jesus himself stands behind the texts being dealt with in a more immediate way than is in fact the case it is easy for Ritschl to make the move from canonical harmonization of diverse theologies to the assumption that such a harmonization is at one and the same time a historical (i.e. as objective as possible) portrayal of Jesus. At this point a simple distinction between the "earthly" and the "historical" Jesus will not now be sufficient. It is thus more appropriate to term Ritschl's picture of Jesus the "Canonical Jesus" [165].

It is evident to any historian of New Testament study that the presentation offered here by Ritschl is a more primitive position of that reached by Martin Kähler in his The So-called Historical Jesus and The Historic Biblical Christ [166]. Ritschl's "Canonical Jesus" corresponds to Kähler's "Biblical Christ" in a very direct way. Kähler's own construal of the relationship between historical-critical study of the

Gospels and theological formulation is not a mere question of the near abandonment of the former in the face of the need for the latter on the basis of acceptance of the Gospel portrayals [167]. It is nevertheless clear that Ritschl's own version of the dilemma leaves a much greater role for the historian than Kähler was prepared to admit. Common to each, however, is the conviction of essential unity in their presentation of Jesus by the Evangelists. Kähler's position proved especially amenable to Bultmann and Tillich, both struggling to come to terms with the problem of how to articulate and find a basis for faith in the face of the historically unreliable nature of the sources. What the post-Bultmannians such as Ebeling, Fuchs and Käsemann have demonstrated, however, is the fact that the truth of the matter lies neither with Bultmann nor Kähler, but somewhere between Ritschl and Kähler [168]. The historical link between Jesus and the kerygma must, in other words, be tested ever anew and demonstrated as clearly as possible, no matter how difficult the exercise, lest the concrete component of Christianity's proclamation (expressed as witness to Jesus the man, from a real present historical context) be wholly lost.

Moving beyond both, however, yet still within the confines of a biblically-controlled dogmatics, Käsemann can see that the diversity of the New Testament is thus not the problem it constituted for Ritschl, but rather a liberation, to the extent that it retains diversity of theological expression within realistic boundaries [169]. In this respect, then, above all, the history of New Testament study has moved the New Testament theologian on to perceive the diversity of the texts as something to be welcomed and utilized as part and parcel of the theological task being undertaken. The recourse, in other words, in using the Gospels in Christology, to any form of harmonized picture of Jesus as a means of supporting the canonical context of Christian theology is a wrong move to make. In this, both Ritschl and Kähler can be opposed. The answer to the question whether Kähler's more inclusive or Ritschl's more selective appeal to "the" "Biblical/Canonical" "Christ/Jesus" should be followed cannot therefore be allowed to have the last word.

4. RITSCHL AND THE PROBLEM OF CHRISTOLOGICAL DIVERSITY IN THE GOSPELS

If our central thesis is correct - that Ritschl in fact operates with a theological picture of Jesus which, though not a simple harmonization of Gospel pictures, may nevertheless be termed the "Canonical Jesus" - then the question of the christological diversity of the four canonical Gospels, and indeed of the New Testament as a whole, naturally arises. For though at a descriptive level the enquiry has merely highlighted what Ritschl is in fact doing, at an analytical and constructive level the question remains; is his approach one which gives any clues as to how to use the Gospels in Christology today? So we must ask; how does Ritschl deal with such diversity? Does he recognize it? If so, does he cope with it adequately? If not, where does this leave him?

The following thesis will be defended; that Ritschl does not ultimately recognize the christological diversity of the Gospels, but that the process of development he underwent in his New Testament study, when related to the persistent theological interest of his work, sees him coping in practice with the phenomenon. This thesis derives from the observations made that a historical-critical analysis of Ritschl's picture of Jesus is insufficient of itself to deal adequately with Ritschl on his own terms. By his emphasis upon the role of the earliest and current Christian communities in the theological process Ritschl has, in other words, already gone beyond his own brief as far as the historical norm for Christology is concerned. This leads, as has been shown, to the abandonment of the historical norm as it stands. Respect for the manner in which Ritschl manages to solve this problem enables his approach to be viewed more favourably than has often been the case. It was a solution which, on the one hand, was respectful of his teacher, Baur, in seeking to follow the path of rigid criticism and, on the other, respected the New Testament canon - thus seeming mere biblicism.

In preparation for an exposition of how Ritschl copes with the phenomenon of the christological diversity of the Gospels, a discussion of Ritschl's handling of the phenomenon of theological diversity in the New Testament in more general terms is appropriate.

164

The main aim of Darrell Jodock's stimulating thesis on F.C.Baur and Albrecht Ritschl is to determine the heart of the controversy between the two figures in the 1850s and to trace the course of Ritschl's theological development with relation to Baur between 1846 and 1857 [170]. Central to his study is the need to determine what each theologian perceived to be the "essence" of Christianity, so that the nature of the continuity throughout the earliest period of Christianity's history could be specified. Only on that basis, maintains Jodock, can precision be given to the content of that norm [171]. Focussing therefore on the two editions of *Die Entstehung der altkatholischen Kirche* his intention is to see how Ritschl deals with the question of continuity between Jesus, the Apostles and Paul [172]. Jodock's conclusion, which is essentially correct, is that Ritschl is concerned to demonstrate a kernel of continuity throughout the main strands of Christianity represented in the New Testament, and that these forms all find their origin in the teaching of Jesus [173].

The differences between the two editions are: i) that the significance of Paul is played down in the second edition; and ii) that the diversity of the traditions from which the main (New Testament) strands were able to mark themselves off are explored further in the later edition, so that, for example, Jewish Christianity is seen as more pluriform, and likewise also Gentile Christianity, the first Apostles (*Urapostel*) and Paul being distinguished from each [174]. With regard to the New Testament itself, however, it is quite clear from Jodock's study that Ritschl follows Baur in perceiving a diversity of traditions, even if there is seen to be a "unity in diversity" at the end of the road.

To Jodock's account should be added the observation that recognition of such diversity was not something which Ritschl maintained only in his earliest years, the period when the Baurian influence upon him was at its strongest. It is true that the impact of Baur's *Tendenzkritik*, and the resulting distinctions made between the Synoptic Gospels, together with the shift of emphasis from the Matthean to the Marcan picture of Jesus, seem more confined to the period up to 1857 [175]. But the distinction between Jesus and the "Apostles" is an expression of such diversity and was a perception which Ritschl never lost [176].

Furthermore, the recognition of the different character of the Fourth Gospel is carried foward, as is the peculiar character of the Epistle to the Hebrews and the diverse theological emphases of Peter, James, Paul and John [177]. But how great is this diversity, according to Ritschl ? More importantly, how *essential* is it ? For sure, it is a recognition of diversity not confined solely to form (e.g. manner of presentation of Jesus) or literary genre, but extends to content [178]. But Ritschl was no redaction critic before his time. For the process of building upon Baur's *Tendenzkritik*, though causing Ritschl to perceive different theological emphases not merely in form but also in content, did not compel him to admit or perceive the existence of wholly diverse theolog*ies* in the New Testament. Beneath all the material in which Ritschl recognizes diversity, there remains, in other words, on his part the firm conviction that even if the New Testament texts do not harmonize on all points, they are nevertheless consistent in their essence. Thus, the methodological premisses worked through by Ritschl in his 1857 work serve also to illustrate his thinking about the New Testament's "unity in diversity". Some examples of how this works out in practice should be cited. It is on this basis that Jewish Christianity is to be distinguished from the thoughts and beliefs of the *Urapostel*, and similarly Gentile Christianity from those of Paul, though clearly each pair is internally related. At stake for Ritschl is the question of the continuity between Paul and the original apostles (*Urapostel*). What is more, the "essential agreement" / "agreement in content" (*wesentliche übereinstimmung*) between the *Urapostel* and Jesus himself needs to be established [179]. This, as Jodock demonstrates, is done in particular with respect to the question of unity of attitude towards the Mosaic Law [180]. Differences between Jesus and Paul *do* appear. Yet these do not appear to be too substantial for Ritschl. It is in the realm of "dogmatic trains of thought" (*dogmatische Gedankenfolge(n)*) that Paul's concept of righteousness "does not directly correspond" (*nicht unmittelbar entspricht*) with Jesus' own. That the two are not too far apart, however, seems the clear implication [181]. Finally one may cite an example quoted by Jodock. Ritschl's change of mind on the use of Hebrews also reflects his concern for the kernel of continuity between the texts of the New Testament [182].

This state of affairs demands critical consideration in the light of the issue under scrutiny in this enquiry. Two aspects should be brought out in particular.

First, it can be asked how substantial any difference perceived by Ritschl actually turns out to be where Jesus himself is concerned. For though the apostles' articulation of faith (their *"theologische Terminologie"*) is to be preferred to the "hints given by Jesus" (*Andeutungen Jesus*), slavish adherance to the latter constituting "misunderstood purism" [183], it is the *form* and not the *content* that is here being spoken of. Jesus could, in short, hardly be superseded theologically [184].

Second, the example of Hebrews cited above raises again the question of the increased role played by the New Testament canon in Ritschl's construal of Christian theology's task and methods. Diversity seems permissible, in other words, but up to certain theological limits.

Ritschl thus twists the issue of canonicity around and focuses not on the sheer presence of a work in the canon of the New Testament but rather on the reasons - even if not explicit - why it is there in the first place [185]. Of the positive reasons for canonicity expressed, it becomes necessary to dwell upon a major reason which lurks on the edge of Ritschl's presentation; the question of christological continuity between the New Testament texts shows itself to be more significant than its incidental mention suggests [186].

Furthermore, once this criterion of canonicity is placed alongside the "insuperability of Jesus" as referred to above and expressed rather in terms of christological normativity, the function of Ritschl's picture of Jesus - understood ambiguously as a "historical" picture - as a christologically normative picture is becoming clear.

Diversity is thus both perceived and permitted by Ritschl in his understanding of earliest Christianity and his reading of the New Testament. This diversity extends even to theological diversity. But to be more precise: it extends to *some* aspects of theological expression. Christological diversity seems ultimately not to be perceived for it is a linchpin of canonicity, and one, furthermore, which has its root, for Ritschl, in Jesus' own understanding of himself and his mission.

The historical backbone for such a firm acquaintance with the words and acts of Jesus as Ritschl laid claim to is no more to hand. As a result, the theological diversity of New Testament writers can now be perceived to extend further than Ritschl himself allowed. Given that this is the case, what happens to Ritschl's construal of the Gospel evidence ? More especially, what effect does this have on the procedure of bringing his work at this point alongside a modern consideration of the topic? It is at this point that the focus can once more be brought upon the question of the christological diversity of the Gospels.

It has already become clear that Ritschl makes use of three of the four canonical Gospels in a quite independent and explicit way. As well as talking in terms of a "synoptic picture" of Jesus - showing a differentiation between John and the first three Gospels - he articulates an understanding of Jesus upon a Matthean and Marcan base at different points in his career. Only Luke receives scant attention after 1847. Ritschl's theological methodology relies heavily upon being able to grasp Jesus historically, however - that is, being able to appeal to the earthly Jesus as the norm of his Christology. When seen in the light of the conclusion reached above - that Ritschl is ultimately unwilling to admit theological diversity in the realm of Christology - it is therefore evident that the claim to be able to gain access to the earthly Jesus through the Gospels is assumed to be the guarantee for such christological harmony.

Perceiving these two aspects of Ritschl's work is not yet to perceive a tension within it. It is quite possible to perceive theological diversity between the Gospels whilst maintaining essential agreement about Christology. Theological diversity may well, for example, be discernible in the realms of eschatology or ecclesiology.

This study has, however, highlighted the fact that there is indeed a tension in Ritschl's work. He depends heavily, in other words, upon the picture of Jesus presented by each of the three Evangelists with which he deals at three salient points in his career. Under Ritschl's construal of the theologian's task, he assumes essential christological harmony with reference to the earthly Jesus whom he believes is accessible through the Gospel material. As the modern reader has seen the gulf open up between earthly Jesus and the Jesus of the different Gospel pictures, the tension in Ritschl's position is clear.

Ritschl's use of three Gospel pictures of Jesus can thus only be understood as his actual encounter with the christological diversity of the canonical Gospels. The concern to interpret the Gospels theologically - related to his interest in the New Testament canon and his resistance to the idea that the writing of a Life of Jesus exhausts what the Gospels say - is therefore the basis on which a positive reception of Ritschl's undertaking is possible.

Such positive reception involves the abandonment of Ritschl's own historical criterion in Christology, which reveals itself ultimately to be: i) a control, or guide, for Christology which it is impossible to set up with any certainty without resorting to a debilitating minimalism; ii) a misreading of the nature of the theological differences between the Gospels. For Ritschl does not see that the "unity of the Gospels", not to be found by reference to an external objective criterion (earthly Jesus), is not, indeed, to be located in some assumed christological harmony. The theology of each Evangelist cannot be focussed, in other words, upon a christological common denominator; what constitutes a theology is much more complex.

That Ritschl knows full well he is dealing with "theological" works is clear. That this aspect of his thinking finds a way into his interpretation is evident from the community emphasis of his approach. These are the foundation-stones in his thinking for what came to fruition half a century later as form-criticism. But Ritschl could not progress so far in his thinking so long as he was moored to the conviction that the earthly Jesus could function as a control for Christian theological reflection in the manner he suggests; such a conviction thus restricts his interpretation of the Gospels and his theology also. His insistence upon the historical norm for his Christology prevents his community emphasis developing into the full recognition of the theological diversity to be found in the Gospels.

The theological appreciation of the Gospels finds a role in his thinking at the points at which he has permitted three Gospels to speak on their own terms and allowed their diversity to impregnate his thought. What Ritschl ends up with in *R u V* is indeed a theological interpretation of Jesus and not one, as the present-day reader can see, ultimately determined solely by historical reference. It is "controlled" as the enquiry above has shown in all but one significant respect - Jesus' vocation - by historical appeal to the extent that the interpreter is seen to have enough historical material to go on to suggest that the interpretation is consistent with the actions and self-understanding of Jesus. But this is the only sort of "control" which can be considered. In highlighting the significance of the Johannine picture of Jesus in the aspect of Jesus which failed the historical-critical test, one is thereby pointing out the illegitimacy of neither the Johannine nor Ritschl's interpretation, but only the fact that it is precisely that; a Johannine interpretation taken up by Ritschl.

In general, however, it can be said that it is the *Marcan* rather than the Johannine picture which is more determinative of Ritschl's Christology, and thus Kingdom, teaching and discipleship are key aspects of Ritschl's own picture of Jesus [187]. The conviction that the Marcan presentation of Jesus is of itself more "historical" leads Ritschl to this position. What is built upon this, though conceived in terms of adherance to the historical norm set by the Marcan picture, is clearly an accommodation to Marcan Christology. Thus, for example, the righteousness (*Gerechtigkeit*) which Jesus embodies in his own actions must be viewed within the understanding of the Kingdom which Jesus proclaims [188].

That Ritschl's approach ultimately does not permit all aspects of his picture of Jesus to be accommodated harmoniously reveals the tension at the heart of his methodology. The Johannine picture is poorly represented in the opening sections of *R u V II* for the simple reason that Ritschl is convinced that the Kingdom of God *was* vital for Jesus himself. Conversely, the Synoptic pictures receive relatively scant attention in the sixth chapter of *R u V III*, where Jesus' understanding of his own identity and mission, and Ritschl's interpretation of the same in terms of obedience to divine vocation and sonship, come to the fore. Clearly there is some sort of link through the categories of sonship and Lordship to support an interpretation of Jesus having a special relationship with God and receiving considerable respect among his contemporaries on this basis. That Ritschl does not dwell upon the Fourth Gospel's portrayal of Jesus as the explicit proclaimer of his identity, however, shows that he does not overuse the Johannine picture. There is a constraint operating upon the acceptance of the Johannine picture in its entirety [189].

Nor is there any attempt to explain the near absence of the Kingdom from the mouth of Jesus in the Fourth Gospel. The result is a collage of juxtaposed pictures pasted together. Ritschl's picture of Jesus - his "Canonical Jesus" - can thus ultimately best be compared to a cubist painting of Jesus in which at first glance the Johannine picture seems prominent, at second (more correctly) the Marcan seems prominent.

Yet in reality he has not mastered the diversity of perspectives, believing his construction to be more life-like than it really is.

A further, and highly significant constraint upon Ritschl's perception of the task of the theologian when faced with diverse Gospel pictures of Jesus must be mentioned. Because the historical aspect of Christology is consistently uppermost in Ritschl's mind and because he therefore fails to treat so much of the Gospel material at a non-historical level - even though he can see quite clearly that the Gospels are more than (objective) history - he leaves his "picture of Jesus" (theological interpretation of Jesus) incomplete.

In practice this means that the exclusion of full consideration of the birth narratives, the miracles, and above all the resurrection is the deficiency of his approach concomitant with his insistence upon the rigid historical norm in Christology with which Ritschl operates. By focussing rather upon the theological task in view, and perceiving to what extent his case rested upon the theologies of the four Evangelists Ritschl would have been better placed to treat such "non-historical" material in a more adequate way. In this way, too, he could have rendered his theological assessment of Jesus more complete [190].

To summarize: Ritschl is open to the possibility of theological diversity in the New Testament. He fails to see that this diversity can extend to Christology. This has restricted his field of vision in this area, producing or caused by (the question cannot be answered conclusively) the close link Ritschl perceives between historical enquiry into the life of Jesus and christological formulation. The link is not, in fact, as close as Ritschl himself maintains. But because Ritschl proves himself to be dependent upon the Gospels' portrayals of Jesus, because he desires to move over and above mere (objective) historical presentation of Jesus, because he seeks to give Christian theology a canonical "shape" and respects the role of the earliest Christian communities in the preservation of Jesus-tradition, Ritschl therefore already incorporates the theologies of the Evangelists into his interpretative process. He thereby begins to demonstrate implicitly how the theologian must deal with christological diversity in the Gospels. Despite this dependence upon aspects of the pictures of Jesus presented by the Evangelists (or at least three of them), and though approaching independent presentations of each Evangelist, Ritschl is still constrained by the fact that he subjects them to too rigorous a historical control. As a result, he excludes consideration of material essential to his intepretative task.

5. SUMMARY

The findings of the critique of Ritschl's picture of Jesus conducted in this chapter should now be summarized.

As became clear throughout the detailed study of the picture itself, the question of the adequacy of Ritschl's understanding and presentation of Jesus is simultaneously a question about the methodological premisses of Ritschl's exposition. It is for this reason that Ritschl's angle of approach is a fruitful avenue of enquiry for the question of the relationship between the study of the "historical Jesus" and the task of theological construction. For this reason also, it was fitting to begin this chapter with some preliminary critical comments concerning Ritschl's use of the Gospels. Because Ritschl's use of the Gospel material ultimately conflicts with the methodology in Christology with which he seeks to operate, it was appropriate to preface the detailed study with words of caution about his approach.

The hidden assumptions with which Ritschl was operating were disclosed. First it was noted how a solution to the Synoptic Problem was correlated with the assumption that the first Gospel to be written, be it Mark or Matthew, possessed generally reliable historical material about Jesus (III.1.1). It was then noted how the conclusion of Marcan priority to which Ritschl eventually came in 1851 brought with it for Ritschl the assumption of the essential historical accuracy of the Marcan framework, the full implications of which were then explored in the separate sections of the detailed study of his picture of Jesus.

The question of Ritschl's increased use of the Fourth Gospel in his later period was also posed (III.1.2). Here it became clear that the matter of Ritschl's greater use proves to be no simple issue. The negative assumption that the increased use is bound up simply with growing awareness of the importance of the New Testament canon was mentioned. It was also suggested, more positively, that Ritschl's thinking about the earthly Jesus underwent a significant change, a change which affected his use of the Gospel material. The fact that the Mosaic Law was no longer seen by Ritschl to be central for Jesus himself (as the evidence of _R u V_ suggests) brought with it a tendency to greater use of John and a reappraisal of the Synoptic evidence. This factor has received little, if any, attention in the discussion of Ritschl's use of the Fourth Gospel.

This observation did not instantly legitimate Ritschl's use of the Gospels. Indeed, the study then conducted showed how, especially with regard to the question of sonship, Ritschl's use of the Fourth Gospel as historical evidence becomes questionable at significant points, once the Synoptic base itself is questioned. But the suggestion at least urged the reader to regard the matter as more subtle and complex than is often allowed. The study of the six aspects of Ritschl's Picture of Jesus expounded in II.3.1. then followed. Ritschl's support for the view that Jesus was a teacher was shown to have firm evidence in the Gospels after historical-critical enquiry, and also wide scholarly support. His linking of Jesus' teaching with the Kingdom of God was also welcomed and strongly supported. The manner of his teaching - in particular with regard to Jesus' relationship with his disciples - was shown to be understood by Ritschl too much on the basis of the Marcan evidence. As such, this particular aspect of Ritschl's construal of Jesus as teacher could not be held after historical-critical enquiry. The centrality of the Kingdom of God in Jesus' words and actions as perceived by Ritschl received support. His understanding of the Kingdom, however, failed to do full justice to the breadth of the material present in the Gospel tradition. In failing to come to terms with the future references, it was felt that he had perhaps collapsed the Kingdom's eschatological dimension into a teleology which related better to the present sayings upon which he concentrated so heavily. His stress upon the present understanding of the Kingdom and Jesus' presence should be welcomed. A difficulty with the word "Founder" was noted. It was seen that when viewed in context in Ritschl's writings the understanding at the level of Gospel-interpretation is clear.

Jesus' Messiahship was understood, correctly, by Ritschl within the Jewish tradition. Though he did not make a systematic study of either the title "prophet" or

"Messiah" this was shown, ironically, to be an advantage. For Ritschl concentrated thereby upon the "prophetic traits" and "messianic consciousness" of Jesus as evident in the activity of Jesus. This same approach could be employed in the evaluation of Ritschl's understanding of sonship. For it was seen how Ritschl's expression of an aspect of the life of Jesus - Jesus' sense of a close relationship with God - received widespread Gospel support without having a firm historical-critical base upon which to rest. The problem of sonship thus not only highlighted the difficulty of verifiability of interpretations of Jesus, but also posed serious questions about the "historical" track which Ritschl had opted to follow. It was seen that of the Synoptic evidence only Mk 14.36 could be held with any degree of certainty to possess something significant for Ritschl's purpose. That Ritschl was already going beyond his (objective) historical brief became clear in the discussion of Jesus' Lordship, where the directness of the link between Jesus and the Christian community found most complete expression. At this point, a legitimate foothold in Jesus' ministry, as presented in the Synoptic Gospels, for Ritschl's understanding of "Lordship" was found to exist. This was seen to be tenable even after historical-critical analysis of the Gospel material had been undertaken. The link with the Christian community (past and present) at this point was nevertheless seen as an important factor, being an expression of Ritschl's persistent desire to construe the picture of Jesus in a manner which was theologically relevant. In the discussion of the vocation of Jesus, it was seen how Ritschl sought to enter into the mind of Jesus, doing so with the aid of the Fourth Gospel's interpretation of Jesus. Though seeking a Synoptic base for his thinking through a particular interpretation of the death of Jesus - as proof of vocation - Ritschl's attempt can be said to have failed. It was clear at this point not only to what extent Ritschl's own theological interest pervades his picture, but also to what extent a Christology must inevitably include inference and interpretation as well as data about Jesus.

The limits of the historical-critical approach in the assessment of Ritschl's picture of Jesus had become clear. Though Ritschl's picture could be corrected in significant respects (e.g. if elements depended solely upon the Marcan framework, then questions could legitimately be posed), the question of truth ultimately posed could not be answered by historical enquiry, by the very fact that Ritschl's picture - though ostensibly built on a historical base - inevitably included within it the interpretative element required of a Christology. This theme was then explored in two different ways.

First the picture of Jesus which Ritschl had produced was seen under the heading of "the Canonical Jesus". Here it was noted to what extent Ritschl built upon the Evangelists' interpretations of Jesus, effectively seeking a harmonization of their interpretations. Similarities were noted with the views of Martin Kähler. This part of the enquiry included within it the observation of the ambiguity of the word "historical", which could be seen to move beyond the meaning understood by Ritschl in his quest for continuity between historical data and christological assertion. There is, in other words, a legitimate use of the word "historical" for the Gospels' portrayals of Jesus and for Ritschl's own in the sense that all the portrayals in question seek to be consistent with known facts.

The second angle of approach was a consequence of the first. Given Ritschl's actual practice of building upon the Evangelists' portrayals of Jesus, the existence of christological diversity was seen to be a problem. After an enquiry looking in more general terms at Ritschl's admission of the existence of theological diversity in the New Testament, it was seen that Ritschl seemed ultimately unwilling to permit theological diversity to extend into the realm of Christology. The manner in which the harmonization of the four Christologies takes effect is on the basis of the historical norm, even if the historical norm includes, as had been shown, elements which could no longer be considered firm evidence. The cost of this approach was the exclusion of much material significant both for a complete understanding of Jesus and for a full appraisal of each Evangelist in his own right.

On the basis of this critique it is possible to draw together the threads relevant to the task of suggesting how Ritschl should be understood as far as the question of the use of the canonical Gospels by the Christian theologian is concerned. The answer to this question constitutes the conclusion of this study.

Notes to Chapter III

1. A conclusion Baur reached using a Hegelian model, whereby Mark was understood to synthesize the Matthean (Jewish) and Lucan (Gentile) tendencies into a neutral form of Christianity.

2. It should be stressed that Strauss and Bruno Bauer apart, there were few voices declaring there was little or nothing in the way of historically reliable material about Jesus to be found in the Gospels. Even F.C.Baur had high hopes for what scrutiny of the Gospel of Matthew (the first Gospel to be written in his estimation) could produce: see esp. Baur 1878 pp23-43 and also the *Vorlesungen über neutestamentliche Theologie* (Leipzig 1864) pp45-121. Further reference to the qualification required to Tuckett's argument is pertinent at this point (see ch I n9 and ch II n89 above). For where there is an assumption that historical material is to be found, together with the assumption that such historical material is of theological relevance (both assumptions being shared by both Baur and Ritschl, though in different ways), then the solution to the problem will inevitably have dogmatic consequences. See, correctly, McGrath 1986 pp74 and 214.

3. Especially as pertaining to words of Jesus. See e.g. Hooker 1970-71 and 1972; Käsemann 1969; Marshall 1977a ch.9 esp. pp200- 211; Stanton 1974a.

4. K.L.Schmidt: *Der Rahmen der Geschichte Jesu* (1919) led the trio of standard Form-Critical works which have proved decisive in the development of the study of the New Testament. Dibelius (1971) and Bultmann (1972) soon followed. Wrede's contribution of 1901 (Wrede 1971) had followed Strauss in pioneering the process of subjecting the Gospel tradition to radical criticism. His more thoroughgoing emphasis upon the theological tendency of an *individual* Evangelist, though far from original - as the work of Baur and Ritschl shows - was decisive because of the manner of his presentation and the climate in which he wrote.

5. E50 p47f.

6. "Matthew's Gospel alone offers no doctrine of the person of the God-man and of faith in him ... "; E50 p48 (my translation).

7. Ritschl 1851 p31.

8. It has already been noted that Ritschl could at times dispense with the Matthean version of an event or saying in his work of 1857 (see e.g. ch II n132).

9. E57 p32 (cf e.g. Hill 1972 p271f v. Beare 1981 pp370-3 on Mt 17.24-7), p34 (cf. e.g. Hill p185 v. Beare p242 on Mt 10.6), pp35 and 41 (cf. Beare 197f on Mt 7.21-3; Hill is less willing than usual to claim an origin of this material in the words of Jesus; Hill p151-3 esp. p152) and passim (for Mt 5.17-20, concerning which

176

Beare suitably summarizes current scholarship: "It is not surprising that then authenticity of all three sentences in Mt 5.17-19 should be challenged." p140, though Beare goes on to accept that v20 may be genuine. Hill's caution leads him to conclude that there is no reason "to deny that at least part of the section reflects the spirit and teaching of Jesus." p117).

10. Above II.3.3.7.

11. McGrath 1986 p58 and p66 n21; see also McCulloh's comments (cf above ch.II n115).

12. J & R III p443. See further e.g. ibid. p436 "His (i.e. Jesus') estimate of himself betrays...a sort of sliding scale in the way he describes his own relation to God, *not only in John*, but also in the other Gospels..." (emphasis added).

13. Above II.3.1. 5 (cf esp. J & R III p449f).

14. J & R III p461 and p476.

15. That is to say, in his later career (see below n22 for documentation of early views about the Fourth Gospel). The expression "main contours" here denotes the two key aspects of Ritschl's picture of Jesus which have been highlighted, i.e. sonship and Kingdom of God. It could, of course, be argued that sonship would never have featured as a major aspect of Ritschl's picture, had he not "rediscovered" the Fourth Gospel. Whilst there is inevitably a case to be made for this argument, its simplicity cloaks full awareness of what is going on. As will become clear below (esp. III.2), it is not a simple matter of Ritschl becoming conservative with regard to the Fourth Gospel, but of revising the conditions under which the Gospel material is used, even if this does impair the "historical" warranting of his theology for which he strives in the sense in which he understands that term. Furthermore, it should be asked whether sonship, even if prominent in the Fourth Gospel, could ever have become a key feature of Ritschl's picture without its having *some* foothold in the Synoptic tradition.

16. *R u V II* pp38, 99f, 244 and 298f.

17. ibid.p36. It should be noted that the issue here is that of the "authenticity in content" (*sachliche Authentie*) and not in word.

18. J & R III p439.

19. *R u V II* p100 (*treue(r) Erinnerung*); ibid p298, where Ritschl refers to John's deviation (*Abweichung*) from the "authentic picture" (*authentisch(en) Bild(e)*) of Jesus provided by the other Gospels.

20. Above n11.

21. Above II.1.5. 3 for comments on the *genre* of E50.

22. For early appraisals made by Ritschl of the Fourth Gospel see e.g. E50 p48, 1851

p19 and E57 p48f n1. Ritschl discloses a less negative approach than Baur, yet seeks to incorporate fully the essential difference between the Synoptics and the Fourth Gospel into his thinking. The roots of the important recognition of the Kingdom's near-absence from the Fourth Gospel are, in short, already to be found (later B.T. p114 and 136; *R u V II* p28 n1).

23. E.g. Troeltsch; above ch. II n107.

24. See Draper 1984 p217f.

25. He could, of course, have pondered on the total absence of the word νομοJ from Mark! Such would, however, have been an *argumentum e silentio* had too much been built upon it.

26. This is the case despite the efforts of e.g. Dodd, Cullmann and J.A.T.Robinson (see above ch. II n137).

27. The picture is thus a "historical picture" in the sense that it is perceived by Ritschl to be a picture of the earthly Jesus. The issue upon which Ritschl here launches himself, without the clarity necessary - the clarity which could be gained post-Kähler - is that of to what extent presenting a picture of the earthly Jesus and interpreting Jesus theologically are ultimately one and the same thing, that is, to what extent it can - or must - be said that the life of Jesus really can only be presented as a theological appraisal. Ritschl gropes for this sort of clarity without being able fully to see all that is entailed. He remains convinced that a "synoptic picture of Jesus" (*R u V II* p41) is obtainable and that furthermore this picture is "historical" (Ritschl 1851 p1) in the sense that it gives us a good idea of what the earthly Jesus was like. See above further n19. The recognition of the theological importance of the earthly Jesus has, however, not yet become distinct from the quest for historical data about Jesus in theological thinking.

28. Caution with terminology is demanded when trespassing upon this minefield of scholarly research. The term "essential correctness" is here instantly, and necessarily, qualified, as it signifies merely that Ritschl's picture, which shows itself to be ultimately a theological picture, will be subjected to one means of assessment. It will be determined, in short, whether his interpretation is at least consistent with what can be known about Jesus historically. No claims are being made at this juncture to the effect that this testing of Ritschl's picture "proves" either the picture itself or the methods which Ritschl uses to produce that picture and to integrate it into his theology.

29. Sanders 1985 p158.

30. J.Weiss 1971; Harnack 1977 esp. pp40-94; Bultmann, to most people's surprise, was able to produce a book entitled *Jesus*, three sections of which (pp23-148 in the 1977 Gütersloh ed.) were devoted to the proclamation of Jesus; see also Bultmann 1952 ch.1 pp3-32 and Primitive Christianity in its Contemporary

Setting (London 1956) pp71-9 and 86-93; Dodd "Jesus as Teacher and Prophet" in Mysterium Christi eds. G.K.A.Bell and A.Deissmann (London 1930) pp53-66; T.W.Manson: The Teaching of Jesus (C.U.P. 1948); Perrin 1967; Hengel 1968, whose statement "...über die Form, in der Jesus selbst der **Lehrer** seiner Jünger war, wissen wir nicht allzuviel." (p89) summarizes the present conclusions reached; Meyer 1979 esp. pp129-153. To this list should probably be added Jeremias' first, indeed only, volume of New Testament theology, subtitled "The Proclamation of Jesus" as the most major recent example of the claim to be able to recover, and use theologically, the teaching of Jesus (Jeremias 1971).

31. E.g. Bultmann 1972 p127f.

32. H.Riesenfeld The Gospel Tradition and its Beginnings (London 1957); B.Gerhardsson Memory and Manuscript (Lund and Copenhagen 1961); and, most recently, Riesner 1981 has followed a similar path.

33. E.g. where Bultmann builds upon the work of Reitzenstein (see esp. Bultmann 1972 pp69-108). See also, recently, and from a literary rather than historical perspective, Robbins 1984 and Talbert 1978.

34. See e.g. the critical work of Hill 1973-4.

35. That the tradition of Jesus as teacher developed can be seen e.g. in Mt 8.25, 17.15 and also Mt 22.36 = Lke 10.25 (cf. Mk 12.32f - this pericope is not, of course, wholly covered by the two-source theory).

36. For the recognition that the "Sermon on the Mount" is a Matthean construction see e.g. Hill 1972 p108, Beare 1981 p125; Fenton 1963 p78. The question of the authenticity of no saying is prejudged by this observation. Only the Matthean creation of Mt 5.1f becomes axiomatic.

37. Mk 12.1-12 is a classic problem (see e.g. van Iersel 1964 esp. pp124-145).

38. Such overconfidence is expressed in particular by Jeremias 1971; see esp. section II.

39. Meyer 1979 p135.

40. See Sanders 1985 section II, esp. ch.6.

41. Above II.3.1. 3 & II.3.1.6

42. E.g. re. Mk 4.26-32 *R u V II* p40 (cf. B.T. p126).

43. Above I.2 and below ch. IV. This present, alternative thesis depends upon the assumption that there is a legitimate reading of Ritschl which approaches his work from a different perspective, i.e. that his system represents a serious attempt to be a Christian theologian faithful to his religious tradition.

44. It is fair to say that Ritschl does not press the designation of Jesus as teacher too

far. The significance of the method of interpretation stated here is thus implicit in Ritschl's own approach, i.e. Jesus did not have to declare "I am a teacher", so much as demonstrate the fact by teaching. Whether this is the case for all aspects of Ritschl's picture and whether this matter can be as clear cut in all cases as it is here must yet be determined.

45. See esp. Chilton 1984 p1; Perrin 1967 p54.

46. Help is clearly given to the interpreter of Ritschl by the position in Ritschl's system in which particular material appears, e.g. *R u V II* §5 and B.T. §13f are presented as expository material whereas e.g. J & R III §§ 6, 34-6, 38f and 53 are clearly part of Ritschl's own theological interpretation. Yet the distinction is a false one, as the latter clearly incorporates the former by interpreting it, and such material as ICR §§ 5-25 and Ritschl 1883 are less easily to be classified. As with the distinction between "fact" and "interpretation", the dividing line is not easy to draw.

47. See Chilton 1984 pp6-26.

48. The choice "eschatological or non-eschatological" constitutes Schweitzer's third "either-or" with respect to the study of the life of Jesus (Schweitzer 1968 p238).

49. Dodd 1961 p38 (cf Sanders 1985 p148f and p381).

50. Evidence subjected to critical scrutiny by Sanders 1985 ch.6.

51. Chilton 1984 p11.

52. "Perrin...realized that it was not enough to say that the kingdom was eschatological, but proleptically present, in Jesus' ministry...although it may sound like a solution, it is really only a statement of the problem." Chilton 1984 p21. Perrin thus moved into the field of literary theory and hermeneutics in the attempt to interpret the Kingdom of God as "symbol" rather than "concept" (1976). Perrin at least recognized the problem and sought to deal with it.

53. The remarkable Matthean form of this saying - where the Kingdom is termed the "Son of Man's" - should, of course, be noted (Mt 16.28). An interpreter approaching Ritschl's work through an education in Gospel criticism which focussed heavily upon the question of the Son of Man is tempted to label Ritschl's own New Testament work as irrelevant on this ground alone. For Ritschl refers to the title infrequently, and when he does shows little real understanding (though can again be excused not having the benefit of the scholarship of relevance in this field which began with Dalman and Bousset, and continued through Bultmann, Cullmann, Tödt and Hahn, to Vermes, Casey and Lindars). In Ritschl's defence, and emphasizing the contingent character of any particular phase of New Testament study, it should be said that the Son of Man may, after a quarter of a century, have had its day as *the* burning issue of New

180

Testament scholarship and that the consensus which may be emerging through the work of Vermes and those influenced by him can be seen to qualify the long-held significance of the term by relativizing its importance.

54. E.g. Mk 9.47, Lke 16.16.

55. See Marshall's moot-point 1978 p702.

56. *R u V II* p30.

57. Sanders 1985 p3-22 for the introductory comments about method.

58. See e.g. Stanton 1974b esp. pp137-71.

59. cf. B.T. p128.

60. Luke should, of course, also be seen as a literary construction. The point being made is that of the question of the historical authenticity of what lies behind individual sections of text. The study referred to is, of course, the work of Schmidt, Wrede and those who took up their conclusions, notably Bultmann (cf above n4).

61. *R u V II* p33f.

62. The question how "new" with respect to Judaism Jesus' understanding of the Kingdom of God actually was must be shelved. See esp. Riches 1980 ch.5; for the Jewish background to the term see e.g. Str./B. I pp172-184, Bousset *Die Religion des Judentums im neutestamentlichen Zeitalter* (Berlin 1906) pp245-250, Evans 1962 p17ff, Lattke 1984, Perrin 1976 pp16-32 and, most extensively, Gray The Biblical Doctrine of the Reign of God (Edinburgh 1979 chs.2-8).

63. See e.g. the revealing quotation in J & R III p387, which reads: "...this religious vocation of the members of the Christian community is prefigured in the person of its Founder, and rests upon his person as its *abiding source of strength* (*als der fortwirkenden Kraft*) for all imitation of him, because he himself made God's supreme purpose of the union of men in the Kingdom of God the aim of his own personal life..." Such material seems to provide evidence for McKinney's thesis that Ritschl's Christology is "exemplarist" (in Hefner 1973a), yet may also permit a more charitable interpretation. Ritschl, in other words, confronts the problem of expressing the lasting influence of Jesus in Christian tradition. To more orthodox critics his statements will seem inadequate; to his more radical critics they will seem to retain too much residual supernaturalism.

64. e.g. ICR §§ 5, 13 and 19.

65. J & R III p400 and (cf. ch.II n255).

66. e.g. ibid. p13.

67. It is, however, true to say that Ritschl does not wholly lose the "otherness" of the Kingdom of God and that interpretations of Ritschl's understanding of the

Kingdom which fail to note this do not do Ritschl justice. See e.g. ICR § 8 p223f. The Kingdom of God is not, according to Ritschl, attained through human striving pure and simple; *R u V II* p34. The priority of God's gracious act is clearly maintained in Ritschl's interpretation of the Kingdom of God; *R u V II* p292f.

68. In other words, the *meaning* of the term "Messiah" ("the anointed one") is being focussed upon, even if the term itself is not used.

69. Baldensperger (*Das Selbstbewußtsein Jesus im Lichte der messianischen Hoffnungen seiner Zeit* 1888) and Holtzmann (*Das messianische Bewußtsein Jesu* 1907) may, more so than Ritschl in this particular sphere, be regarded as transitional figures, pointing to the overlap between the interest in Jesus' "inner life" (Holtzmann) and the growing concern to locate Jesus' life and work within the historical, social and religious milieu within which he lived (Baldensperger), a concern better represented by J.Weiss (1892= E.T. 1971), Bousset (1892= E.T. 1906a) and Wrede (1901= E.T. 1972).

70. See e.g. esp. E50 pp47, 48, 49 and 51.

71. Holtzmann, like Ritschl, depended heavily on Mark. See Holtzmann 1863 pp469-96 esp. p493f (cf also Kümmel 1973 p151f).

72. But note Bultmann's phraseology, which reveals that he works with a very specific understanding of Messiahship (1952 p27).

73. "By and large, the position in Judaism at the time of Jesus seems to have been as follows: 'Messiah' was the general, collective symbol of the salvation promised by God. It did not denote particular, concrete understandings of personal ways and means (of being Messiah). All Jews were able to condense their highest ideals and hopes into this symbol. 'Messiah' was, so to speak, a formal rather than a material category." Leivestad 1982 p256.

74. Rowland 1985a p179f; esp. p180.

75. See Cullmann 1959 p117ff; Rowland 1985a p180ff.

76. E.g. Holtzmann 1863 pp484-494 (extracts in Kümmel 1973 p152ff). The contemporary recognition of Jesus' acceptance of suffering must be classed as a more metaphorical understanding of Messiahship, interpreting Jesus' role as Son of Man and Servant of God rather than the term "Messiah" itself in the context of Jesus' known activity. Cf e.g. Cullmann 1959 chs. 3 and 6 esp. pp159-164; Rowland 1985a pp182-7 esp, p187.

77. Rowland 1985a p182.

78. See esp. Ritschl 1851 pp30-33, but also J & R III p436. The distinction between Ritschl's and Holtzmann's discussions of the argument for Marcan priority should be noted (i.e. Ritschl rejects the proto-Mark theory).

79. "... (A) systematic and internally consistent presentation of the very core of (the) Gospel (hi)story"; ibid. p31(my translation).

80. See, further, the discussion of Ritschl's understanding of Jesus as prophet directly below.

81. E.g. Schillebeeckx 1983 pp115-271; Sanders 1985 pp110-9.

82. Rowland 1985a p178 together with the whole discussion about "the Old Testament in the New" and particularly Jesus' own relationship to Old Testament traditions, of which Chilton's A Galilean Rabbi and His Bible (London 1984) counts as one particularly fascinating example.

83. See the complementary comments on Messiahship made by Leivestad 1982 p243.

84. Rowland 1985a pp175-8.

85. Cullmann 1959 ch.2 pp13-50.

86. He moves quickly to what are deemed specific ascriptions of the title "prophet" to Jesus (ibid p31).

87. See now esp. Sanders' way of construing the problem e.g. 1985 pp91-5.

88. Luke differs more in the detail of the wording of the transfiguration saying (Lke 9.35) and Matthew appears to assimilate the Baptism saying to his transfiguration material (Mt 17.5).

89. Yet whether "the start" is Jesus or the early Church could not be determined.

90. Van Iersel's attempt (cf above n37) to determine the existence of a "core" going back to Jesus is ingenious, but fails due to the author's belief that he can perceive words of Jesus when encountering Semitisms (e.g. p133). Even so, the hypothetical character of the whole enterprise, even if correct, precludes use of the passage as firm evidence for this enquiry.

91. Its offence and the concomitant fact that it could thus not be invented (Taylor 1966 p522; Stauffer 1982 p39), in addition to a textual argument (Cranfield 1959 p410; Metzger 1975 p62), can be set in opposition to the recognition that the Son's subordination to the Father is a common New Testament theme. That the "Day of the Lord" tradition, plus the tradition of the angels' limited knowledge about details of the end-time, could have played a role in the creation of such a saying in the early Church need therefore not be doubted (Taylor p522).

92. Taylor 1966 p383.

93. Mt 10.32 looks as though it has undergone revision by Matthew's hand (cf Cranfield 1959 p283).

94. Esp. Vermes 1967; see above n61.

95. That is to say, the Aramaic observations permit the apparent distinction between Jesus and the Son of Man to present no great difficulty. Considerations of the eventual significance of the Greek υιοĵ permit the realization of potential misunderstanding and/or overinterpretation in the process of translation from Aramaic to Greek.

96. E.g. Nineham 1963 p305.

97. Metzger 1975 p110.

98. Even leaving aside the question whether Jesus calling God "Father" in the Gospels veils a reference to God as "abba", there is nevertheless a dispute as to the frequency within Judaism of references to God as Father in any form (e.g. Vermes v. Hahn in Vermes 1976 p210ff and 264f; Jeremias v. McCasland in Jeremias 1967a p15). But the authenticity of the saying need not be doubted.

99. The question of the authenticity of the context can be shelved. *"Could* Jesus have said it ?" - or perhaps more appropriately: "could the early Church have coined it without precedence ?" - is the more searching question. See Jeremias 1967a esp. p54ff and Vermes 1976 p210 and n88 p264.

100. Though he admits one such reference to God as "abba" in b.Ta'an 23b (1967a p61).

101. By adding two more references (cited in Dunn 1980 p280 n97). One of these is quoted in full in Hengel 1976 p45 n89.

102. Hill 1972 p136.

103. Cranfield 1959 p433.

104. Vermes 1976 p211. This is especially so given that Vermes requires his own translation of m.Ber 5.1 to prove his point (Danby's translation reads "that they might direct their heart toward God" The Mishnah Oxford 1933 p5, rather than "in order to direct their hearts towards their Father in heaven"). On this whole question, see most recently, J.Barr 1988.

105. Dunn 1980 p27.

106. Cf. e.g. Beare 1981 p171. The simplicity of the Lucan form is quite striking. This suggests that Lke is striving to preserve something much simpler, more direct and out of step with liturgical habit. It may therefore be at least possible to suggest that "abba" lies behind the Lucan form here.

107. This narrative invites speculation. It may, of course, be a perfectly authentic saying around which an elaborate and fictitious story has been spun, for the saying contains nothing more than any pious Jew could have said. But clearly the narrative intends to say more and a firm conclusion as to the independence

or original meaning of the saying is beyond reach.

108. Lke 6.36, 9.26, 10.21f, 11.2, 13, 12.30, 32, 22.39, 22.42, 23.34, 23.46 (plus 24.49).

109. E.g. Mt 12.50, 20.23, 26.29, 26.42. This is admitted even by Jeremias (1967a p31).

110. cf. e.g. Bultmann on Lke 22.29: 1972 p158f.

111. ο πατηρ υμων is found in all cases except Lke 11.13 where ο πατηρ is found. The exception is interesting, though may point in either one of two opposing directions: i) simplifying a "simple" form of address (cf Lke 11.2) and thus a more authentic form; ii) bearing witness to the crystallization of the forms ο πατηρ and ο υιοͽ in later strata.

112. i.e. even if redactional colouring of a basic saying is clearly recognizable, the latter discloses nothing extraordinary.

113. Bultmann 1972 p160.

114. Hengel 1974b must be mentioned at this point. Hengel demonstrates quite convincingly the complex interplay between cultures which began long before the 1st century C.E.. It is interesting to note that Bultmann's provoking of interest amongst New Testament scholars for parallels between religious traditions (his debt to the History of Religions School) should produce those who challenge his whole understanding in this respect as too narrow. Never has Büchner's comment through the words of Danton in _Dantons Tod_ proved more true: "_Die Revolution ist wie Saturn, sie frißt ihre eigenen Kinder._" Bultmann's understanding of Judaism comes under siege now, of course, from a more subtle perspective (if not by subtle means) namely that of E.P.Sanders (e.g. in Paul and Palestinian Judaism London 1977). Black and Jeremias in particular have probed the Aramaic hinterland of the New Testament writings.

115. Marshall 1978 pp430-8 esp. p432.

116. ibid. p433.

117. Cf. above ch.II n230.

118. See e.g. Barrett 1972b p71f; Schnackenburg 1968 p154ff.

119. It should be noted that problems of priority and precise relationship between the four Gospels do not need to be solved for this conclusion to stand. The simple fact that three witnesses are in rough agreement against a single very different witness suggests such a conclusion.

120. Cf. e.g. Stanton 1973 p40: "Recent attempts to grapple with christological themes in the New Testament have concentrated rather too rigidly on christological titles."

121. The greatness of Bousset's 1913 work Kyrios Christos (Bousset 1970) is often recognized (e.g. Neill 1964 p163f; Morgan 1973 p12). Its publication can be said to mark a turning-point in the development of New Testament Christology.

122. In this case, an ambiguity emerges, i.e. whether God or Jesus is meant (e.g. Mt 4.7, 10).

123. This can be explained by Luke's seeming familiarity with the LXX.

124. Such a state of affairs is the legacy of Hengel's work (cf. n114) and the healthy scepticism towards the sayings material displayed in the work of Sanders (1985), the latter constituting a reaction to the over-optimism of the likes of Jeremias (cf above n38).

125. Cf n120 above.

126. E.g. J & R III p406.

127. ibid.; also ibid. p446 and ICR §13.

128. See e.g. Mk 1.22; and also III.2.2 above on.

129. The discussion of "moral superiority" is related to, though not identical with, the issue of Jesus' uniqueness. Interesting comments are made on this question by Sanders (1985 p320). Sanders recognizes that "uniqueness" is not a historical category.

130. Cf. above n63.

131. See above III.1.2.3.

132 J & R III p456f. Jn 14.30, 15.19, 16.33 and 18.36 are worthy of note in this regard.

133. Accepting the fact that to function as a norm, the criterion selected is inevitably restrictive in that its purpose is to exclude - in this case - interpretations regarded as invalid. The point being made here, however, is that Ritschl has broached the subject of a norm for Christian theology, yet has failed - in some resepcts at least - to allow the theology (theologies) of early Christianity to be properly represented in his haste to build in a historical criterion of judgment for that theology.

134. The neo-Kantian concern to relate human and divine wills in religion can be seen e.g. in Lotze (Outlines of the Philosophy of Religion London 1887 §§ 44, 46, 61 and 81).

135. i.e. one cannot appeal to specific data to prove whether or not Jesus was being obedient to God; even when words and acts of Jesus are known, an interpretative step is involved. Sartre's comment comes to mind: "If a voice speaks to me, it is still I myself who must decide whether the voice is or is not that of an angel." (Existentialism and Humanism London 1973 p31). Though not inevitably

susceptible to Sartre's own interpretation in every respect, the observation does highlight the difficulty of interpreting human motivation, a difficulty which has a bearing on the christological problem here being considered.

136. E.g. Ogden 1982 pp67-72 and esp. Ogden's critique of Mackey in 1984 pp157-165.

137. McIntyre 1966 pp115-119 and 124ff. Consider McIntyre's comment: "...if the psychological model is to be discarded, then modern christology is on the verge of reintroducing its own brand of docetism." (p124) and the programmatic statement: "So genuinely...was the humanity of Christ presented by the school of liberal theology that there was no going back upon this insight. Perhaps this assertion might now have to be defended in face of the dehistoricizing tendencies of modern theological scepticism..." (p125f).

138. Schweizer 1971 p83.

139. J & R III p462f.

140. R u V II p100.

141. And may, indeed, not be aware of the fact.

142. His interest in Abelard, e.g., is worthy of note: J & R I § 6. Paul Fiddes Past Event and Present Salvation (Darton, Longman and Todd: London 1989) represents a notable recent attempt to reappriase Abelard's theology of the atonement.

143. In the sense that as they stand, they cannot necessarily be seen to derive from Jesus see e.g. esp. Mk 8.35ff (cf. Schweizer 1971 p176f and Nineham 1963 p230 on v35) and Mk 10.45 (10.45b possibly being an addition; cf. Nineham 1963 p280f.).

144. Ritschl deals with Jesus' suffering but does not pick up the potential importance of the term "Son of Man" in this regard (cf. B.T. p160ff.). Even allowing for the fact that the Son of Man question has been over-stressed in the past thirty years, it cannot simply be ignored in this context (see above n53).

145. The question of the potential difference between the Synoptists and the Fourth Evangelist on the Son of Man cannot be answered here; see e.g Barrett 1972 p72f and Schnackenburg 1964-5 or 1968 pp529-42.

146. This aspect of Ritschl's work is perhaps itself an indicator of contingent factors at work upon the industry of the New Testament theologian; what is topical collides with the concern for what is true. The "Son of Man" had not really been "discovered" at that time (despite Baur's 1860 essay in ZWT).

147. See esp. Bultmann 1972 p93f and p111.

148. Bammel and Moule (eds.) 1984; Sanders 1985 esp. chs.10-11; Watson 1985.

149. i.e. through the drawing of parallels to the phenomenon in the ancient world (see Hengel 1981).

150. This may perhaps be considered the modern "history of religions" approach in the sense that it presents a corrective to Ritschl's own efforts (cf *R u V II* p80ff), and builds upon the work of Ritschl's turn-of-the-century critics. In other respects though, of course, Hengel and Bousset are far apart.

151. Knox 1967 p88.

152. Ritschl's interest in Abelard has been cited already (above n142). His critique of the doctrine of the two natures (*J & R III* pp399 and 407ff) should also be mentioned, as should the many critics of Ritschl who have questioned his orthodoxy (e.g. Orr, Garvie)!

153. McIntyre 1966 p42f: "At the centre of every christological statement is an historical statement endeavouring to make its escape. When the historical statement fails to appear, we may well ask ourselves whether we really have been dealing with a christological statement." Ogden (above n136) would perhaps not dispute this statement, though might demand further definition of what is meant by "historical" here, requiring of it an "existential-historical" rather than an "objective-historical" (i.e. past-referential) meaning. Perhaps the only satisfactory solution is to suggest that *both* are entailed in a christological statement, the believer binding his/her fate to that of Jesus by being a follower.

154. E.g. negatively through the exclusion of miracles, the resurrection; positively by the application of detailed comparative study. On the question of canonicity, below III.3.

155. See, however, further below III.4.

156. Sections III.3. and 4. below. The current reader of the Gospels can, of course, be more generous in allowing christological diversity to come into play. (S)he can see that the admittance that the Gospels are not historical texts, the recognition of the importance of the earthly Jesus for Christian faith, the difficulty of perceiving the earthly Jesus by historical-critical means and the recognition of the New Testament canon's importance do not together constitute a need to press for the New Testament's doctrinal unity. On this basis, it is possible to explore the term picture of Jesus; i.e. the ambiguity of the phrase can be used as a starting-point for a discussion about how the "historical Jesus", the use of the four Gospels and the task of New Testament theology relate to each other.

157. Childs 1984 ch.10 (pp157-209). Inevitably, Childs leaves more room for such differences, given the respective contexts in which each interpreter works.

158. See above n28.

159. See summary of III.2..

160. Or, more accurately, Gospel pictures (see further below III.4). See also Hefner 1972 p29 and Jodock 1969 p273.

161. Frei (1974) introduces this term into his discussion of the emergence of the discipline of hermeneutics vis-a-vis the rise of historical criticism. Its relevance here is clear. The Gospels border on the objective-historical in view of their form, yet might not stand up to rigorous historical-criticism. Whether or not they are "true" is not a question to be answered by verifying (or not, as the case may be) the people or events to which they ostensibly refer. This use of "historical" relates to Harvey's "perspectival-image or memory-impression of Jesus" (1967 p266f and 268-75).

162. Leaving aside the question of whether there are more than four "pictures" represented in the Gospels (i.e. a picture of Jesus in "Q", or in a "Gospel of Signs" within the Fourth Gospel).

163. See esp. the introduction to *R u V II* for Ritschl's views on the canon's importance (cf above II.1.2 and 1.3). Morgan (1973 p10) construes Ritschl's views from the standpoint of Ritschl's negative critics in the History of Religions School.

164. Not only in the New Testament but throughout Christian tradition.

165. This is not a term which Ritschl uses. It is introduced here simply for the sake of clarity in the argument.

166. Kähler 1964. One decisive difference between Kähler and Ritschl should, however, be stressed. In focussing on the breadth of the Gospel tradition (including miracles and resurrection) Kähler has drawn out more fully the implications of Ritschl's position. The scholar interpreting with the benefit of hindsight is left to speculate whether Ritschl would have approved of such a development, or revised his thinking in order better to accommodate the insights of historical research which he deemed so important.

167. The caricature is seen to derive primarily from Bultmann (though perhaps unjustly so), yet certainly the Bultmann school has appealed to Kähler via Bultmann; see Link 1975 p8f. Kähler's influence on Tillich is also important; e.g. Tillich 1957. Tillich wrote the foreword to the first (1964) English edition of Kähler's work on Jesus.

168. Ebeling 1963b and 1963c; Fuchs 1964; Käsemann 1964 and 1969.

169. Käsemann 1972-3 and esp. 1984 p60f.

170. Jodock 1969.

171. ibid. esp. ch.7.

172. ibid. chs.2-6.

173. Though note Jodock's construal of the relationship between Jesus and his followers in Ritschl's early work: "...it is not the picture of Jesus that serves as proof for the accuracy of the antithesis (i.e. between Paulinism and Jewish Christianity), but the antithesis that serves as proof for the accuracy of the picture of Jesus." (1969 p35).

174. ibid p204 and p205ff.

175. When the personal break between Baur and Ritschl took place and what significance it may have had (Jodock 1969 esp. ch.4; Hefner 1972 p24f; Harris 1975 pp108-11) are pertinent questions. Yet even without firm answers to these questions, it is safe to suggest that Ritschl was reaching his own conclusions about the nature and history of earliest Christianity in the mid-fifties, conclusions which were made public in E57.

176. See e.g. the juxtaposition of §§ 31 and 32 in *R u V II*.

177. Even allowing for the fact that the Fourth Gospel is used much more by Ritschl in his later years   (cf above III.1.2);   see *R u V II* pp269-99.

178. i.e. theological differences are admitted.

179. E57 p51.

180. Jodock 1969 p201ff.

181. E57 p49f and p51.

182. Jodock 1969 p223f.

183. J & R III p3.

184. The implications of this observation are, of course, considerable, encapsulating the nature (and the problem) of Ritschl's historical-theological appeal to the person of Jesus.

185. Above II.1.3., where the importance of the Old Testament background for the canonicity of New Testament texts for Ritschl is referred to. This is ostensibly Ritschl's main argument for New Testament canonicity (*R u V II* p14), though others are mentioned (e.g. argument of antiquity; apostolicity - though this is seen to be of itself insufficient and metaphorical). See, however, next note.

186. The footnote inserted by Ritschl in the introduction to *R u V II* is of the utmost importance (R u V II p14f). Here he adds to the understanding of the Old Testament essential agreement in the realm of Christology as the backbone of his argument for the presence of these particular books in the New Testament. Referring the reader to a line of argumentation followed in E57 p307, it becomes clear that, for Ritschl, recognition of the Old Testament's authority presupposes belief in Christ.

187. Yet what is notably absent from Ritschl's use of Mark (miracles, passion-predictions, resurrection) should be stressed and brought alongside the comments made about the distinction between Kähler and Ritschl at this point (above n166).

188. It is also worthy of note that despite the 1857 Marcan emphasis, the Kingdom of God - though now more prominent in Ritschl's exposition - is not yet the key theme it later clearly became in Ritschl's own theology. On Ritschl's over-dependence upon Mark's Gospel see, finally, below IV.3. Ritschl here succumbs to the "oldest is best" fallacy. The oldest stratum is, of course, not necessarily more theologically accurate. Ritschl's use of Mark is not, in other words, to be rescued on similar terms.

189. This is perceived by Ritschl to be objective-historical though may, of course, be shown to be Marcan (though the two are not mutually exclusive).

190. This constitutes the nub of the issue as far as continuity with Kähler or Ritschl is concerned.

Chapter IV

Reappraising Ritschl:

Ritschl's Picture of Jesus and the Task of New Testament Theology

On the basis of the exposition and critique of Ritschl's position just conducted, in particular his picture of Jesus, it is now possible to determine what consequences follow for understanding Ritschl as a Christian theologian seeking to interpret the canonical Gospels theologically.

Five short sections consider three aspects of particular importance under the following headings: historical study and theological interest; Jesus and the Kingdom of God; Jesus as the Son of God. Framing these summary sections will be an introductory section which revisits the question of the definition of "biblical theology" and a summary section which draws together the findings of the study as a whole.

1. "BIBLICAL THEOLOGY" REVISITED

Though the wider issue of the theoretical relationship between different theological disciplines has remained marginal to this present study, it was necessary in the expository section of the enquiry to locate Ritschl's work on the Gospels and his picture of Jesus within his overall theological task. It is therefore fitting also to suggest in what way, if any, the enquiry has a consequence for the understanding of Ritschl's theology as "biblical theology".

I sought to show that Ritschl's theology is best understood as a christocentric New Testament theology (II.1. esp. II.1.4). This contention was then demonstrated further through the process of relating aspects of his Gospel study, as finding expression in his picture of Jesus, to themes in his theology as a whole (II.3.3). To these expository contentions can now be added the findings of the critique.

Ritschl's study of the Gospels has shown itself to be still more intrinsic to his theology as a whole than was suggested upon the basis of the recognition of the simple and direct relationship between the earthly Jesus and Ritschl's theology. For, as the disclosure of how Ritschl's picture of Jesus is constructed revealed, it is clear that major themes in Ritschl's theology (e.g. Sonship, Righteousness, Vocation) owe more to the theology of particular Evangelists than to the earthly Jesus himself. The importance of taking the question of a theologian's enquiry into the "historical Jesus" and his use of the Gospels together is thus demonstrated. If the findings of the critique in this respect are correct, however, they only confirm the basic assumption with which this study has operated, namely that respect for Ritschl's biblical study is essential for a full and proper understanding of Ritschl's theology.

The view that "any account of Ritschl's theology that does not take his biblical work seriously must therefore be regarded as suspect and its conclusions treated with caution" can be supported [1]. The present study has thus confirmed Draper's more methodological enquiry through scrutiny of a particular aspect of Ritschl's biblical work - his study of the Gospels. Ritschl's biblical work is to be seen as relating directly to his overall undertaking in theology.

2. HISTORICAL STUDY AND THEOLOGICAL INTEREST

A particular feature of the present enquiry has been the relationship between historical study and theological interest. At the heart of the enquiry has been the question of how the Christian theologian makes use of the historical-critical method in his/her attempt to construct a theology. This question is clearly paramount where the issue of the use of the New Testament, or any particular part of it, by the theologian is concerned. Ritschl's own theology as a New Testament theology confronts this issue directly. His approach was seen to be one which sought to make full use of the historical method, whilst retaining the theological concern which Ritschl believed had been lost by his teacher F.C.Baur, the reaction against whom determined much of what Ritschl came to conclude.

The application of historical method found its most stark application in Ritschl's interest to locate historically reliable material about Jesus. Ritschl maintained this interest throughout his career. The theological interest came to the fore especially in Ritschl's increasing awareness of the importance of the New Testament canon for Christian theology. The present study has attempted to show, however, that these two manifestations of the respective interests - historical and theological - should not be seen as the sole expressions of these interests. The interests should not be allowed to be polarized in this way. For, as the enquiry conducted attempted to show, Ritschl perceived the question of a theological interest in the life of Jesus to be more intrinsically bound up with the life of Jesus than such polarization would suggest. In this sense, therefore, historical and theological concerns coincide.

It is now apparent that Ritschl misunderstood the relationship between the earthly Jesus and the communities which wrote about him and interpreted him. Nevertheless, it is clear that the relationship between historical and theological concerns at this level - the level of the life of Jesus and people's perception of and reaction to that life - is more complex than is often supposed. In seeking to make the "purely historical" data about Jesus a very rigid norm for christological assertion Ritschl has been shown to be mistaken. Ritschl misunderstood the relationship between fact and interpretation as evidenced in the Gospel tradition [2]. But Ritschl's theological interest in the life of Jesus did prevent the question of truth disappearing from view. In his discovery of the theological role to be played by the New Testament canon, he was building into his system a second norm which could define the limits of permissible theological interpretation even after the abandonment of his rigidly historical norm. Though this may have had the effect of restricting the range of his own historical enquiry, it nevertheless gave expression to his concern for theological construction and, perhaps, implicitly suggests a manner in which Ritschl's approach may yet prove helpful.

As it stands Ritschl's "Canonical Jesus" is untenable. For even in the comparatively narrow context of the interpretation of the Gospels, the question of pluralism is not far away. The understanding of the four Gospels as four distinct interpretations of Jesus, which cannot readily be harmonized into a single whole, presents the Christian

194

interpreter with the problem of deciding upon a criterion by which one might choose the most adequate picture. But in drawing attention to the dual concerns of historical enquiry and canonical context within the brief of constructing a theological appraisal of the life of Jesus, Ritschl may be indicating a feature of Christian theology which must remain at the heart of the critical task.

Furthermore, in seeking to delve beneath the surface of Ritschl's presentation of Jesus and using the category of "picture of Jesus", this present study has attempted to suggest both how Ritschl himself dealt with the problem of the christological diversity of the Gospels - even if ultimately inadequately - and how a current interpreter might best proceed [3].

The enquiry has, in short, tried to show the way in which these two key elements in Ritschl's approach - historical study and theological interest - are represented in his engagement with the question of the interpretation of the life of Jesus. It becomes apparent that respect for both elements is needed in order to do justice to Ritschl's procedure.

3.   JESUS AND THE KINGDOM OF GOD

Ritschl will remain known for his concentration upon the Kingdom of God [4]. Because of the most recent work in this field he will begin to be known as the figure who brought about the shift in approach to the discussion of the meaning of the Kingdom of God [5]. His reminder that discussion of the term must reckon with Jesus' own usage if it is to receive its appropriate Christian coinage will remain, in other words, a vital insight. This general conclusion has been confirmed by this present enquiry. The conclusion can, however, be made more precise.

Though it was shown that Jesus can be said with some certainty to have proclaimed the coming of the Kingdom of God, the meaning of the term "Kingdom" and the time and manner of its "coming" are not easy to determine, either as far as Jesus' own understanding or that of the Evangelists is concerned. For this reason, though Ritschl stressed the need for the Christian interpreter of the Kingdom-concept to reckon with Jesus' own understanding, he clearly underestimated the interpretative difficulties involved.

The present enquiry revealed Ritschl's dependence upon the Marcan presentation of Jesus for his own understanding of the concept "Kingdom". This feature of Ritschl's picture of Jesus demonstrates very well the extent to which the process of theological interpretation of the life of Jesus entails encounter and engagement with the theologies of the Evangelists to a degree which Ritschl did not perceive.

It could with some justification be maintained that Ritschl's construal of the Marcan understanding of the Kingdom-concept might yet be salvaged on the grounds that it represents a continuity of Christian interpretation with a part of the original Christian tradition as found in the canonical writings. In other words, it employs the theology of a particular Evangelist (in this case Mark) in a manner which this study has suggested is inevitable.

The problem with this position is that it is difficult to support the precise understanding for which Ritschl opts in the face of the fullest available Gospel evidence (that is, the witness of the other Evangelists and the breadth of the material dealing with the Kingdom in the Gospels). At this point, therefore, where there is sufficient reason to suppose that something which was truly of Jesus can be glimpsed in the Gospel tradition, the historical-critical approach has made a contribution to theological understanding by enabling the Christian interpreter to distinguish in general terms the main thrust of Jesus' proclamation from the use made by an Evangelist (in this case, Mark). In concrete terms; Ritschl's over- dependence upon Mark (one should perhaps even say on one strand of Mark) at this point must be ruled out as illegitimate, and is demonstrably so by its failure to interpret adequately the "future" Kingdom-sayings.

The fact remains that Ritschl's attempt to interpret the Gospel material was a specific methodological step in the construction of a theological system. The rejection of Ritschl's interpretation of the Kingdom of God must therefore, to be fair to Ritschl, offer a more adequate understanding of the Kingdom and demonstrate its dependence upon the Gospel material in a more comprehensive manner. Failing that, the rejection must explain how a different interpretation not supported in some manner by reference to the Gospel material could abandon the methodological premisses which Ritschl perceives to be essential in the Christian theological process.

The closeness of the relationship between _R u V II_ and _J & R III_ thus becomes evident in a very concrete way at this point. Furthermore, it becomes clear in a very direct way that _J & R III_ cannot legitimately be understood or interpreted without reference to _R u V II_. For the respective volumes preserve the practical application of this aspect of Ritschl's understanding of the Christian theological task with respect to the Kingdom of God. The implications of this observation for the study of Ritschl's theology are again clear. As a model for the understanding of Ritschl, this manner of approach urges the system which Ritschl creates to be viewed in the more integrative fashion in which it was conceived and constructed.

4. JESUS THE SON OF GOD

In considering this, the second major aspect of Ritschl's picture of Jesus as highlighted in the exposition and critique conducted earlier, it becomes still more evident how the integrative conception of Ritschl's theology must be dealt with. The angle of approach in this case must, however, be slightly different.

In the same way that Ritschl understood himself to be encountering Jesus' own conception of the Kingdom of God in expounding the Marcan understanding, so he confuses once more an interpretative understanding of Jesus with Jesus' own understanding of himself and his mission. He does this by assuming that the latter is more easily determinable through the former than is in fact the case. Thus, in the discussion of the sonship of Jesus it became evident that Ritschl was too ready to take on trust the presentation of Luke, more so Matthew and to a still greater degree John, in believing Jesus to have understood himself as Son of God in a special way. On closer inspection, and in the light of the critique conducted, this tendency of Ritschl's carries a number of implications.

First, once the Gospel tradition has been subjected to historical criticism, it is not as apparent as it was in the case of the discussion of the Kingdom of God, that some of the material discussed does ultimately derive from Jesus. The sheer extent of the interpretative material present when one considers this aspect of the Gospel pictures of Jesus thus becomes clear.

Second, the degree of dependence upon the Fourth Gospel is inevitably greater at this point. This second specific aspect of Ritschl's picture of Jesus raises the question of the relationship between historical enquiry and theological interest in a different way. In contrast to the discussion on the Kingdom of God, Ritschl does not have the tried and tested support of the historians on his side but has, rather, the witness of the history-like Gospel accounts which are interpretative to a still greater degree at this point. Ritschl does, however, have more widespread support within the Gospel tradition for this interpretative construal of Jesus' relationship to God. In this sense, therefore, he has a more solid base of appeal than he had for the particular understanding of the concept "Kingdom" that he possessed.

The theological problem thereby posed is; to what extent does a Christian theologian rest content simply with the criterion of "continuity with the Gospel tradition" which seems to be here at work? Ritschl's supposition, of course, was that the historical reference to the earthly Jesus, included within the appeal, guaranteed the legitimacy of the continuity. The problem emerges with fullest force once that historical reference is questioned, a situation in which the Christian interpreter of the Gospels now finds him-/herself.

The most adequate solution to this problem respects Ritschl's supposition whilst moving beyond it. It is necessary to combine an openness to historical data with the acceptance that the Gospel interpretations are taken on trust. In suggesting, however, that the interpretations are taken on trust, it is necessary to be fully aware that one cannot possibly affirm all aspects of each picture [6]. The advantage, therefore, of isolating "aspects" of a picture of Jesus is that the approach is a way of breaking down an interpretation into constitutive elements without resorting to the mere compilation of a catalogue of titles, an approach now shown to be deficient [7]. The sonship of Jesus can thus be taken on trust, not as a description of a metaphysical status or as a title denoting a ready-made category into which Jesus could be fitted, but as a description which best expressed the intimacy of Jesus' relationship to God. Ritschl may, in short, not be far wrong in concentrating on and developing this aspect of the Gospel tradition through his exposition.

As stated above the balance between data and interpretation has shifted somewhat from the discussion of the Kingdom of God. The important observation which must be made, however, is not that theological interpretation must first isolate data in order to interpret it, but that the interpretative process deals with both data and interpretation together. This observation pertains both to what is interpreted (in this case the Gospels) as well as to what is produced (which is not just an interpretation but includes within it an historical link - to Jesus at one pole, to the interpreter him-/herself at the other) [8].

The study of Ritschl's picture of Jesus has highlighted the importance of this awareness. In fact, Ritschl himself has erred too much on the side of the exploration of the historical referent in the theological process. This is perhaps not unrelated to his tendency to stress teleology over eschatology, the present/presence of the Kingdom over its future/coming. The historicality of Christianity gains the upper hand.

But Ritschl's Christian understanding does not ultimately collapse into sheer narrative though it recognizes the importance of Christianity's historicality. His pervasive theological interest ensures that the reflective, interpretative process remains vital to the task of Christian theology. In this, the awareness of the fluctuating relationship between data and interpretation at different points in the Christian tradition is preserved.

A full understanding of Ritschl, therefore, involves the recognition of this awareness. It involves the recognition that the emphasis upon the sonship of Jesus does not simply describe, but seeks to express a truth about the motivation of Jesus as one who effected the work of God in his own action in a special way. In this way Ritschl jeopardizes, ultimately detrimentally, the norm of historical verifiability which he sought to build in to his Christology, yet does not compromise the question of truth which he perceived at the heart of theological reflection.

5. THE USE OF THE GOSPELS AND METHOD IN CHRISTOLOGY

The enquiry into Ritschl's picture of Jesus is best be summarized as an encounter with Ritschl's use of the Gospels as a Christian theologian. As became evident throughout the course of the critique, there exists a hiatus between Ritschl's method in theory and in practice. Though the former was conceived as the construction of a Christology built according to a rigid historical norm and to be located at the heart of his theological system, the latter demonstrated the extent to which Ritschl's approach was, in fact, concerned far more with the question of theological continuity. At the heart of the answer to this question lay the matter of the use of the Gospels in the creation of a theologically adequate understanding of Jesus, an answer which drew only in part upon the historical task implicit in it. It was seen, further, how the interest in the New Testament canon related to this concern with the question of theological continuity.

The findings of this present enquiry are best summarised as follows:
Ritschl's theology is a christocentric New Testament theology. Its Christocentricity draws particular attention to his use of the Gospels, given that it is in these particular New Testament writings where the question of the relationship between the earthly Jesus and Christian theological reflection is paramount. Ritschl's concern to permit historical method to play its full role in the process of christological reflection involves a heavy emphasis upon historical data about Jesus. His theological interest does not, however, permit mere cataloguing of such data to serve as the theological appraisal of Jesus which Christian theology requires. On that basis his "picture of Jesus" was expounded and studied.

"Picture of Jesus" is a term which retains the ambiguity present in Ritschl's theology. The term proves useful even after greater clarification of the process of Christian theological reflection has been gained. Though deficient in the extent to which he overstated the achievements and value of the historical method in the process of Christian theological reflection with respect to the person of Jesus, Ritschl's reminder of the historical and theological dimensions to the task of the interpretation of Jesus in Christian reflection need stressing both for a full appreciation of Ritschl's own approach and more generally for a more complete understanding of Christian theological method.

His Christocentricity serves as a model which raises the pressing question to what extent Christian theology must inevitably have Christology at its heart. As a direct consequence of this approach arises the question whether a New Testament theology must begin, or at least ultimately relate back in some way to the Gospel material.

Ritschl's focus on the Gospels resulting from his Christocentricity fails, however, to encounter the problem of christological diversity. It must, therefore, be in particular in this respect that his approach be subject to correction. That correction, rather than abandonment, is possible can be seen from the fact that his Christology survives the abandonment of its rigid historical norm. This survival occurs because of the fact that Ritschl's ultimate dependence upon the theologies of the Gospels can be demonstrated, a dependence which in turn offers a suggestion as to how the theological diversity present in the Gospels may be made use of by the theologian.

Notes to Chapter IV

1. Draper 1984 p241.
2. This may be expressed as Ritschl's failure to distinguish adequately between the objective-historical and the existential-historical dimensions to the christological task. It is, however, ultimately Ritschl's respect for the latter which makes his approach interesting.
3. The term "picture of Jesus" is neither new nor unambiguous. Link offers one of the most helpful approaches to its use through the work of Kähler (Link 1975 esp. pp248-55). See also R.Slenczka (1967 esp. pp85-91 and pp236-52). This approach to the theological appraisal of the life of Jesus also relates to recent work by Pelikan (1985), Sloyan (1986) and Wessels (1990). Pelikan eschews calling his study a theological study. But his work undergirds the thesis which lies implicit in this present study; that Christologies, as self-involving, are culture-related, if not culture-bound. It is perhaps no accident that such an approach should emerge from a study of Ritschl (on this see Niebuhr 1952). That the charge that Ritschl sold out to his culture cannot be allowed to have the last word is suggested by the conclusions of this study, which wishes to locate cultural (and thus also theological) diversity already within the New Testament, hence "pictures of Jesus". Wessels deserves praise for asking the tough theological question about the potential limits of christological pluralism (1990 ch.VI).

4. Cf. e.g. Perrin 1963 pp13-16 and 1976 p66; Lundström 1963 pp3-9, to cite only the more general surveys; Ritschl specialists are fully aware of Ritschl's importance at this point.

5. Chilton 1984 p5ff.

6. For the simple reason that the Gospels are not to be harmonized theologically, let alone historically. This is true of the Synoptic Gospels as separate Gospels as well as the Synoptics over against the Fourth Gospel. See further n3 above.

7. Cf above III n120.

8. See e.g. J & R III p392; this relates to the points made in n2 above.

Bibliography

1. PRIMARY LITERATURE

Albrecht Ritschl

Published Works:

1845   Review of Dietlein: *Das Urchristenthum* (T.J. 4, pp547-561)

1846   *Das Evangelium Marcions und das kanonische Evangelium des Lucas* (Tübingen)

1847   *Das Verhältnis der Schriften des Lucas zu der Zeit ihrer Entstehung* (T.J. 6, pp293-304)

1850   *Die Entstehung der altkatholischen Kirche* (Bonn)

1851   *Ueber den gegenwärtigen Stand der Kritik der synoptischen Evangelien* (T.J. 10, pp480-538; reprinted in *Gesammelte Aufsätze* pp1-51; Freiburg i.B. and Leipzig 1893)

1857   *Die Entstehung der altkatholischen Kirche* (2nd ed.; Bonn)

1858   *Ueber die methodischen Principien der Theologie des Herrn Dr. v.Hofmann* (A.K.Z. 37, cols. 353-364)

1860   Review of H.J.Holtzmann: *Kanon und Tradition* (T.S.K. 33, pp571-597)

1861   *Ueber geschichtliche Methode in der Erforschung des Urchristenthums* (J.D.T. 6, pp429-59; reprinted in F.C.Baur: *Ausgewählte Werke* vol.V, pp469-99; Stuttgart 1975)

1862   *Einige Erläuterungen zu dem Sendschreiben: ,Die historische Kritik und das Wunder'* (H.Z. 8, pp85-99; reprinted in F.C.Baur: *Ausgewählte Werke* vol.V, pp521-37; Stuttgart 1975)

1866a   Review of C.Tischendorf: *Wann wurden unsere Evangelien verfaßt?* (J.D.T. 11, pp353-56)

1866b   Review of C.Wittichen: *Die Idee Gottes als des Vaters* (J.D.T. 11, pp560-2)

1871   *Ueber die Methode der älteren Dogmengeschichte* (J.D.T. 16, pp191-214; reprinted in *Gesammelte Aufsätze* pp147-169; Freiburg i.B. and Leipzig 1893)

1872   A Critical History of the Christian Doctrine of Justification and Reconciliation (Edinburgh; = *Die christliche Lehre von der Rechtfertigung und Versöhnung : Erster Band*; Bonn 1870)

204

1875   *Zum Verständnis des Prologs des johanneischen Evangeliums* (T.S.K. 48, pp576-582)

1876   Review of F.Bleek: *Einleitung in das Neue Testament* (J.D.T. 21, pp314-320)

1878   Christian Perfection (Bibliotheca Sacra 35, pp656-80; =*Die christliche Vollkommenheit* [1st ed.]; Göttingen 1874)

1880   "Prolegomena" to The History of Pietism (E.T. of the Prolegomena to *Geschichte des Pietismus* Erster Band; Bonn [a revised version of the 1877 article in Z.K.G. pp1-55]; in Hefner 1972 pp53-147)

1881   Theology and Metaphysics (E.T. of *Theologie und Metaphysik* Bonn; in Hefner 1972, pp151-217)

1881-2 *Aus Ritschls Dogmatik-Kolleg* (extracts from Ritschl's Dogmatics lectures as noted down by his son, Otto Ritschl; published in R.Schäfer 1968 pp186-206)

1882   *Rechtfertigung und Versöhnung* Vol.2 (2nd ed.; Bonn)

1883a   *Rechtfertigung und Versöhnung* Vol.3 (2nd ed.; Bonn)

1883b   *Reich Gottes* (in R.E.P.T.K. [2nd.ed.] Band 12, pp599-606; Leipzig)

1885   *Welt* (in R.E.P.T.K. [2nd.ed.] Band 16, pp742-48; Leipzig)

1886   Instruction in the Christian Religion (E.T. of *Unterricht in der christlichen Religion* [3rd ed.] Bonn; using material from the first edition, in Hefner 1972, pp221-291)

1887   Festival Address on the Four-Hundredth Anniversary of the Birth of Martin Luther: Nov.10th 1883 (E.T. of *Festrede am vierten Seculartage der Geburt Martin Luthers - 10.November 1883* published in *Drei akademische Reden*, Bonn; in David Lotz 1974 pp187-202)

1889   *Die christliche Lehre von der Rechtfertigung und Versöhnung Band 2: Der biblische Stoff der Lehre* (3rd ed.; Bonn)

1902   The Christian Doctrine of Justification and Reconciliation [The Positive Development of the Doctrine] (E.T. [2nd ed.] of *Rechtfertigung und Versöhnung Band 3*, 3rd ed., Bonn 1888; T & T Clark, Edinburgh)

Unpublished work:

1877-8 *Biblische Theologie des Neuen Testaments* (manuscript of lecture notes for Ritschl's Göttingen lectures delivered in the Winter-Semester, Eck-Nachlaß No.10 at the *Universitätsbibliothek* Giessen)

2. SECONDARY LITERATURE (SELECTED)

The list contains all works referred to in the notes of this study, together with other selected titles which proved particularly helpful in its preparation.

Kurt Aland
  1962   The Problem of the New Testament Canon (London)
  1978   (ed.) *Synopsis Quattuor Evangeliorum* (10th ed.) (*Deutsche Bibelstiftung*, Stuttgart)

G.W.Anderson
  1970   Canonical and Non-canonical (ch.6 in The Cambridge History of the Bible vol 1. eds. P.R.Ackroyd & C.F.Evans; C.U.P.)

E.Bammel and C.F.D.Moule (eds.)
  1984   Jesus and the Politics of His Day (C.U.P.)

W.R.Barnett
  1976   Historical Relativism and Christology in the thought of Wilhelm Dilthey and Albrecht Ritschl (unpublished Ph.D thesis Chicago)
  1979   Historical Understanding and Theological Commitment (J.R. 59 pp195-212)

James Barr
  1973   The Bible in the Modern World (London)
  1974   Trends and Prospects in Biblical Theology (J.T.S. pp265-282)
  1976a Biblical Theology,
  1976b Revelation in History,
  1976c Scripture, Authority of (articles in I.D.B. Suppl.Vol. pp104a-111b, 746a-749a and 794a-797b; Nashville)
  1983   Holy Scripture: Canon, Authority, Criticism (Oxford)
  1988   "Abba, Father" and the Familiarity of Jesus' Speech, in, Theology 91 (1987-88) pp173-179

C.K.Barrett
  1972   The Gospel According to St. John (2nd ed.; London)
  1984   Jesus and the Word (in *Rudolf Bultmanns Werk und Wirkung* ed.B.Jaspert, pp81-91; Darmstadt)

Karl Barth
  1961   Evangelical Theology in the Nineteenth Century (in The Humanity of God pp9-32; London)
  1962a Unsettled Questions for Theology Today
  1962b The Word in Theology from Schleiermacher to Ritschl,

206

(in <u>Theology and Church: Shorter Writings 1920-1928</u>, pp55-73 and 200-216; London)

1972   Ritschl (ch.29 in <u>Protestant Theology in the Nineteenth Century</u>; London 1972)

David L.Bartlett
1983   The Shape of Scriptural Authority (Philadelphia)

R.Bauckham
1978   The Sonship of the Historical Jesus in Christology (S.J.T. 31 pp245-260)
1985   The Son of Man: 'A Man in My Position' or 'Someone'? (J.S.N.T. 23 pp23-33)
M.Baumotte (ed.)
1984   *Die Frage nach dem historischen Jesus* (Gütersloh)

W.Bauer (plus W.F.Arndt, F.W.Gingrich and F.W.Danker)
1979   A Greek-English Lexicon of the New Testament and Other Early Christian Literature (2nd.ed. Chicago and London)

F.C.Baur
1860   *Die Tübinger Schule und ihre Stellung zur Gegenwart* (2nd ed.; now in *Ausgewählte Werke* vol.V., Stuttgart 1975, pp293-465)

J.Baur
1987   *Albrecht Ritschl - Herrschaft und Versöhnung* in <u>*Theologie in Göttingen*</u> pp256-270; Göttingen)

F.W.Beare
1981   The Gospel according to Matthew (Oxford)

Robert F.Berkey and Sarah A.Edwards (eds)
1982   Christological Perspectives (New York)

Bruno Berndt
1959   *Die Bedeutung der Person und Verkündigung Jesu fur die Vorstellung vom Reiche Gottes bei Albrecht Ritschl* (Diss.Tübingen)

P.Billerbeck (and H.L.Strack)
1969   *Kommentar zum Neuen Testament aus Talmud und Midrasch* (Band 1; 5th ed.; München)

Matthew Black
1969   The 'Son of Man' Passion Sayings in the Gospel Tradition

(Z.N.W. 60 pp1-8)

Hendrikus Boers
1979   What is New Testament Theology ? (Philadelphia)

G.Bornkamm
1960   Jesus of Nazareth (London)

Wilhelm Bousset
1906   Jesus (London and New York)

C.E.Braaten and R.A.Harrisville (eds.)
1964   The Historical Jesus and the Kerygmatic Christ (New York)

Edgar S.Brightman
1917   Ritschl's Criterion of Religious Truth (in A.J.T. 21, pp212-224)

Herbert Braun
1965   The Problem of a New Testament Theology (J.T.C. 1 pp169-183)
1968   The Meaning of New Testament Christology (J.T.C. 5 pp89-127)

Rudolf Bultmann
1925   *Das Problem einer theologischen Exegese des Neuen Testaments*
        (in Z.Z. 3 pp334-357; now in A.D.T. II, pp47-72; Munich 1963)
1952   Theology of the New Testament Vol.1 (London)
1955a   The Theology of the New Testament Vol.2 (London)
1955b   Essays Philosophical and Theological(London)
1958   Jesus Christ and Mythology (New York)
1961   Existence and Faith (London)
1969   Faith and Understanding (London)
1972   The History of the Synoptic Tradition (Oxford)
        (= 2nd German edition of 1931 + 1962 *Ergänzungsheft*)
1984   New Testament and Mythology (Philadelphia)

Richard Paul Busse
1984   The Implicit Metaphysical Scheme of Albrecht Ritschl's Theology
        (Th.D.thesis: Lutheran School of Theology at Chicago)

D.G.A.Calvert
1983   From Christ to God (London)

Hans von Campenhausen
1972   The Formation of the Christian Bible (Philadelphia)

D.A.Carson
    1981   Historical Tradition in the Fourth Gospel: After Dodd, What ? (in Gospel
           Perspectives II eds. R.T.France and D.Wenham, pp83-145, Sheffield)

P.M.Casey
    1976   The Son of Man Problem (Z.N.W. 67 pp147-154)
    1985   The Jackals and the Son of Man : Matt.8.20/ Luke 9.58
           (J.S.N.T. 23 pp3-22)

J.H.Charlesworth
    1979   The Concept of the Messiah in the Pseudepigrapha
           (in A.N.R.W. II.19.1 ed.W.Haase pp188-218, Berlin and New York)

Brevard S.Childs
    1984   The New Testament as Canon (London)

Bruce Chilton (ed.)
    1984   The Kingdom of God (London)

J.P.Clayton (ed.)
    1976   Ernst Troeltsch and the Future of Theology (C.U.P.)

J.B.Cobb Jr.
    1975   Christ in a Pluralistic Age (Westminster, Philadelphia)

Hans Conzelmann
    1969   An Outline of the Theology of the New Testament (London)

C.E.B.Cranfield
    1959   The Gospel According to St.Mark (Cambridge)

Oscar Cullmann
    1956   The Plurality of the Gospels as a Theological Problem in Antiquity (in
           The Early Church pp40-56)
    1959   The Christology of the New Testament (London)
    1975   The Johannine Circle (London)

Don Cupitt
    1972   One Jesus, many Christs ? (in S.W.Sykes and J.P.Clayton eds.,
           pp131-144)

W.D.Davies
1964   The Setting in the Ministry of Jesus (ch.6. in The Setting of the Sermon on the Mount; C.U.P.)

Daniel L.Deegan
1962   Albrecht Ritschl on the Historical Jesus (S.J.T. 15, pp133-150)
1963a Martin Kähler: Kerygma and Gospel History (S.J.T. 16, pp50-67)
1963b The Ritschlian School, The Essence of Christianity and Karl Barth (S.J.T. 16, pp390-414)
1964   Albrecht Ritschl as Critical Empiricist (J.R. 44, pp149-60 = S.J.T. 18, 1965, pp40-56)

Leonard De Moor
1970   The Ritschlian View of Revelation (E.Q. 42, pp93- 106)

Martin Dibelius
1931   Jesus in Contemporary German Theology (J.R. 11, pp179-211)
1971   Die Formgeschichte des Evangeliums (Tübingen, 6th ed. = 3rd ed. of 1959; E.T. From Tradition to Gospel New York 1935 = 2nd German ed. of 1933)

C.H.Dodd
1932   The Framework of the Gospel Narrative (Ex.T. 43, reprinted in New Testament Studies Manchester U.P. 1953 pp1-11)
1961   The Parables of the Kingdom (London)
1963   Historical Tradition in the Fourth Gospel (C.U.P.)

Jonathan L.Draper
1984   The Place of the Bible in the Theology of Albrecht Ritschl (unpublished Durham PhD. thesis)

Avery Dulles
1966   Response to Krister Stendahl's 'Method in the Study of Biblical Theology' (in The Bible in Modern Scholarship ed.J.P.Hyatt pp210-6, London)

David L.Dungan
1975   The New Testament Canon in Recent Study (Interpretation 29 pp339-351)

J.D.G.Dunn
1975   Jesus' Filial Consciousness (Ch.2. in Jesus and the Spirit; London)
1977   Unity and Diversity in the New Testament (London)
1980   Christology in the Making (London)

210

G.Ebeling
   1955   The Meaning of 'Biblical Theology' (J.T.S. 6,pp210- 225; also in
             Word and Faith pp79-97)
   1963a The Significance of the Critical Historical Method for Church
             and Theology in Protestantism
   1963b Jesus and Faith
   1963c The Question of the Historical Jesus and the Problem of Christology
             (essays in Word and Faith pp17-61, pp201-246 and pp288-304; London)

Owen E.Evans
   1962   Kingdom of God, of Heaven (I.D.B. vol 2 pp17-26; Nashville)

Cajus Fabricius
   1909   *Die Entwicklung in Albrecht Ritschls Theologie von 1874 bis 1889 nach*
             den verschiedenen Auflagen seiner Hauptwerke dargestellt (Tübingen)

Edward Farley
   1968   Jesus Christ in Historical and Non-Historical Schemes
             (Perspectives 9, pp61-79)
   1975   Ecclesial Man (Philadelphia)
   1982a Ecclesial Reflection (Philadelphia)
   1982b Scripture and Tradition (in King and Hodgson eds., pp35-61)

W.R.Farmer
   1961   A 'Skeleton in the Closet' of Gospel Research (B.R. 6, pp18-42)
   1976   The Synoptic Problem (2nd ed.; Dillsboro, North Carolina)
             (esp.chs 1-3)

John C.Fenton
   1963   Saint Matthew (Harmondsworth)

F.S.Fiorenza
   1978   The responses of Barth and Ritschl to Feuerbach (S.R. 7, pp149-166)

Ellen Flesseman-van Leer
   1964   *Prinzipien der Sammlung und Ausscheidung bei der Bildung des Kanons*
             (Z.Th.K. 61 pp404-420)

R.N.Flew
   1934   Ritschl (ch.21 in The Idea of Perfection in Christian Theology, Oxford)

W.Foerster (and G.Quell)
   1958   Lord (Key Words; London)

A.D.Foster
1965   Albrecht Ritschl (in A Handbook of Christian Theologians
       eds.D.G.Peerman and M.E.Marty, pp49-67)

Hans Frei
1974   The Eclipse of Biblical Narrative (New Haven and London)
1975   The Identity of Jesus Christ (Philadelphia)

Ernst Fuchs
1964   Studies of the Historical Jesus (London)

R.H.Fuller
1965   The Foundations of New Testament Christology (London)

V.P.Furnish
1964-5 The Jesus-Paul Debate: from Baur to Bultmann
       (B.J.R.L. 47, pp342-381)

John G.Gager
1974   The Gospels and Jesus: Some Doubts about Method
       (J.R. 54, pp244-272)

Alfred E.Garvie
1918   Ritschlianism (in Encyclopaedia of Religion Ethics ed. James Hastings,
       vol.10 pp812-820; Edinburgh)

Clifford Geertz
1973   Religion as a Cultural System (ch.3. in The Interpretation of Cultures,
       New York)

Brian A.Gerrish
1968   Theology and the Historical Consciousness (McCormick Quarterly 21,
       pp198-213)
1984   A Prince of the Church (London)

J.P.Givens
1902   The Ritschlian Conception of Christian Revelation and the Sacred
       Scriptures (B.D.thesis,Chicago)

James K.Graby
1966   The Problem of Ritschl's Relationship to Schleiermacher
       (S.J.T. 19, pp257-268)

Colin E.Gunton
1983   Yesterday and Today: A Study of Continuities in Christology (London)

Gustavo Gutierrez
1974   A Theology of Liberation (London)

Ernst Haenchen
1965   *Albrecht Ritschl als Systematiker*
        (in *Gott und Mensch*, pp409-475; Tübingen)

Ferdinand Hahn
1969   The Titles of Jesus in Christology (London)

Georg Ludwig Hahn
1854   *Die Theologie des Neuen Testaments* (Leipzig)

Kenneth Hamilton
1965   Revolt Against Heaven (Exeter)

Adolf von Harnack
1977   *Das Wesen des Christentums*
        (new edition: *Siebenstern Taschenbuch*; Gütersloh)

Horton Harris
1975   The Tübingen School (Cambridge)

A.E.Harvey (ed.)
1985   Alternative Approaches to New Testament Study (London)

Van Austin Harvey
1967   The Historian and the Believer (London)

B.L.Hebblethwaite
1972   The Appeal to Experience in Christology
        (in S.W.Sykes and J.P.Clayton eds. pp263-278)

Philip Hefner
1961   Albrecht Ritschl and His Current Critics (L.Q. XIII, pp103-112)
1962   Baur versus Ritschl on Early Christianity (C.H. 31, pp259-278)
1964   The Role of Church History in the Theology of Albrecht Ritschl
        (C.H. 33, pp338-55)
1966   Faith and the Vitalities of History (New York)
1971   Concreteness of God's Kingdom: a Problem for the Christian Life
        (J.R. 51, pp188-205)

1972   Albrecht Ritschl: Three Essays (Philadelphia)
1973a   (ed.) Ritschl Symposium (papers presented at the Symposium at the
        Lutheran School of Theology at Chicago in January 1973; unpublished)
1973b   Crashing the Nationality Barrier in Theology (Review of Claude Welch:
        Protestant Theology in the Nineteenth Century Vol.1; Interpretation 27,
        pp212- 216)

Martin Hengel
    1968   *Nachfolge und Charisma* (Berlin)
    1971   Was Jesus a Revolutionist ? (Philadelphia)
    1974   Judaism and Hellenism (London)
    1975   The Son of God (London)
    1977   Crucifixion (London)
    1981   The Atonement (London)

A.I.C.Heron
    1980   A Century of Protestant Theology (London)

Wilhelm Herrmann
    1927   Systematic Theology (London)
    1966a   *Schriften zur Grundlegung der Theologie Band 1* (Munich)
    1966b   *Der geschichtliche Christus der Grund unseres Glaubens*
            (in Z.Th.K. 2, 1892; also in 1966a pp149-185)
    1966c   *Christlich-Protestantische Dogmatik* (1909)
            (in 1966a, pp298-358, esp.pp333-38)
    1967   *Die Bedeutung der Geschichtlichkeit Jesu für den Glauben*
            (=T.L.Z. 37,1912) (in *Schriften zur Grundlegung der Theologie*
            Band 2, pp282-89; Munich)
    1972   The Communion of the Christian with God
            (=E.T. 1906 of German original 1903; London)

A.J.B.Higgins
    1969   Is the Son of Man Problem Insoluble ? (in *Neotestamentica et Semitica*
            eds. E.Ellis and M.Wilcox, pp70-87; Edinburgh)

David Hill
    1972   The Gospel of Matthew (London and Grand Rapids)
    1973-4 On the Evidence for the Creative Role of Christian Prophets
            (N.T.S. 20, pp262-274)

Peter C.Hodgson
    1966   The Formation of Historical Theology (New York)

1968   (ed.) Ferdinand Christian Baur on the Writing of Church History
(New York)

R.Hofmann
1877   *Apokryphen des Neuen Testamentes*
(in R.E.P.T.K. [2nd ed.] vol.1, pp511-529; Leipzig)

Carl R.Holladay
1983   New Testament Christology: Some Considerations of Method
(N.T. 25, pp257-278)

H.J.Holtzmann
1863   *Die Synoptischen Evangelien: Ihr Ursprung und Geschichtlicher
Charakter* (Leipzig)

Morna Hooker
1970   Christology and Methodology (N.T.S. 17, pp480-88)
1972   On Using the Wrong Tool (Theology 75, pp570-81)
1979   Is the Son of Man Problem really insoluble ? (in Text and Interpretation
eds. E.Best and R.McL.Wilson, pp155-168; C.U.P.)

M.Hooker and C.Hickling (eds.)
1975   What About the New Testament (London)

J.L.Houlden
1983   Biblical Theology (N.D.T. pp69-71)
1986   Connections (London)

Hans Hübner
1976   *Das Gesetz als elementares Thema einer Biblischen Theologie ?*
(KuD 22, pp250-76)
1983   *Sühne und Versöhnung* (KuD 29, pp284-305)

B.M.F.van Iersel
1964   *,Der Sohn' in den synoptischen Jesusworten* (Leiden)

Joachim Jeremias
1963   The Sermon on the Mount (Philadelphia)
1967a Abba (in The Prayers of Jesus pp11-65; London)
1967b *Die älteste Schicht der Menschensohnlogien* (Z.N.W. 58, pp159-172)
1971   New Testament Theology Vol.1 (London)

Paul Jersild
    1962a Natural Theology and the Doctrine of God in Albrecht Ritschl and
            Karl Barth (L.Q. XIV pp239-257)
    1962b Judgment of God in Albrecht Ritschl and Karl Barth
            (L.Q. XIV pp328-346)

Darrell Jodock
    1969   F.C.Baur and Albrecht Ritschl on Historical Theology (Ph.D.Diss. Yale)

Martin Kähler
    1870   Review of B.Weiss: *Lehrbuch der biblischen Theologie des*
            Neuen Testaments (T.S.K. 43, pp576-607)
    1897   *Biblische Theologie* (in R.E.P.T.K. 3rd.ed., ed.A.Hauck vol.3
            pp192-200; Leipzig)
    1964   The So-Called Historical Jesus and the Historic, Biblical Christ
            (Philadelphia)

Ernst Käsemann
    1963   Introduction to F.C.Baur: *Ausgewählte Werke*
            (Band 1, ppviii-xxv; Stuttgart)
    1964   Essays on New Testament Themes (London)
    1967   *Vom theologischen Recht historisch-kritischer Exegese*
            (Z.Th.K 64, pp259-281)
    1969   Blind Alleys in the "Jesus of History" Controversy
            (in New Testament Questions of Today pp23-65; London)
    1970   (ed.) *Das Neue Testament als Kanon* (Göttingen)
    1972-3 The Problem of a New Testament Theology (N.T.S. 19, pp235-45)
    1984   Differences and Unity in the New Testament
            (Concilium 171: Different Theologies, Common Responsibility -Babel
            or Pentecost ? eds. C.Geffré, G.Gutierrez and V.Elizondo, pp55-61;
            Edinburgh)

Julius Kaftan
    1897   *Dogmatik* (Freiburg, Leipzig and Tübingen)

Gordon D.Kaufman
    1971   What Shall We Do With the Bible ? (Interpretation 25, pp95-112)
    1979   An Essay on Theological Method (2nd ed.; Missoula)
    1981   The Theological Imagination (Philadelphia)

Leander Keck
    1972   A Future for the Historical Jesus (London)

H.C.Kee
   1977   Jesus in History (2nd ed.; New York)

David H.Kelsey
   1975   The Uses of Scripture in Recent Theology (London)
   1980   The Bible and Christian Theology (J.A.A.R. 48, pp385-402)

J.H.S.Kent
   1982   The End of the Line ? (London)

Frank Kermode
   1979   The Genesis of Secrecy (London)

R.H.King and P.C.Hodgson (eds.)
   1982   Christian Theology (Philadelphia)

J.D.Kingsbury
   1979   The Gospel in Four Editions (Interpretation 33, pp363-75)

Robert Emil Koenig
   1953   The Use of the Bible in Albrecht Ritschl's Theology and the Significance
           of His Method for Today (unpublished PhD. Diss. Chicago)

H.Köster
   1971   One Jesus and Four Primitive Gospels
           (in Trajectories Through Early Christianity pp158-204; Philadelphia)

John Knox
   1967   The Humanity and Divinity of Christ (C.U.P.)

Hans-Joachim Kraus
   1970   Die Biblische Theologie: Ihre Geschichte und Problematik
           (Neukirchen-Vluyn)

Werner Georg Kümmel
   1973   The New Testament (London)
   1974   Theology of the New Testament (London)
   1975   Introduction to the New Testament (London)

Nicholas Lash
   1980   Up and Down in Christology
           (in eds.S.W.Sykes and D.Holmes eds., pp31-46)

Ragnar Leivestad
1971-2 Exit the Apocalyptic Son of Man (N.T.S. 18, pp243-267)
1982   Jesus - Messias - Menschensohn: Die jüdischen Heilandserwartungen
       zur Zeit der ersten römischen Kaiser und die Frage nach dem
       messianischen Selbstbewußtsein Jesu
       (in A.N.R.W. II 25.1., pp220- 264)

B.Lindars
1975-6 Re-enter the Apocalyptic Son of Man (N.T.S. 22, pp52-72)
1983   Jesus Son of Man (London)
1985   Response to Richard Bauckham: The Idiomatic Use of Bar Enasha
       (J.S.N.T. 23, pp35-43)

Hans-Georg Link
1975   Geschichte Jesu und Bild Christi (Neukirchen-Vluyn)

James C.Livingston
1971   The Ritschlian Theology and Protestant Liberalism
       (ch.9 in Modern Christian Thought : From the Enlightenment
       to Vatican II; New York)

David W.Lotz
1974   Ritschl and Luther (Nashville)
1980   Albrecht Ritschl and the Unfinished Reformation H.T.R. 73,
       pp337-372)

D.Lührmann and G.Strecker (eds.)
1980   Kirche (Tübingen)

G.Lundström
1963   The Kingdom of God in the Teaching of Jesus
       (Edinburgh and Richmond, Virginia)

Harvey K.McArthur
1969   From the Historical Jesus to Christology
       (Interpretation 23, pp190-206)

G.W.McCulloh
1973   Christ's Person and Life-Work in the theology of Albrecht Ritschl:
       with special attention to the Munus Triplex (Ph.D. Chicago)

Sallie McFague
1983   Metaphorical Theology (London)

A.McGrath
   1986   The Making of Modern German Christology
          (esp. chs 3 and 4; Blackwell, Oxford)

John McIntyre
   1966   The Shape of Christology (London)

J.P.Mackey
   1979   Jesus: the Man and the Myth (London)

H.R.Mackintosh
   1937   Types of Modern Theology (chs.1-3 & 5; London)

Martin McNamara
   1983   Palestinian Judaism and the New Testament (Wilmington, Delaware)

John Macquarrie
   1963   Twentieth-Century Religious Thought (London)
   1986   Theology, Church & Ministry (London)

G.Maier
   1977   The End of the Historical-Critical Method (St.Louis)

C.Marsh
   1989   Defining Christianity after Ritschl: History, Theology and the
          "Picture of Jesus" in Late Nineteenth Century Protestant Thought
          (in Papers of the (AAR) Nineteenth Century Theology Working
          Group Vol.XV eds. S.Briggs and R.P.Busse; Berkeley, California)

I.H.Marshall
   1967   The Divine Sonship of Jesus (Interpretation 21, pp87-103)
   1977a I Believe in the Historical Jesus (London)
   1977b (ed.) New Testament Interpretation (Exeter)
   1978   The Gospel of Luke (Exeter)

Henry Menke
   1903   The Ritschlian Conception of Jesus and Some Implications Involved
          (B.D.thesis, Chicago)

Otto Merk
   1972   Biblische Theologie des Neuen Testaments in ihrer Anfangszeit
          (Marburg)
   1984   (ed.) Schriftauslegung als theologische Aufklärung (Gütersloh)

Bruce M.Metzger
1975   A Textual Commentary on the Greek New Testament
       (corrected ed.; London and N.Y.)

Norman Metzler
1971   The Ethics of the Kingdom (unpublished Ph.D. Munich)

Ben F. Meyer
1979   The Aims of Jesus (SCM: London)

Friedrich Mildenberger
1981   *Geschichte der deutschen evangelischen Theologie im 19. und 20.*
       Jahrhundert (Stuttgart)

Robert Morgan
1973   The Nature of New Testament Theology (London)
1976   Expansion and Criticism in the Christian Tradition
       (in M.Pye and R.Morgan eds., pp59-101)
1976-7a A Straussian Question to "New Testament Theology"
       (N.T.S. 23, pp243-265)
1976-7b F.C.Baur's Lectures on New Testament Theology
       (Ex.T. 88, pp202-6)
1979   The Hermeneutical Significance of the Four Gospels
       (Interpretation 33, pp376-388)
1980a Günther Bornkamm in England (in D.Lührmann and G.Strecker eds.,
       pp491-506; Tübingen)
1980b *Non Angli sed Angeli*: Some Anglican Reactions to German Gospel
       Criticism (in S.W.Sykes and D.Holmes eds., pp1-30)
1984   *Theologische Auslegung im angelsächsischen Bereich*
       (in O.Merk ed., pp34-40)
1985   Ferdinand Christian Baur (in Nineteenth Century Religious Thought
       in the West Vol.1 eds. N.Smart, J.P.Clayton, P.Sherry and S.T.Katz,
       pp261-289; C.U.P.)

Robert Morgan and Michael Pye (eds.)
1977   Ernst Troeltsch: Writings on Theology and Religion (London)

W.F.Moulton and A.S.Geden (plus H.K.Moulton)
1978   A Concordance to the Greek Testament (5th ed; T & T Clark,
       Edinburgh)

D.L.Mueller
1969   An Introduction to the Theology of Albrecht Ritschl (Philadelphia)

Gotthold Müller
  1971   *Spekulation-Ethizismus-Kerygmatismus : Haupttypen moderner
         Christologie* (T.Z. 27, pp117-134)

Archie L.Nations
  1983   Historical Criticism and the Current Methodological Crisis
         (S.J.T. 36, pp59-71)

Stephen Neill
  1964   The Interpretation of the New Testament 1861-1961 (London)
         [now expanded by N.T.Wright The Interpretation of the New
         Testament 1861-1980 Oxford 1988]

E.Nestle and K.Aland
  1979   *Novum Testamentum Graece* (26th ed.Stuttgart)

H.R.Niebuhr
  1952   Christ and Culture (London)

Dennis E.Nineham
  1963   Saint Mark (Harmondsworth)

C.J.Nitzsch
  1854   *Biblische Theologie* (in R.E.P.T.K. vol.2, pp219-225;
         Stuttgart and Hamburg)

Schubert M.Ogden
  1976   The Authority of Scripture for Theology
         (Interpretation 30, pp242-261)
  1982   The Point of Christology (London)
  1984   Rudolf Bultmann and the Future of Revisionary Christology
         (in *Rudolf Bultmanns Werk und Wirkung* ed.B.Jaspert, pp155-173;
         Darmstadt)

James Orr
  1893-4 Albrecht Ritschl (in Ex.T. 5, pp534-39)
  1898   The Ritschlian Theology and the Evangelical Faith (London)

David Pailin
  1976   Authenticity in the Interpretation of Christianity
         (in M.Pye and R.Morgan eds., pp129-159)

Wolfhart Pannenberg
1968   Jesus - God and Man (London)

G.Parsons
1979   Reappraising Ritschl (Modern Churchman 22, pp109-117)

Jaroslav Pelikan
1985   Jesus Through the Centuries (New Haven and London)

K. Penzel
1968   Will the Real Ferdinand Christian Baur Please Stand Up?
        (J.R. 48, pp310-323)

Norman Perrin
1963   The Kingdom of God in the Teaching of Jesus (London)
1967   Rediscovering the Teaching of Jesus (London)
1976   Jesus and the Language of the Kingdom (London)

M.Pye and R.Morgan (eds.)
1976   The Cardinal Meaning (The Hague)

H.S.Reimarus
1971   Fragments (E.T. of two of the Wolfenbüttel Fragments
        1777-8; London)

H.G.Reventlow
1984   The Authority of the Bible and the Rise of the Modern World
        (London)

J.K.Riches
1972   What is a 'Christocentric' Theology ? (in S.W.Sykes and J.P.Clayton,
        pp223-238)
1980   Jesus and the Transformation of Judaism (London)

James Richmond
1978   Ritschl: a Reappraisal (London)

Rainer Riesner
1981   *Jesus als Lehrer* (Tübingen)

J.Ringleben (ed.)
1990   *Gottes Reich und menschliche Freiheit* (Göttingen)

H.Ristow and K.Matthiae (eds.)
1961   *Der historische Jesus und der kerygmatische Christus* (Berlin)

Otto Ritschl
1892   *Albrecht Ritschls Leben I* (Freiburg i.B.)
1896   *Albrecht Ritschls Leben II* (Freiburg i.B. and Leipzig)

Vernon K.Robbins
1984   Jesus the Teacher (Philadelphia)

James M.Robinson
1959   A New Quest of the Historical Jesus (London)

J.Roloff
1973   *Auf der Suche nach einem neuen Jesusbild* (T.L.Z. 98, cols.561-572)

Christopher Rowland
1985a Christian Origins (London)
1985b Reading the New Testament Sociologically: An Introduction
       (Theology 88, pp358-64)

George Rupp
1977   Culture-Protestantism : German Liberal Theology at the Turn of the
       Twentieth Century (Missoula)

Michael Ryan
1966   The Function of the Discipline of History in the Theological
       Interpretation of Albrecht Ritschl (unpublished PhD. Drew
       University)

E.P.Sanders
1985   Jesus and Judaism (London)

P.Schäfer
1974   *Die Torah der messianischen Zeit* (Z.N.W. 65, pp27-42)

Rolf Schäfer
1964   *Das Reich Gottes bei Albrecht Ritschl und Johannes Weiss*
       (Z.Th.K. 61, pp68-88)
1968   *Ritschl: Grundlinien eines fast verschollenen dogmatischen Systems*
       (Tübingen)

K.H.Schelkle
1973   *Jesus - Lehrer und Prophet* (in *Orientierung an Jesus* ed.

P.Hoffmann, pp300-308; Freiburg)

Daniel Schenkel
1852   *Die Aufgabe der biblischen Theologie* (T.S.K. 25, pp40-66)
1869   A Sketch of the Character of Jesus (London)

Edward Schillebeeckx
1983   Jesus: an Experiment in Christology (London)

Adolf Schlatter
1905   *Atheistische Methoden in der Theologie (Beiträge zur Förderung
        christlicher Theologie* 9, pp229-250; reprinted in *Zur Theologie des
        Neuen Testaments und zur Dogmatik* pp134-140; Munich)

F.D.E.Schleiermacher
1928   The Christian Faith (E.T. of *Der christliche Glaube,* 2nd ed.1830;
        Edinburgh)
1958   On Religion (E.T. of *Ueber Religion* 3rd ed., 1893; New York)
1970   Brief Outline on the Study of Theology (E.T of *Kurze Darstellung des
        theologischen Studiums,* 1830; Virginia)
1975   Life of Jesus (E.T. of 1832 lectures first published in 1864;
        Philadelphia)
1978   Hermeneutics: The Handwritten Manuscripts (E.T. of 1959 ed. of
        manuscripts; Missoula)

C.F.Schmid
1870   Biblical Theology of the New Testament (Edinburgh)

K.L.Schmidt
1928   *Formgeschichte* (R.G.G. 2nd ed.,vol.2,cols.638ff)

R.Schnackenburg
1964-5 *Der Menschensohn im Johannesevangelium* (N.T.S. 11, pp123-137)
1968   The Gospel according to St.John vol.1 (New York and London)

Siegfried Schulz
1972   *Die neue Frage nach dem historischen Jesus* (in *Neues Testament und
        Geschichte* eds. B.Reicke and H.Baltensweiler, pp33-42; Zürich)

Albert Schweitzer
1968   The Quest of the Historical Jesus (New York)

224

Eduard Schweizer
1960 The Son of Man (J.B.L. 79, pp119-29)
1971 The Good News according to Mark (London)
1976 The Good News according to Matthew (London)

J.L.Segundo
1985 The Historical Jesus of the Synoptic Gospels
      (Maryknoll, Melbourne and London)

Alan P.F.Sell
1979 Ritschl Appraised: then and now (R.T.R. 38, pp33-41)
1986 Theology in Turmoil (Grand Rapids)

H.B.Sharman
1943 Son of Man and Kingdom of God (New York and London)

Reinhard Slenczka
1967 Geschichtlichkeit und Personsein Jesu (Göttingen)

Gerard S.Sloyan
1986 The Jesus Tradition (Mystic, Connecticut)

James D. Smart
1979 The Past, Present and Future of Biblical Theology (Philadelphia)

Jon Sobrino
1978 Christology at the Crossroads (Maryknoll)

L.Stählin
1889 Kant, Lotze and Ritschl (Edinburgh)

Graham Stanton
1972 The Gospel Traditions and Early Christological Reflection
      (in S.W.Sykes and J.P.Clayton eds., pp191- 204)
1973 On the Christology of Q (in Christ and Spirit in the New Testament
      eds S.S.Smalley and B.Lindars, pp27-42; C.U.P.)
1974a Form Criticism Revisited (in M.Hooker and C.Hickling eds.,
      pp13-27)
1974b Jesus of Nazareth in New Testament Preaching (C.U.P)
1983 The Interpretation of Matthew (London)

Ethelbert Stauffer
1982 Jesus, Geschichte und Verkündigung (in A.N.R.W. II.25.1

ed.W.Haase, pp3-130)

Lothar Steiger
1961   *Die Hermeneutik als dogmatisches Problem* (Gütersloh)

Georg Eduard Steiz
1858   Review of Albrecht Ritschl: *Die Entstehung der altkatholischen Kirche* 2nd ed (A.K.Z. 37, cols.1153-66)

Krister Stendahl
1966   Method in the Study of Biblical Theology (in The Bible in Modern Scholarship ed. J.P.Hyatt, pp196-209; London)

Hans-Herbert Stoldt
1980   History and Criticism of the Marcan Hypothesis (Edinburgh)

D.F.Strauss
1977   The Christ of Faith and the Jesus of History (E.T. of *Der Christus des Glaubens und der Jesus der Geschichte*, Berlin 1865; Philadelphia)

Georg Strecker
1969   *Die historische und theologische Problematik der Jesusfrage* (Ev.Th. 29, pp453-476)
1975   *Das Problem der Theologie des Neuen Testaments* (in Das Problem der Theologie des Neuen Testaments ed. G.Strecker, pp1-31; Darmstadt)
1980   *"Biblische Theologie"* ? (in D.Lührmann and G.Strecker eds., pp425-45)

Peter Stuhlmacher
1970   *Kritische Marginalien zum gegenwärtigen Stand der Frage nach Jesus* (in *Fides et communicatio* eds. D.Rössler, G.Voigt and F.Wintzer, pp341-361; Göttingen)
1975   *Schriftauslegung auf dem Wege zur biblischen Theologie* (Göttingen)
1979   *Vom Verstehen des Neuen Testaments* (Göttingen)

A.T.Swing
1901   The Theology of Albrecht Ritschl (New York)

S.W.Sykes
1972   The Theology of the Humanity of Christ (in S.W.Sykes and J.P.Clayton eds., pp53-71)
1982   (ed.) England and Germany: Studies in Theological Diplomacy (Frankfurt)

1984   The Identity of Christianity (London)

S.W.Sykes and J.P.Clayton (eds.)
1972   Christ, Faith and History (C.U.P.)

S.W.Sykes and D.Holmes (eds.)
1980   New Studies in Theology I (London)

Charles H.Talbert
1978   What is a Gospel ? (London)
1979   The Gospel and the Gospels (Interpretation 33, pp351-62)

Vincent Taylor
1933   The Formation of the Gospel Tradition (London)
1966   The Gospel according to St.Mark (2nd ed. London)

Ronald F.Thiemann
1981   Revelation and Imaginative Construction (J.R. 61, pp242-263)

Paul Tillich
1957   Systematic Theology Vol.2 (London and Chicago)

H.Timm
1967   *Theorie und Praxis in der Theologie Albrecht Ritschls und Wilhelm Herrmanns* (Gütersloh)

David Tracy
1981   The Analogical Imagination (London)

Ernst Troeltsch
1902   *Die Absolutheit des Christentums und die Religionsgeschichte*
        (reprinted by *Siebenstern Taschenbuch Verlag*; Munich and
        Hamburg 1969)
1913   The Dogmatics of the *"Religionsgeschichtliche Schule"* (A.J.T. 17,
        pp1-21; now also in Religion in History Edinburgh 1991, pp87-108)
1971   *Über historische und dogmatische Methode in der Theologie*
        (reprinted in G.Sauter [ed.]: Theologie als Wissenschaft, pp105-127;
        Munich) [now translated in Religion in History Edinburgh 1991,
        pp11-32)
1977   Writings on Theology and Religion (see R.Morgan and M.Pye)
1980   The Place of Christianity among the World Religions (previously
        unpublished 1923 lecture, in Christianity and Other Religions
        eds.J.Hick and B.Hebblethwaite, pp11-31; Glasgow)

Christopher M.Tuckett
  1979   The Griesbach Hypothesis in the Nineteenth Century
         (J.S.N.T. 3, pp29-60)
  1983a The Revival of the Griesbach Hypothesis (C.U.P.)
  1983b (ed.) The Messianic Secret (London)

Geza Vermes
  1967   The Use of BarNash/Bar Nasha in Jewish Aramaic
         (in An Aramaic Approach to the Gospels and Acts by Matthew
         Black, 3rd ed., pp310-328; Oxford)
  1976   Jesus the Jew (orig.edition 1973; London)
  1983   Jesus and the World of Judaism (London)

Philipp Vielhauer
  1965   Gottesreich und Menschensohn in der Verkündigung Jesu
         (in Aufsätze zum Neuen Testament pp55-79; Munich)

Hans Vorster
  1965   Werkzeug oder Täter Zur Methodik der Christologie
         Albrecht Ritschls (Z.Th.K. 62, pp46-65)

Christian Walther
  1961   Typen des Reich-Gottes-Verständnisses (chs. 2,7 and 8; München)

F.Watson
  1985   Why Was Jesus Crucified? (Theology 88, p105ff)

Bernhard Weiss
  1882   Biblical Theology of the New Testament vol.1
         (E.T. of 3rd German ed. of 1879; Edinburgh)
  1883   The Life of Christ vol.1 (Edinburgh)

Johannes Weiss
  1901   Die Idee des Reiches Gottes in der Theologie (Giessen)
  1971   Jesus' Proclamation of the Kingdom of God
         (E.T. of 1st ed. of 1892; London)

Claude Welch
  1972   Protestant Thought in the Nineteenth Century Vol.1 (London)
  1985   Protestant Thought in the Nineteenth Century Vol.2
         (New Haven and London)

228

Anton Wessels
1990   Images of Jesus (London)

Stephan Weyer-Menkhoff
1988   *Aufklärung und Offenbarung* (Göttingen)

W.D.Whan
1909   The Person and Work of Christ in the Theology of Ritschl
        (M.A. thesis, Chicago Div. School)

C.M.Williamson
1972   Did Ritschl's Critics Read Ritschl ?
        (E.Q. 44, pp159- 168 and 234-246)

W.Wrede
1971   The Messianic Secret (E.T. of 1901 text; Cambridge and London)

Paul Wrzecionko
1964   *Die philosophischen Wurzeln der Theologie Albrecht Ritschls*
        (Berlin)

Eduard Zeller
1860   *Die Tübinger historische Schule* (H.Z. 4, pp90-173)
1861   *Die historische Kritik und das Wunder* (H.Z. 6, pp356-373, reprinted
        in F.C.Baur: *Ausgewählte Werke* vol.V, pp501-519; Stuttgart 1975)

J.A.Ziesler
1983   New Testament Theology (N.D.T. pp398-403)

Index

230

Clayton, J.P., 11 [22]
Community (see "Church / (Christian) Community")
Conzelmann, H., 98 [81]
Cranfield, C.E.B., 182 [93], 183 [103]
Criterion, 25, 50, 55, 72, 78, 115, 121-3, 127, 143, 149f, 152, 155, 168, 185 [133]
Cross, F.L., 96 [54, 55], 97 [67]
Cubism, 169
Cullmann, O., 103 [137], 106 [173], 137f, 177 [26], 179 [53], 181 [75, 76], 182 [85, 86]

Dalman, G., 179 [53]
Davies, A., xviii
Deegan, D.L., 5, 11 [24, 28]
Demythologizing, 130
Dibelius, M., 174 [4]
Disciples (also: Discipleship), 59ff, 84, 124, 127, 132, 169
Diversity, xviii, 52, 101 [110], 103 [140], 104 [141], 108 [213], 113 [279], 157f, 161f, **163-171**, 174, 185 [133], 187 [156], 188 [160, 162], 193f, 197, 200, 200 [3]
Dodd, C,H., 103 [137], 124, 129f, 177 [26], 178 [30], 179 [49]
Draper, J.L., 5-7, 11 [23], 14, 16, 94 [19, 23, 24], 95 [31], 96 [49, 54], 99 [91], 101 [105], 104 [152], 177 [24], 192, 200 [1]
Dunn, J.D.G., 2, 10 [10], 93 [3], 99 [84], 141, 183 [101, 105]

"Early Catholicism", 2
Ebeling, G., 162, 188 [168]
Ehrenfeuchter, E., 97 [66]
Epistemology, 11 [25], 101 [103, 105]
Eschatology, 1, 129-131, 133-5, 140, 167, 179 [48], 198
"Essence of Christianity", 164

Ethics, xvii, 5, 15, 63f, 86-90, 113 [274], 129
Evans, O.E., 180 [62]
Ewald, H., 99 [87]
Experience, xvi, xix

Fabricius, C., 102 [118]
Faith, 19f, 23, 25, 91, 104 [142], 109 [224], 187 [56]
Faithfulness, 90
Farmer, W.R., 2, 10 [9], 99 [88, 89]
Fenton, J.C., 178 [36]
Fiddes, P., 186 [142]
Foerster, W., 106 [173]
Form Criticism 168, 175 [4]
Foster, A.D., 5, 10 [7], 11 [24]
Frei, H., 160, 188 [161]
Fuchs, E., 162, 188 [168]

Gabler, J.P., 95 [31]
Garvie, A.E., 10 [1, 3], 101 [105], 187 [152]
Gentile Christianity, 30, 83, 142, 164, 175 [1]
Gerhardsson, B., 124, 128, 178 [32]
Gerrish, B.A., 102 [119]
God (general), xviii, xix, 62, 71, 87, 89, 111 [254], 146, 150-2, 157, 176 [12], 180 [63], 181 [67, 73], 185 [122], 197f
  as Love, 62
  as Father, 58f, 62f, 65, 70, 83, 85, 105 [157], 106 [185], 111 [248], 138-43, 145, 151f, 183 [98, 100]
  wrath of, 34
Gospels (general), xvi, 3, 6-9, 12, 24, 26-9, 34f, 37, 39-42, **43-55**, 56f, 59f, **70-83**, 87, 89f, 92, 101 [115], 104 [142], 107 [197], 110 [241], 113 [272, 278], **114-22**, 123f, 127-130, 134, 137f, 151f, 156f, 159, 162f, 167f, 170ff, 174, 175 [2, 4], 176 [12, 19], 179 [53], 184 [119], 187 [156], 188 [166], 191f,

234

Norm, Normativity, xvi, xviii, xix, 24f, 28, 33, 40, 45, 51, 54f, 57, 71-3, 78, 97 [62], 101 [111, 112], 108 [213], 117, 119f, 123, 129, 144f, 147, 149, 151, 158-61, 163, 166-9, 185 [133], 193, 199f

Obedience, (see "Jesus, as Obedient One")
Ogden, S.M., 186 [136], 187 [153]
Old Testament, 16, 21-3, 69, 108 [205], 182 [82], 189 [185, 186]
Ontology, xvii, xx
Orr, J., 101 [105], 187 [152]

Pannenberg, 2, 10 [11], 93 [4]
Parables, 125ff, 139
Parsons, G., 10 [16]
Paul, Pauline epistles/theology, 3, 6f, 19, 28, 30f, 33f, 39f, 53, 87, 91, 99 [83], 104 [144], 113 [278], 164f
Pelikan, J., xviii, 200 [3]
Perfection, 63
Perrin, N., 106 [186], 112 [265], 124, 178 [30], 179 [45, 52], 180 [62], 201 [4]
Peter, Petrine tradition, 30, 99 [83], 113 [278], 165
Pietism, 6, 13, 15, 41, 94 [11]
Philosophy, philosophy of religion, 1f, 5, 11 [25], 13, 28, 36, 41, 101 [103], 129
Pluralism, xviii
Positivism, 36
Principles, xvi
Proclamation, 46, 66, 107 [188], 124, 132f, 137

"Quest of the Historical Jesus" (also: "Quest for Jesus"), 8, 26, 29, 42, 44, 49, 54, 73

Rauschenbusch, W., 94 [18]
Realism, 100 [99]

Reconciliation, 87
Redaction Criticism, 103 [128], 127
Redemption, 85f
Reductionism, 1
Reformation, 5f, 15, 19, 22
"Religionsgeschichtliche Schule" (see "History of Religions School")
Reischle, M., 94 [17], 102 [119]
Reitzenstein, R., 178 [33]
Religion, religious, 16, 24f, 52, 96 [45, 46, 47, 51], 97 [62], 104 [142], 108 [205]
Resurrection, 170, 187 [154], 188 [166], 190 [187]
Revelation, xvi, 90, 96 [46]
Riches, J.K., 96 [54], 108 [206], 180 [62]
Richmond, J., 5, 10 [16], 11[21, 23, 26, 27], 13, 93 [7], 97 [65], 99 [88]
Riesenfeld, H., 124, 128, 178 [32]
Riesner, R., 178 [32]
Righteousness, 76f, 81, 83, **90f**, 109 [223], 113 [274, 278], 116, 127, 165, 169, 192
Ringleben, J., 5, 10 [16], 11 [23]
Ritschl, O., 27, 34, 95 [31, 42], 97 [65, 66], 98 [68, 69, 71, 77], 100 [93, 96, 102]
Robbins, V.K., 178 [33]
Robinson, J.A.T., 103 [137], 177 [26]
Robinson, J. M, 104 [146]
Rowland, C., 135, 137, 181 [74, 75, 76, 77], 182 [82, 84]
Ryan, M., 113 [267]

Sanders, E.P., 99 [85], 128, 131, 177 [28], 178 [40], 179 [49, 50], 180 [57], 182 [81, 87], 184 [114], 185 [124, 129], 186 [148]
Sartre, J-P., 185 [135]
Schäfer, R., 5f, 11 [23], 14, 94 [9], 95 [38], 96 [51], 99 [91]
Schillebeeckx, E., 182 [81]

DDS